THE LAMENT FOR ART
■ DERMOT BOLGER

'A love-poem to the City of Dublin, to its people, its streets, its housing estates, but above all to that indomitable Dublin spirit that is as unique as it is indefinable.' (*Sunday Tribune*) 'You won't see a better first Irish play this year.' *Guardian*

LOW IN THE DARK
■ MARINA CARR

'Her purpose apparently is to confirm the false promises of motherhood, and to dismantle many of the myths associated with it . . . one of the most exciting, new and absolutely original aspects of Carr's writing is the manner in which the sexism of language and religious imagery is exposed . . . Marina Carr is a playwright to be watched.' *Sunday Tribune*

MISOGYNIST
■ MICHAEL HARDING

In rehearsal for its premiere as this volume went to press, Harding's play, strongly influenced by religious and folk ritual, is an extraordinary near-monologue lavish supplemented by erotic imagery, video and large choirs of spoken voices. Harding has been hailed as 'one of the most significant new Irish writers of his generation.' *Sunday Tribune*

THE HAMSTER WHEEL
■ MARIE JONES

'What happens to a marriage when one partner is incapacitated . . . and becomes completely dependent upon the other? Marie Jones's new play for Charabanc takes a scalpel to this frequently ignored social issue, probing deep into those dark marital recesses that people just don't talk about . . . A powerful, wholly theatrical experience . . .' *Irish Times*

Other Volumes in the International Collection

KATHARINE BRISBANE (Ed)
Australia Plays
New Australian Drama
Jack Davis No Sugar; **Alma De Groen** The Rivers of China;
Michael Gow Away; **Louis Nowra** The Golden Age;
David Williamson Travelling North
1-85459-056-1

ALASDAIR CAMERON (Ed)
Scot Free
New Scottish Plays
John Byrne Writer's Cramp; **John Clifford** Losing Venice;
Anne Marie Di Mambro The Letter-Box; **Chris Hannan**
Elizabeth Gordon Quinn; **John McKay** Dead Dad Dog;
Rona Munro Saturday at the Commodore;
Tony Roper The Steamie
1-85459-017-0

BARBARA DAY
Czech Plays
Modern Czech Drama
Vaclav Havel Tomorrow! **Ivan Klima** Games;
Josef Topol Cat on the Rails;
Daniela Fischerova Dog and Wolf
1-85459-074-X

MICHAEL GLENNY (Ed)
Stars in the Morning Sky
New Soviet Plays
Alexander Chervinsky Heart of a Dog;
Alexander Galin Stars in the Morning Sky;
Alexander Gelman A Man with Connections;
Grigory Gorin Forget Herostratus!
Ludmila Petrushevskaya Three Girls in Blue
1-85459-020-0

STEPHEN GRAY (Ed)
South Africa Plays
Drama from Southern Africa
Anthony Ackerman Somewhere on the Border
Maishe Maponya The Hungry Earth
Susan Pam-Grant Curl up and Dye
Paul Slabolepszy Over the Hill;
Pieter-Dirk Uys Just Like Home
1-85459-148-7

THE CRACK IN THE EMERALD

■ NEW IRISH PLAYS

THE LAMENT FOR ARTHUR CLEARY
■ DERMOT BOLGER

LOW IN THE DARK
■ MARINA CARR

MISOGYNIST
■ MICHAEL HARDING

THE HAMSTER WHEEL
■ MARIE JONES

SELECTED AND INTRODUCED BY
■ DAVID GRANT

N
H
B

NICK HERN BOOKS
London

A **Nick Hern Book**

The Crack in the Emerald first published in 1990
as an original paperback by Nick Hern Books

Second edition reprinted 1994 by Nick Hern Books,
14 Larden Road, London W3 7ST

Typeset in Baskerville by Action Typesetting Ltd, Gloucester
Printed in Great Britain by Athenaeum Press Ltd,
Gateshead, Tyne & Wear.

A CIP catalogue record for this book is available from
the British Library

ISBN 1 85459 237 8

Contents

Given the chance to update this introduction after five years, it is reassuring that, a few administrative details apart, the only major thing to have to report is that the reputation of all four writers continues to grow. Marina Carr's latest play, *The Mai*, is being produced at the Peacock Theatre for the 1994 Dublin Theatre Festival. Michael Harding has enjoyed considerable success at the same theatre with *Hubert Murray's Widow*. Dermot Bolger, though concentrating mainly on prose, still writes regularly for the theatre. Marie Jones's output has been prolific with numerous plays for television and radio (including a television version of *The Hamster Wheel* as well as several stage plays, among them an adaptation of Gogol's *The Government Inspector*). The only real qualification to my previous note relates to my assertion that *Misogynist* could not be a monologue. In fact, the writer revived the piece as a solo performance with the well-known actor Tom Hickey, and toured widely throughout rural Ireland to enormous success. There could be no greater contrast in scale than that between its Abbey premiere and the performance I witnessed at the back room of a pub in Black Lion on the Cavan-Fermanagh border. Such is the enduring resilience and versatility of Irish drama!

David Grant,
September 1994

Introduction

The intention behind this collection of new plays is to display the range and quality of playwrights in Ireland today, and to assert the continuing vitality of an Irish writing tradition, forever under threat of being ossified by the museum instinct of popular perceptions. It's an old Irish aphorism that the best heroes are dead ones. Thus Sheridan and Goldsmith, Shaw and Wilde, Yeats and Synge, Behan and O'Casey have established a firm place in the Irish psyche. And now sadly, Samuel Beckett has taken his place in that illustrious Hall of Fame. Their pictures are regularly to be seen on posters, postcards and (ah, the surest test of all) in half the pubs of Dublin.

There are living playwrights to be sure – Brian Friel, Hugh Leonard, Tom Murphy, Thomas Kilroy, John B. Keane, Frank McGuinness and Tom MacIntyre even maybe. But public recognition as a (capital I) 'Irish' (capital P) 'Playwright' is a cautious and a fickle thing.

The irony, of course, is that not only is this (admittedly fairly arbitrary) list of recognised living Irish Playwrights far from complete, reflecting the common tendency to exclude women and (almost more heretical) writers from the North. It fails to take account of a truly enormous group of talented younger or less established playwrights, many of whom have succeeded, against all the odds, in getting their work into production, and four of them into this book. Such is the strength of writing for the theatre in Ireland today that it has been possible to make our selection exclusively from plays by Irish writers receiving their first production in Ireland within the space of one year (as it happens, from one Dublin Theatre Festival to the next). Even then, the selection is not exhaustive, but the chosen plays do reflect the extraordinary diversity of modern Irish theatre, and the way in which tradition enjoys an active partnership with innovation.

One of the plays, Dermot Bolger's *The Lament for Arthur Cleary* brings a fresh and challenging new voice to the perennial preoccupation of Irish drama with Emigration.

Two of the plays (Michael Harding's *Misogynist* and Marina

Carr's *Low in the Dark*) can be seen in the context of the more recent trend in Ireland towards largely image-based plays like *The Great Hunger*. But each writer is exploring their own quite distinct response to this development, and at the same time reaffirming the continuing importance of words.

Two of the writers are women, but that indicates no more than the growing importance of women in every aspect of Irish theatre.

Only one of the writers is from Northern Ireland, suggesting perhaps a shift of initiative back to the South after the heady days in the early 80s and the late flowering of what is sometimes known (pejoratively perhaps) as 'Troubles Drama'. Marie Jones's play (*The Hamster Wheel*) is all the more important in that it represents the most significant move so far in Northern Irish theatre writing away from that particular genre.

All the plays are concerned with intimate human relationships. This may be to say no more than that each play is a drama. But the particular insights in each case are unique, and uniquely Irish (be it Northern, Southern, contemporary or abstract). And just as they are unique they are profoundly universal.

CASTING AN IMAGE

Although with quite distinct styles, Michael Harding and Marina Carr can helpfully be grouped together within this collection as writers working mainly in a non-naturalistic style. Irish theatre has always been a broadly based affair, and we need only cite Yeats and Beckett to affirm that naturalism has not been the prevailing rule. There has been a recent surge of experiment on the Irish stage, in which the balance between word and image has been explored, with powerful implications for the nature of the use of words themselves. A series of collaborations between actor Tom Hickey, writer Tom MacIntyre and director Patrick Mason created the climate in which other theatrical imaginations could be unleashed, and Michael Harding and Marina Carr have two of the most original imaginations in Irish Theatre today.

Harding's work is strongly influenced by religious and folk ritual. Himself a former priest, the perceived anti-clericalism of his award-winning play, *Una Pooka*, set around the visit to Ireland of Pope John Paul II, caused considerable controversy when it was produced at the Peacock Theatre last year, but the overall intentions of his work seem much more concerned with understanding the nature of humanity in its broadest sense, rather than focusing on any specific aspect of it. His first play, *Strawboys*, drew strongly on harvest and fertility rites, and a community play, *The Waking of Brian Boru*, presented in Ennis earlier this year created a contemporary context for the ancient Mummers play.

Harding seems fascinated, however, as much by new as by traditional resources for the theatre, and has shown special interest both in the use of video and of large choirs of spoken voices. Both feature strongly in *Misogynist*. This is emphatically not a monologue, although the language is almost entirely given over to the one actor. The context of symbols, music and technology that Harding creates around the central performer are as essential to the play as the language itself.

Philosophy, rather than religion seems to be the principal influence on Marina Carr's writing. On the page, *Low in the Dark* with its coded character names, its terse language, and its abstract themes, seems firmly in the tradition of the Theatre of the Absurd. Beckett comes most strongly to mind. And in performance the same immediacy of human emotion shines through that is often an almost unexpected feature of productions of Beckett plays.

As with *Misogynist*, Marina Carr's central theme is gender, and to that extent the two plays make interesting companions. Harding's play is deliberately couched in maleness. *Low in the Dark's* bias is less firmly slanted, but the all too rare phenomenon in Irish drama of the female voice is loudly to be discerned. While Marina Carr's raw materials are all familiar if diverse (from classical references like Pallas Athene to Playtex bras) the overall effect is of total originality and spontaneity.

HOME AND ABROAD

If, as I suggest, *Misogynist* and *Low in the Dark* are both exemplary of a renewed spirit of formal innovation in Irish Theatre, *The Lament for Arthur Cleary*, though more traditional in theme, is no less remarkable for the manner in which it came to be written. All plays undergo a process of development and change in rehearsal, but this play can be seen to have been quite exceptional in the degree of collaboration that existed between writer Dermot Bolger, director David Byrne, and dramaturg Maureen White. This increasing readiness to see the final crafting of the play as a collaborative process is certainly one of the most exciting developments in Irish theatre.

The Lament for Arthur Cleary began life as a long poem in which Dermot Bolger (already a well-known novelist and publisher) transposed the old story of Arthur Leary to modern Dublin. A Catholic Irish nobleman returns to Ireland in penal times when Catholics are not permitted to own a horse above a certain value. Refusing to sell his horse at the required price, Leary is killed. Bolger's present day parallel concerns a returning emigrant and the horse becomes a powerful motor cycle. The final outcome is the same.

The poem attracted the attention of David Byrne, then working with Wet Paint, a company specifically constituted to present theatre to a young audience in the more disadvantaged areas of Dublin. This brief necessarily dictates the kind of work the company produces. It must be relevant, accessible and quite robust. The theme of the poem was certainly appropriate, but its delicacy made it seem at first sight an unlikely choice. The particular excitement about the piece of theatre that resulted derived in large measure from the refusal of all concerned to patronise their audiences, or to compromise their work. In many ways, indeed, it was more challenging than much of the work presented in more conventional contexts.

The occasional use of masks, a very fluid transition of actors from one character to another and the intermittent and sinister intrusion of the border guard presented no difficulty in practice for an audience that was for the most part not theatrically sophisticated.

Thematically, the play is as contemporary as it is timeless. Emigration has been a regular preoccupation of recent Irish theatre. Brian Friel's *Philadelphia, Here I Come* and Tom Murphy's *Conversations on a Homecoming* are just two examples that spring to mind. But *Arthur Cleary* is unusual for its Dublin setting. The rural melancholia familiar on Irish stages gives way to urban anger. And the European dimension seems more topical now than the more usual American connection.

THE NORTHERN DIMENSION

Politics apart, the practical effect of the Border on Irish Theatre has been its separate development in the North and the South. Marie Jones in Belfast, therefore, comes from a different artistic and cultural environment to the other writers in this collection. That is not to say that there have been no writers from Northern Ireland to have actively contributed to theatre in the South –

Denis Johnston and Saint-John Ervine to name but two. But there has also long been a northern theatre with its own distinct identity. Often this has shown a radical emphasis, as with Sam Thompson's shipyard play, *Over the Bridge*, which the establishment tried to suppress, and it is to this latter tradition that Marie Jones may more appropriately be seen to belong.

In recent years, a dominant, though by no means exclusive, concern of the Northern Irish Theatre has been to come to terms with 'The Troubles'. For most of the 70s, writers were perhaps too close to be able to address the subject constructively, and the most effective comment was often humorous and satirical. Then, towards the end of the decade, there seemed suddenly to be a flowering of 'Troubles Drama' with writers like Graham Reid, Christina Reid and Martin Lynch at last providing perceptive and thoughtful analyses of the political situation from a wider social and cultural perspective.

Against this background, five actresses, including Marie Jones, frustrated at how few opportunities for work seemed to exist in Northern Ireland set up the Charabanc Theatre Company, and with playwright Martin Lynch and director Pam Brighton, researched and collaboratively wrote *Lay Up Your Ends*. This play addressed an issue that seemed to the Company of far more fundamental importance to women in Belfast than 'The Troubles' – the experience of women whom they interviewed of life in the 1930s in the linen industry, of the coming of Trades Unions, and by extension of the role of women in Northern Ireland life in general. The production was a triumph.

Charabanc went on to research and produce five more plays touring to Britain, to Russia and the United States and throughout Ireland. They also managed to avoid becoming ghettoised as a feminist company, establishing themselves as the most progressive force in modern Northern Irish Theatre. By this stage, Marie was an established playwright, and while the Company's work was still collaborative, she was undertaking the majority of the writing. Commissions followed from other companies, including Belfast's new Theatre-in-Education Company, Replay, for which she has now written two plays.

The Hamster Wheel represents a quantum leap away from previous Charabanc productions, although it too is based on extensive interviews and research. It addresses a set of troubles as real and as serious as Northern Ireland's political ones, but which get nowhere near the same kind of attention. It also asserts Marie Jones's position as a playwright of the first order. Where her previous work has rejoiced in boldly drawn characters and

unrestrained humour, here the characters are rounded and
emotionally deep. The humour is still there, and the washing
machine repair man's monologue is a superb example of the mix
of tragedy and comedy that is at the heart of the best of Irish
drama. But the members of the family having to cope with the
shock of Norman's illness are all firmly fleshed out. In particular,
the play captures the strengths and weaknesses of the 'Ulster
Male' and, for that matter of the 'Ulster Female'. The characters
are individual, but they are also tellingly typical.

THE MEANS OF PRODUCTION

One thing that the North and the South have in common are the
prevailing commercial realities that stack the odds against new
plays being considered for production. Outside the context of the
Belfast and Dublin Festivals, new work is generally regarded as
an unacceptable risk, and even they are finding it harder to
sustain their commitment to new work year by year.

For those unfamiliar with Irish Theatre, it may be helpful to
survey in outline its structure in the two parts of the island. In
Northern Ireland, there is only one production management
working throughout the year, the Lyric Theatre in Belfast. This
has always presented itself as a 'Poets' Theatre', and has
managed to keep new work in its programme, in spite of
constantly shrinking resources. For many years, they contributed
the only new drama to the Belfast Festival. Currently they seem
keen to offer at least one new play a season. The other notable
managements, apart from Charabanc and Replay are Theatre
Ulster (a creature of the Northern Ireland Arts Council, which
tends to stick to the standard repertoire, but which did recently
mount a very successful stage abridgement of Graham Reid's
Billy Plays, which on television had first brought Kenneth
Branagh to prominence), and the Derry-based Field Day Theatre
Company, founded by Stephen Rea and Brian Friel, with whose
work they are particularly associated.

In the Republic, by contrast, the most significant recent trend
has been towards decentralisation. Dublin continues to be the
most important production base, with the National Theatre's
two stages (the large Abbey and the smaller Peacock Theatre),
the prestigious Gate Theatre (currently noted for its high
production standards, but more often programming Irish classics
than new work), and the Gaiety and Olympia Theatres, like the
new Andrew's Lane and Tivoli Theatres, (both of which have

opened within the last three years) nowadays rarely taking
production initiatives themselves, but available for hire by a
growing number of independent managements. Where the
veteran Phyllis Ryan's Gemini Productions used to stand
virtually alone, there are now Rough Magic, Groundwork,
Playwrights and Actors, The Passion Machine and many more.
There is no shortage, either, of smaller-scale independents like
Co-Motion and Pigsback, and more specialised companies such
as TEAM Educational Theatre Company and, of course, Wet
Paint, who are often among the readiest of all to tackle new
work. Finally there is the annual Dublin Theatre Festival, which
in addition to being a producer in its own right, facilitates the
showcasing of work by other managements. It is with satisfaction
I record that two of the plays in the present collection have been
presented within either the 1989 or 1990 Theatre Festival
programmes, though I would stress that this was only incidental
to their being selected.

The real change in recent years, however, has been the
emergence of an important regional dimension. Druid Theatre in
Galway led the way, but they have now been joined by the Red
Kettle Theatre Company in Waterford, the Island Company in
Limerick, and Seven Woods in Sligo. There is even the Yew
Theatre Company in the tiny Mayo town of Ballina who last
year gave the stage premiere of Christina Reid's *My Name, Shall I
Tell You My Name*, a production that was later seen at London's
Young Vic. Cork, as the second largest city in the Republic has
a surprisingly sparse theatre life, but the Local Authority are
currently addressing the whole question of arts provision there,
and we may expect significant developments in the near future.
In the meantime, the Meridian Theatre Company, has emerged
with a growing reputation that is based largely on new
indigenous writing.

Amid all this regional variety, only Meridian and Druid
regularly produce new work. Each is emblematic of one end of a
spectrum, within which the Dublin theatres and managements
can also variously be placed. Meridian is a new company, and
depends for its core funding on a government employment
scheme. Druid, conversely, is so well respected and established
that it can expect regular funding on a more or less realistic
level. This gives them confidence to bring on and programme
new work. But both companies also share that essential
additional ingredient – the determined conviction that without
new writing, Irish Theatre is destined to become moribund.

It is fashionable but necessary in Ireland to continue to

grumble at the paucity of resources available for the development of new writing for the Theatre. And there is no doubt that so evidently rich a national resource deserves more adequate support. In particular, there is no recognition of the need for commissioning money to allow writers to take risks. All too often a commission is seen as an advance on royalties, and there is widespread misunderstanding that a commissioned play that is not at once produced has somehow failed. In practice, most writers put in the initial work on a play in the hope of being able subsequently to exploit it. It is a thing of wonder that so many good plays get written at all. Once written, there is often a need for practical experiment with a director and actors before a stageable text emerges. In a context where money for production is so scarce, this argument is seldom persuasive in securing the resources necessary to help the writer complete the work.

For this reason, I choose to conclude with a heartfelt acknowledgement of the various producers who allowed the four plays in this collection to achieve production. Interestingly, these were not exclusively the larger managements, but were as various as the plays themselves, ranging from the National Theatre ('the Abbey') who have championed Michael Harding's work, to the ad hoc Crooked Sixpence Company, which with the help of the Project Arts Centre first brought Marina Carr's work to the public stage. These and the other two companies involved, Charabanc (*The Hamster Wheel*) and Wet Paint (*The Lament for Arthur Cleary*) all deserve our thanks for the commitment and encouragement that have so signally enriched the growing heritage of Irish drama.

David Grant
July 1990

THE LAMENT FOR ARTHUR CLEARY
■ DERMOT BOLGER

Dermot Bolger was born in Finglas, North Dublin, in 1959. His first two novels of Dublin life, *Night Shift* and *The Woman's Daughter*, received the AE Memorial Award, the Macaulay Fellowship and the Sunday Tribune Arts Award. His third novel, *The Journey Home*, was a best-seller in Ireland when published by Viking in 1990.

The author of five collections of poetry, Bolger's first play, *The Lament for Arthur Cleary*, was one of the major hits of the 1989 Dublin Theatre Festival and received the Stewart Parker BBC Award. His second play, *Blinded by Light*, was presented by the Abbey Theatre, Dublin, on their Peacock stage in 1990.

Dermot Bolger is editor of Raven Arts Press, one of Ireland's most radical publishers, and is a member of the Arts Council of Ireland.

For David Byrne and Maureen White

Characters

ARTHUR CLEARY, a Dubliner in his late twenties.
The GIRL, his girlfriend who goes to live with him.
The FRONTIER GUARD
The PORTER   } all of whom play a variety
The FRIEND (a woman) } of interchanging roles.

The Lament for Arthur Cleary was first performed by Wet Paint Arts as part of the Dublin Theatre Festival at The Project Arts Centre on 18 September 1989. The cast was as follows:

ARTHUR CLEARY	Brendan Laird
GIRL	Hilary Fannin
FRONTIER GUARD	Owen Roe
PORTER	Berts Folan
FRIEND	Lynn Cahill

Directed by David Byrne
Dramaturg, Maureen White
Stage Director, Sinead Connolly
Designed by Ned O'Loughlin
Music by Gerard Grennell
Costumes by Maire Tierney

ACT ONE

As the first strains of music begin, the actors file slowly out onto the stage. The FRIEND, *the* FRONTIER GUARD *and the* PORTER *in that order stand at the back of the stage with sticks in their hands.* ARTHUR CLEARY *goes to sit on a small box in the front right hand corner and the* GIRL *takes centre stage. There is a raised wooden platform (about six feet high and two feet across) in the centre of the stage and a barrel at the far right where the* FRIEND *is standing. When the* GIRL *begins to recite, her voice is echoed by a recording of itself over the music which grows in tempo.*

GIRL. My lament for you Arthur Cleary
   As you lay down that crooked back lane
   Under the stern wall of a factory
   Where moss and crippled flowers cling,

   I cupped your face in my palms
   To taste life draining from your lips
   And you died attempting to smile
   As defiant and proud as you had lived.

The stage goes black and across the music comes the sharp banging of sticks on both the drum and the wooden supports of the backdrop. They grow in fury until they're almost drowned by the scream of pipes in the soundtrack. There is sudden silence. In the growing dim light we can discern the three figures who are each holding a death mask over their faces and standing poised with sticks raised. After they have each spoken once they will slowly converge on ARTHUR *sitting on the box and the* GIRL *who is sleeping uneasily, twisting in dreams under a white cloth at his feet. Each sentence is accompanied by a sharp thud of a stick.*

PORTER (*resigned*). It's dead Arthur, don't you know it's dead?

FRIEND (*defiant*). When did we ever care about them, son? When did we ever?

FRONTIER GUARD (*menacingly*). Decide Cleary. With me or against me.

FRIEND (*spiteful*). You'd go off with him, that old cripple.

She slaps her stick against the barrel beside her on the last word. They move forward, chanting phrases from their sentences which are slightly jumbled into each other but sufficiently spaced to be distinctive. There are a number of sharp bangs of sticks as they approach which unnerve ARTHUR. *The* PORTER *laughs mockingly in a low tone. They gather behind* ARTHUR *and with one final thud, this time on the box he is sitting on, they raise their sticks in a fan behind his back. At this final thud the* GIRL *jerks awake and sits bolt upright, her back against* ARTHUR, *the sheet clutched protectively against her.* ARTHUR *reaches down, soothing her.*

ARTHUR. Bad dream love, just a bad dream.

The GIRL *looks at him as though coming back to her senses and then stares forward.*

GIRL. I'm frightened, Arthur. I dreamt it again.

ARTHUR. The same one? Can you remember it?

She tries to think and shakes her head.

GIRL. No, but it was the same one. It's always gone when I wake but I know it. I know the fear in it. Like the fear of nothing else.

Pause.

Let's go Arthur, now, while we've still time.

ARTHUR (*half amused/half soothing*). Go away? Listen love, I've finally come home. This is our home. Nobody can take it from us. Home. Say it.

GIRL (*nervously*). Home?

ARTHUR (*firmly*). Home.

GIRL (*less tentatively*). Home.

ARTHUR (*firmly*). Home.

His arm nestling her head, they lie back slowly as they repeat the word. The lights go down into blackness.

ARTHUR & GIRL (*firmly*). Home.

A new music begins, eerie, unsettling with the hint of the noise of trains. A spotlight switches on, held by the FRONTIER GUARD. *It flickers over the stage.*

FRONTIER GUARD. Check the wheels!

PORTER. For what?

FRONTIER GUARD (*dismissively*). Just do it!

From behind the raised platform the PORTER *switches on his torch. Its beam moves up and down the wooden bars in front of which* ARTHUR *stands in semi-darkness with a green passport in his hand. The* FRONTIER GUARD *enters behind him.*

FRONTIER GUARD. Passport please.

ARTHUR *turns.*

ARTHUR. Oh, sorry. (*He hands him his passport which the* FRONTIER GUARD *opens and examines.*)

FRONTIER GUARD. Ah Irish. Irish. Boom-boom! Eh! (*He laughs.*)

ARTHUR. Yeah. Boom-bleeding-boom.

The FRONTIER GUARD *hands him back his passport.*

FRONTIER GUARD & PORTER (*ironically as they circle with torches*).

We are green, we are white,
We are Irish dynamite!

ARTHUR. Eh, do you mind me asking? Where am I now? Which side of the border am I on?

FRONTIER GUARD (*stops and shrugs his shoulders*). What difference to you Irish? I see you people every day, you're going this way, you're going that way, but never home. Either way you're a long way from there.

ARTHUR (*nods his head towards the window*). What's he looking at the wheels for?

FRONTIER GUARD. Looking for? It is the rules, Irish. He does what he is told. If you ordered him to look for a snowball in a fire he would sit staring all night.

FRONTIER GUARD *laughs as he stares out at the* PORTER *walking with the torch, then turns abruptly, snapping back into his official voice.*

FRONTIER GUARD. We will go on soon.

He exits as the PORTER *comes around to* ARTHUR'*s side of the platform, still shining the torch up and down.*

ARTHUR. What difference does it make? (*He looks up and down.*) Another limbo of tracks and warehouses. Could be anywhere. (*He gives a half laugh.*) Except home.

PORTER (*looking up and shining the torch directly at his face*). How can you leave a place when you're carrying it round inside you, Cleary? .

ARTHUR (*moving to the window and staring down at him in astonishment*). How do you know my name? I don't know you.

PORTER. You don't know nothing.

He switches the torch off and scurries forward to set up the wooden box on the front left of the stage. The FRIEND *comes striding forward in confident pose towards the box. The* FRONTIER GUARD *and the* GIRL *have gathered together in front of the raised platform, where the* PORTER *joins them, and have begun clapping as soon as the torch was switched off, while* ARTHUR *has moved to one side, stooped as if listening to a radio. The* FRIEND *clears her throat and then silences the others with a grand sweep of her hand. She stares in front of her. There is applause scattered throughout her speech, which she halts by the use of her hand.*

FRIEND (*in a smooth, politician's voice*). Although we are a small nation in this great community, our heritage abounds with saints, with poets, with dreamers. Though we in Government are realists, first and foremost. We know we cannot all live in this one island. But we are not ashamed. Young people are to Ireland what champagne is to France! Our finest crop, the cream of our youth, nurtured from birth, raised with tender love by our young state, brought to ripeness and then plucked! For export to your factories and offices. Fellow European ministers, we are but a small land with a small role to play in this great union of nations. But a land with a great history. Long before Columbus set sail in 1492, long before Amerigo Vespucci gave his name to that great continent.

Applause takes on rhythmic effect.

Our missionaries in their boats of animal hide had already discovered the new world. Through all of the dark ages we have gone, fought to spread the word of God among you.

OTHERS *bless themselves.*

To petition you for arms to repel our invader –

OTHERS *join hands and grimace.*

To fight your wars. Once more we entrust to you the flower of our youth, not black –

OTHERS. Oh no.

FRIEND. Or yellow –

OTHERS. Oh no.

FRIEND. But white –

OTHERS. Oh yes.

FRIEND. Not illiterate –

OTHERS. Oh no.

FRIEND. Or backward –

OTHERS. Oh no.

FRIEND. But qualified.

OTHERS. Oh yes.

FRIEND. Not migrants –

OTHERS. Oh no.

FRIEND. Or illegals.

OTHERS. Oh no.

FRIEND. But as equal Europeans.

OTHERS, *great applause.*

FRIEND. We know they are ready to take their place, we know you will not turn your back on them.

ARTHUR *moves his fingers as if on a dial, freezing the* FRIEND *in her pose, and there is the crackle of a radio between stations, the hiss of foreign accents and a brief blare of music fading into static again. The* PORTER *now moves forward to stand behind him. He speaks in the voice of an old Turk.*

PORTER (*as old Turk*). It's no good trying to find home on a radio, Irish.

ARTHUR *clicks the radio sharply off.*

PORTER. You should go.

ARTHUR. You think it's that simple?

PORTER. I know it's not. (*Laughs.*) And after a time you can only go there in your mind. Because when you go back you can feel ... the distance, eh. The big town just a squalid

village, the big man ... what's that you call him ... a crock
of shit. You say nothing, but you know and ... wait till you
see Cleary ... the big men, the bosses, they know you know.

ARTHUR (*laughs ruefully*). Are you not sick of here, Toras?

PORTER. Here? (*Laughs.*) Here I have a bed with three others,
a locker, a piece of wall for my photographs, a Yugoslav
woman who serves me meals without a smile. No, I carry
home with me ... in my wallet.

ARTHUR. How long has it been?

PORTER (*coughs*). I cough and it hurts. If I go, the doctors on
the border may not let me back here. Eighteen months more
and I will have the money to go home with honour. Home to
stay. (*He coughs again and spits.*) Home to die. My young
nephew, he can come in my place and have the money, the
bed, the pin-ups, the locker. You're still young Irish, why you
never out on the town anymore?

ARTHUR. I prefer my own diseases.

PORTER. You talk like an old man Cleary.

ARTHUR. I'm tired. I feel like one.

The FRONTIER GUARD *stomps his way across to them.*

FRONTIER GUARD. Those Slavs are not worth shit. Another
one sick coughing with the dust. They're given masks if they'd
only wear them.

ARTHUR. The masks slow them down. Then you dock them
for not reaching their quotas.

FRONTIER GUARD. Who asked you? You Irish moan. Soft,
lazy white skin! I need a real man who's not afraid of work.
Double time for this shift. Eh, Toras!

ARTHUR. Toras, you're crazy. You're just off an eight-hour
shift. Rest yourself.

PORTER. Tomorrow I rest, Cleary, tonight I earn.

The PORTER *trots off to stand behind the* FRIEND.

ARTHUR. He's an old man before his time. You're killing him.

FRONTIER GUARD (*short laugh*). I don't need to, Irish. He's
killing himself. (*His tone hardens.*) You've no stomach for it here
Irish, then you should go home.

ARTHUR (*half to himself*). Yeah, I just might one of these days. A few jars in O'Connell Street, then down the Rock Salmon Club where I'd be safe from the likes of you.

FRONTIER GUARD (*mocking laugh*). Don't you know by now, Irish? (*Chilling tone.*) I work the door.

He clicks his fingers and the FRIEND *comes back to life.*

FRIEND. And now my fellow minister will give a brief discourse on night life in Dublin. Thank you.

She steps down and the PORTER *lifts her round into the centre of the stage where she and the* GIRL *begin to dance to the disco beat which is growing louder. The* PORTER *lifts the box away to one side and then walks slightly drunken over to the far side of the stage. The* FRONTIER GUARD *clicks his fingers, checks his suit and stands self-importantly beside the raised platform as lights begin to spin so that the stage becomes awash with speckled light suggesting a night club. In the corner, the two girls are seen checking their make-up and miming a conversation with themselves. The* FRONTIER GUARD *is passive, self-assured. He puts an arm out as though blocking the doorway, well aware of his strength. The* PORTER *backs away and then approaches, nervous, gazing up at the doorway. He stops. The* FRONTIER GUARD *ignores him. The* PORTER *moves closer.*

PORTER. What's it like inside. Mister?

The FRONTIER GUARD *unfolds his hands and looks down at him. He speaks slowly as if to a child but also like a seedy Soho doorman.*

FRONTIER GUARD. Everything you ever dreamed of. Girls hot for it, lining the walls, leather mini-skirts, thighs like long stalks of barley waiting to be harvested.

PORTER. It's that good, is it?

FRONTIER GUARD. It's better.

PORTER. So, eh, I suppose . . . is there . . . eh, any chance . . . ?

FRONTIER GUARD. Ever hear of Matt Talbot's first miracle?

PORTER. Eh, no.

FRONTIER GUARD. Brothers they were, out in Ballybough. Three of them. Dockers. Down the kips in Monto every weekend. All three of them contracted it. (*Pause.*) The pox!

Worst dose imaginable. Only one cure you know. (*He raises two fingers sideways to form a scissors and makes a cut down at the* PORTER's *zip. The* PORTER *jumps back.*) Matt Talbot was their only hope. He says to them 'go down to the Liffey before dawn every morning for a week, strip naked, cover yourselves in muck and beg God for forgiveness'.

He pauses.

PORTER. And were they cured?

FRONTIER GUARD (*tone changing as he advances*). No! And the first miracle of Matt Talbot was that they didn't murder the little runt afterwards. And it would take a second bloody miracle by him to get the likes of you in here. So get the hell away from this door!

The PORTER *retreats as* ARTHUR *approaches.* ARTHUR *watches him back off and looks at the* FRONTIER GUARD *who shrugs his shoulders.*

FRONTIER GUARD. Kids! (*Looks at him again.*) Think they own the world after a pint of Harp. You looking for something?

ARTHUR *looks over the* FRONTIER GUARD's *head, tracing an outline with his hand.*

ARTHUR. A fish used to be there.

FRONTIER GUARD (*looking at him*). So were the Vikings.

ARTHUR (*pointing*). No, you can still see the outline of the sign.

FRONTIER GUARD (*looking up*). Jaysus you can too. That wasn't today or yesterday.

ARTHUR. The Rock Salmon Club. Used to be my regular. Great bands, poxy name.

FRONTIER GUARD. Yeah, I remember it. That was what . . . God, it's closed over ten years now. Went there a few times myself. Never thought I'd wind up working on the door. I was barred from it often enough. Well, you know yourself.

ARTHUR. Will you stop. I'd me skull busted in here once. They closed the gaff for a while after. What's it now?

FRONTIER GUARD. Bop de bop bop (*Moves his hands to make shapes.*) around the handbags. Under twelves with adults. Have you been away or what?

ARTHUR.Yeah. For too long I think. Thought this place might be the same.

FRONTIER GUARD. Just kids now, disco beat. You're welcome to have a look.

ARTHUR. Naw, you're alright. Thanks anway. I'll see you round.

FRONTIER GUARD. Yeah, good luck. (*Looks over* ARTHUR's *shoulder and talks to himself.*) Ah, here we go, the terrible twins.

As ARTHUR *wanders off the two* GIRLS *have appeared.*

GIRL. Oh God, it's him. Not here, Sharon. Let's go somewhere else.

FRIEND. Where then?

GIRL. Anywhere. I hate him.

FRIEND. Just to be nice to him, only takes a minute and you're in. You rub him up wrong.

GIRL (*shudders*). It's him rubbing me up I hate.

FRIEND. So listen, what are our choices, what do you fancy doing? Stand around the streets all night . . .

The PORTER *passes and leers at her. He roars.*

FRIEND. . . . get a bus home, sit with your da, take up knitting.

GIRL (*imitating knitting movements*). Alright, I'll go in. But you first.

FRIEND (*warning her*). And you keep your trap shut, do you hear. You get us in enough bloody trouble.

They approach the FRONTIER GUARD.

FRONTIER GUARD. Well girls. Anything I can do for you? Suggestions? Requests?

FRIEND. You couldn't try letting us in for a change, Frank?

FRONTIER GUARD. Might have to frisk you first, girls. Need to protect my punters.

FRIEND. You're not the only nightclub in this street.

FRONTIER GUARD. The only one that serves under twelves like you. Does your da know you're out . . . wearing that? So how about it . . . one kiss?

The PORTER *has joined the queue behind the* GIRL. *The* FRIEND *looks back at him.*

FRIEND. Your boyfriend might get jealous. Come on, Frank, please, it's cold.

FRONTIER GUARD. You could try wearing clothes . . . those skimpy things, flaunting yourselves. No, I'd have a moral objection.

FRIEND. Come on, Frank, please.

FRONTIER GUARD. The Brownies meeting is over, girls. Past your bedtime.

FRIEND. You know us, Frank, you let us in last week. We even have comps. We got them in the pub.

She produces two cards which she hands to him.

FRONTIER GUARD. How's your little moody friend tonight? Still stuck up. (*Looks past* FRIEND *at* GIRL *and eyes her.*) So do you call that a dress or an undress?

GIRL. I see why they call them monkey suits.

FRONTIER GUARD *looks past her at the* PORTER, *who grins.*

FRONTIER GUARD. What do you want Chink? No seagulls for your curry in here. Try Dollymount Strand. Go on.

PORTER. Just want to dance, what's it to you?

FRONTIER GUARD. Come up here, and we'll see if you're as yellow as your skin. Back to your own country, boy.

PORTER. I was born here.

FRONTIER GUARD (*tone quieter*). Come here a second, sonny, I won't hurt you.

PORTER *approaches.*

PORTER. What?

FRONTIER GUARD *flicks him around and twists his arm behind his back.*

FRONTIER GUARD. You weren't born anywhere. You were hatched out in the sun.

He shoves him and the PORTER *half stumbles, half falls off stage.*

FRONTIER GUARD. Well, girls . . .?

GIRL. Bastard.

FRIEND (*hissing to* GIRL). Shut up. (*To* FRONTIER GUARD.) Frank, come on, we've . . .

FRONTIER GUARD (*snaps*). Get out of my sight. Now!

FRIEND. Apologise to Frank.

GIRL. I will not.

> GIRLS *back away arguing to left as* ARTHUR *approaches from right.* FRONTIER GUARD *turns.*

FRONTIER GUARD. You back again?

ARTHUR. I'll take you up on that offer.

FRONTIER GUARD. What?

ARTHUR. See the gaff . . . memories.

> FRONTIER GUARD *shrugs his shoulders.*

FRONTIER GUARD. Ah, listen, I'd have second thoughts. You'll get nothing in there except odd looks.

ARTHUR. Not looking for anything.

> *The* GIRLS *have been miming a discussion at back of stage during last few pieces of conversation.*

FRONTIER GUARD. I'm not supposed to allow jeans, for a start.

ARTHUR. Old time's sake, mate.

> *The* PORTER *appears behind the two* GIRLS. *He throws a shape and grins.*

PORTER. Howya girls?

GIRLS (*together*). Fuck off.

> *They approach the door again and queue behind* ARTHUR.

FRONTIER GUARD (*points*). And the sweat shirt, not allowed. Strict rule that, you need a shirt to get in here now.

> ARTHUR *looks behind at the* GIRLS *queuing.*

ARTHUR. So if I had a shirt . . . any shirt?

FRONTIER GUARD. There'd be no problem.

ARTHUR (*turning to FRIEND*). Hey, do us a favour. Lend us your blouse for a moment.

FRIEND. Shag off, will you. (*Calls.*) Frank?

ARTHUR (*to* GIRL). How are you? I'll give it back to you inside.

GIRL. What would I wear?

ARTHUR. Straight swap. (*He grins.*) Come on. Chance it.

He peals off his tee-shirt and holds it out to her. The GIRL *looks at her* FRIEND *and then back at him before she unbuttons her blouse and hands it to him.*

ARTHUR. Thanks.

He puts it on and buttons it up. Turns.

ARTHUR. Bit tight, but it will do. Well . . . any other objections?

FRONTIER GUARD. What the . . . don't get fresh with me, right. I work out every day.

ARTHUR. Weights?

FRONTIER GUARD. Weights, press-ups, sprints, you name it. So watch yourself.

ARTHUR. Can you . . .? Naw, it's a bit hard.

FRONTIER GUARD. Do what? I can do it.

ARTHUR. Naw, it's . . . tough.

FRONTIER GUARD. Don't get fresh. Two hours a day. I can do it.

ARTHUR. Press the back of your left hand flat against your left shoulder. You need to be superfit, mind you.

FRONTIER GUARD. Bullshit, I'll show you.

He begins to press his hand backwards.

ARTHUR. Right against the shoulder.

The GIRL *looks at him and begins to grin. The* FRIEND *hushes her.* ARTHUR *steps past through the doorway. The* FRONTIER GUARD *is now standing in cartoon camp-gay position.*

The PORTER *drunkenly approaches behind his back, looks at him and staggers on through the doorway.*

FRONTIER GUARD (*snapping hand down as he realises he's been had*). Cheeky bastard. He won't get out so easy. I'll wait till Tommy comes on. We'll sort him. (*Turns to the* GIRLS.) What do you want now?

FRIEND. Frank. She didn't mean it . . . what she said. Can we get in?

FRONTIER GUARD (*nods his head towards door*). Go on.

The FRIEND *slips past him and as the* GIRL *is about to follow,* FRONTIER GUARD *puts his hand out to block her.*

FRONTIER GUARD (*to* FRIEND). Go on. I just want a few words with your friend here in the silly jacket.

GIRL. Sharon, don't. Wait.

FRONTIER GUARD. Go on, she'll be in in a minute. Go on or I'll bar you.

The FRIEND *vanishes.* FRONTIER GUARD *turns to the* GIRL.

FRONTIER GUARD. Think you're smart, do you? Anything else you want to take off? Don't let me stop you.

GIRL. No, I'm . . . (*Almost whisper.*) sorry.

FRONTIER GUARD. What did you say?

GIRL (*quietly*). Said, I'm sorry.

FRONTIER GUARD. Can't hear you.

GIRL. I'm sorry for what I said.

FRONTIER GUARD. You be nice to Frank and Frank will be nice to you. (*Puts his arm around her as she tries to wriggle free.*) One kiss for Frank, show that we're pals.

GIRL. Listen, I have to join my friend.

FRONTIER GUARD. She'll wait. Just one. On the cheek, go on. (*Holds her firmer.*)

GIRL. Please.

FRONTIER GUARD. One.

She reluctantly kisses him slightly on the cheek and shivers. She darts from his arms and tries to avoid his hand as she gets past.

FRONTIER GUARD. All the same you girls. See you on the way out, love.

She passes through the door as the music soars. ARTHUR *and the* FRIEND *come forward.* ARTHUR *has the blouse in his hand.*

FRIEND. Go on, give it back to her.

ARTHUR *throws her blouse across to her.*

FRIEND. Give him his thing. God knows what germs . . .

The GIRL *takes off sweat-shirt, waits a minute then throws it across to* ARTHUR. *They look at each other for a moment before the* FRIEND *pulls her away.*

FRIEND (*whispering*). Jesus, you almost blew it again. I'm sick of getting you out of scraps.

GIRL. But he . . .

FRIEND. Leave him for Tommy and Frank.

They are caught up in the sweep of music and the PORTER *and the* FRONTIER GUARD *bounce forward, holding masks and dancing. The* GIRLS *join them, swaying back and forth with masks. The music dips slightly as* GIRLS *stop and, holding the masks at arms length, confer briefly.*

GIRL. What's he like?

FRIEND. Big-headed. You know what they say, big head, small . . .

She gestures with her hands and they laugh, starting to sway again to the louder music. ARTHUR *has re-emerged from the back of the stage to stare around him. His eye finally stops on the* GIRL *and he walks towards her. He taps his mask on her shoulder. The* GIRL *sees him and flicks the mask away. She stands in an aggressive stance. Her* FRIEND *is looking over her shoulder at her. The music dips again.*

ARTHUR. Excuse me.

GIRL. What do you want?

ARTHUR. Just to dance.

GIRL. Why?

ARTHUR. I didn't know you needed a reason when I used to dance here.

GIRL. You do now. They're going to get you, you know. Frank's just waiting for his mate to come in.

ARTHUR. I'll be gone before then. Only wanted a look. Used to dance here once. Come on, one dance.

GIRL (*doubtful*). One dance?

She nods suddenly and they begin to dance. She tries to size him up as they dance.

GIRL. You're old for in here . . . are you married?

He laughs and shakes his head.

GIRL. If me mate sees me with you again she'll think I'm after your pension.

ARTHUR. Who gives a toss what people think?

They continue dancing for a moment.

GIRL. You dance well for an old fellow.

ARTHUR. Black-and-Tans taught us the steps when I was young.

She laughs and they begin to move together. They are drawn closer together but the GIRL pulls back again for a moment before being drawn onwards in the dance.

GIRL. You were funny . . . with Frank . . . the hand.

ARTHUR. Yeah, one day his prince will come. (*Pause.*) From One Hour Photo.

She laughs.

ARTHUR. Saw an old Turk do it to a German foreman. Whole factory line stopped work, everybody cracking up. Eventually the foreman joined in as well . . . then they split the old Turk's head open.

As the music stops they are left cold, paralysed for a moment in their stances. Her FRIEND calls over to her.

FRIEND. Kathy!

The GIRL looks back at her FRIEND, suddenly embarrassed.

FRIEND. Are you coming – (*points.*) Or what?

The FRIEND is staring at ARTHUR. She looks back at the mask in her hand and flicks it away as her voice grows protective.

FRIEND. Come on, will you!

The GIRL *suddenly shrugs* ARTHUR'*s hand from her shoulder.*

GIRL (*in a low voice to* ARTHUR). No, it's crazy.

ARTHUR. What?

GIRL. Find somebody your own age.

ARTHUR. Age isn't important. Only for horses and greyhounds. Listen . . .

GIRL (*confused, crying out*). Please. Can't you see. It *is* for me!

ARTHUR (*stepping back*). I'm sorry. I didn't . . . I'm sorry.

She turns to walk back towards her FRIEND *and they exit as the music begins again and* ARTHUR *moves backwards away from her, looking older now, turning and walking tiredly away towards the back of the stage. The music suddenly stops and the four* DANCERS *turn as one and rush towards the front of the stage, shouting together the word* TAXI! ARTHUR *joins end of queue as the voices jumble together.*

PORTER. No, he's not getting sick, he always walks like that.

FRONTIER GUARD. I was here first, mate. Shove over there.

FRIEND. Please, Clondalkin, there's two of us.

GIRL (*back at* FRONTIER GUARD). Quit pushing, will you.

PORTER. Just up to . . . shag it.

They watch the taxi move off into the distance. GIRL *sees* ARTHUR *and edges back towards* FRIEND. ARTHUR *glances at her as he walks away.*

FRIEND (*joking*). You need a minder. Bleeding geriatric he was. Are you trying to get us a bad name? I mean he has the free travel and all, but . . .

GIRL. Ah just leave him alone, will you.

FRIEND. Ah well, at least you could have brought him home to meet your da unlike those two punks we met last week.
Himself and your da could have had a great time reminiscing about the Emergency and rationing . . . (*Sings.*)

God bless de Valera and Sean McEntee
They gave us the black bread
And the half ounce of tea . . .

GIRL. Give over, Sharon, he beat the creep you were dancing
  with.

FRIEND. At least my fellow had his own teeth.

GIRL. Sharon, you make everything so . . .

She stops moving and speaking when she suddenly glimpses ARTHUR *in
the distance.*

FRIEND. I'd love a burger.

Stage dissolves into burger hut scene with voices together.

PORTER. Double Kuntucky vomit burger with stale fries. I'm
  only messing, honest. Ah no, leave me alone.

FRONTIER GUARD. I'm waiting here half the night.

FRIEND. Shift your hand or I'll burst you.

GIRL. I don't want a burger, Sharon.

ARTHUR (*standing back from the queue*). Fuck this.

ARTHUR turns to exit and we see the GIRL *turn and glimpse him before
the lights focus on* ARTHUR. *The* GIRLS *follow him out. He mimes
pulling a jacket tighter around himself, leans on the wall of the quay, facing
the audience and sighs as he stares down. Once or twice, he shakes his head.*

GIRL. Sharon, there he is by the river. Just wait for me . . . a
  minute.

FRIEND. Don't be thick, Kathy, come on will you.

GIRL. I just want to say goodbye to him.

FRIEND. There's Jimmy's parked outside the Savoy, he'll give us
  a lift. I'm going now.

GIRL (*as* FRIEND *moves*). Sharon . . .

She hesitantly begins to approach ARTHUR. *She pauses at his back
as he tries to clear his ears and then taps him on the shoulder. She jumps back
as he turns. He raises his hand to his head and shakes it again.*

GIRL. You got out OK, I was worried . . .

ARTHUR. What, the bouncer? I'd called his bluff first time.

GIRL (*looking at him*). Are you . . . ?

ARTHUR (*after a moment*). The disco. It's the hissing . . . like being
  underwater for a while when you come out.

GIRL. You mustn't be used to it.

ARTHUR. I'm not. It's been a long time since I was in there.
And it was all live music then. I was there the night the police
raided it when The Chosen Few were playing. I was only
fourteen, but I was there. I saw Gallagher with the Impact and
Skid Row . . .

GIRL (*with increasing incomprehension*). Who?

ARTHUR (*he looks at her*). Skid . . . (*He stops.*) Just bands.

GIRL. Oh.

He looks out towards the audience. She follows his eyes.

GIRL. The river, it's nice at night, disguised like.

ARTHUR. Do they still tell you at school, about O'Connell
Street? The widest street in Europe, they used to say.

GIRL. (*surprised at question*). Don't know. (*Shrugs her shoulders.*) I
never listened to them.

ARTHUR. 'The widest street.' I used to believe them. That
same old Turk said it to me once, about this village. But it's
true of here too.

GIRL (*puzzled*). What is?

ARTHUR. It's all smaller, different when you return. Look at
it . . . O'Connell Street. Just like some honky-tonk provincial
plaza. Everywhere closed except the burger huts, all the buses
gone, everyone milling around drunk, taking to the glittering
lights like aborigines to whiskey. Just like some provincial kip
I've seen dozens of. (*He pauses.*) But it all seemed so grand
once. As a kid I remember . . . being choked up, staring down
at it, as far as the eye could see . . . as a treat from the Pillar.

GIRL. The what?

ARTHUR. Nelson's.

GIRL. Jesus, I wasn't born when that was . . . (*Suddenly
embarrassed.*) Sorry, it must make you feel . . .

ARTHUR (*quietly*). No, I deserve it. I'm talking too much.

GIRL. I keep doing that, don't I.

ARTHUR. No, you're right.

GIRL (*hesitantly*). I didn't mean to hurt you.

ARTHUR. Go on back. You'll meet somebody.

GIRL. No. I've had enough. I hate it. My friend's annoyed with me anyway, she's gone on.

ARTHUR. How will you get home?

GIRL. I'll get a taxi. I have the money.

ARTHUR. I'll take you home if you let me.

The GIRL *looks at him uncertainly.*

GIRL. Have you a car?

He grins and shakes his head as they begin to walk towards the right.

ARTHUR. No, we're out of miracles – there was a run of them earlier. I've a motorbike, bought it when I came home. Broke me, but shag it. Couldn't afford one when I was growing up. Always swore I'd get one, roar down all the lanes I knew as a kid. It's stupid I suppose. Bread and margarine till I get work, but you'd get a pain in your hole being sensible. Do you want to risk it?

GIRL. I survived the dancing clones. I'd say I'll survive it. It has an engine at least?

ARTHUR. This thing would take you across the Sahara desert.

GIRL. Will it get us to Clondalkin?

ARTHUR. Jaysus, I'd sooner chance the Sahara desert, but we'll give it a bash. Here, mind your man.

The PORTER *has been leaning on the barrel at right of stage. He sways forward, wheeling it, singing, then plonks it down, leans on it and looks at them.*

PORTER. Giz a cigarette, go on, will you.

ARTHUR. Sorry mate, I haven't any.

PORTER. Go on, giz . . .

The PORTER *stares down at the barrel while* ARTHUR *leads the* GIRL *over towards where the bike is parked and the* FRONTIER GUARD *and* FRIEND *emerge from the left.*

FRONTIER GUARD. Ruined the play, darling. There was no need to say that at the interval, just because he was wearing jeans at the theatre.

FRIEND. All I asked him was why wasn't he out minding the cars.

FRONTIER GUARD (*producing car keys*). He was a member of the audience, love. He was just wearing jeans.

FRIEND. Well he looked like the lad in the cap you gave the 50p to.

FRONTIER GUARD. Oh, my God!

He walks the length of the stage, searching, then turns and darts back way he has come. The FRIEND *follows him.*

ARTHUR (*avoiding the drunk* PORTER *again*). The bike is here by the monument.

There is a structure at the back of the stage which suggests a bike. A mask in the shape of a helmet is chained to the base of it. The drunk PORTER *wanders back to them.* ARTHUR *bends down about to pick it up and hand it to her.*

PORTER. Is the last 19 gone?

ARTHUR (*bending down for the helmet*). Gone gone, mate. It's after twelve.

PORTER. The last 22?

ARTHUR. They're all gone.

PORTER. The 16s or the 3s?

ARTHUR (*straightening*). All the buses are in bed. It's safe to cross the road.

The drunk PORTER *has swayed across the stage, catching hold of a raised platform which almost falls on his head.* ARTHUR *takes it from him so that it lies on its side.*

FRONTIER GUARD. Oh, my God, darling?

FRIEND. What?

FRONTIER GUARD. The Volvo? The new Volvo is gone?

FRIEND. Oh, darling.

FRONTIER GUARD (*to* ARTHUR). You there, excuse me. My new Volvo, gone, It was there, did you see . . . ?

ARTHUR. No, I'm sorry mate. Just after coming along.

PORTER (*to* ARTHUR). What's wrong with him? What's up?

ARTHUR (*bending again for the helmet*). His flash Volvo. It's gone.

PORTER (*moving over to* FRONTIER GUARD). Your last rolo? It's gone. Here, I'll give you a hand looking. You look there ...

He begins to search while FRONTIER GUARD *and* FRIEND *stand back in horror from him. They walk off and the* PORTER *follows them.*

PORTER. Here, I'll take a lift off you.

ARTHUR *bends to take the helmet and hands it to the* GIRL.

GIRL. Have you only one helmet? What about you?

ARTHUR. Take it.

The GIRL *looks at it in his hands and then takes it and raises it over her head as her recorded voice begins to speak. They sit astride the bike and the lights move to suggest speed with slots of white as they pass beneath lamp-posts.*

GIRL's *voice.*

I accepted it like a pledge
And my arms circled your leather jacket
Your hair blown into my face
We raced up the quays towards my estate

Down a lane choked with scrap
Among the rust eaten ghosts of lorries
Within sight of my father's house
Is where I first loved Arthur Cleary

The engine dies with the last line of the poem. The GIRL *gets off the bike and turns to face* ARTHUR. *He goes to help her remove the helmet but the she steps back, defining her territory. She takes the helmet off, waits a moment, then throws it over to him. She fixes her hair and looks at him. They are both silent as if in their private thoughts.* ARTHUR *leans on the edge of the platform.*

ARTHUR. That disco. I was stupid to go back. It used to be my regular. It was crazy to think the same people might be there, but they all seem to have vanished. It was one of the few places I knew that was still standing. I suppose they're all married by now. Mortgages, ulcers, overdrafts. Far from dancing on their minds.

GIRL. Where were you?

ARTHUR. Places . . . all much the same, you forget the names.

GIRL. Glad to be back?

ARTHUR. Just got to get my bearings. You know, feels like only months I was away and yet you keep turning corners and what should be there isn't there. Sorry, I really am talking too much.

GIRL. No.

ARTHUR. Great place to talk, that's how I remember it. Meeting people, hours passing, evenings, winding up in rooms still talking. Funny – say hello to people now they look at you. Think it's all I've said in the last week – ten fags, milk, the paper, *zwei Brötchen und einige Käse* – they look at you like you've ten heads – oh Jaysus, sorry, a scabby sliced pan please.

GIRL. You're funny.

ARTHUR. How do you mean?

GIRL. Don't know . . . different. (*Pause.*) Why'd you come back to this kip?

ARTHUR. I belong in this kip. It's like at the end of a night, you know, you have to go home.

GIRL. You're welcome to it. If I had a chance I would be gone tomorrow. Anywhere – just out of here. Somewhere anonymous, the freedom of some city where if you walked down the longest street not one person would care who you are or where you're from.

ARTHUR. That can be lonely too.

GIRL. You can live with loneliness. You can't live here. (*She climbs awkwardly onto the top of the barrel and looks at him.*) You're different somehow, you're still breathing. Maybe because you got out. Sometimes . . . don't laugh . . . sometimes I think they've sucked all the air out of this city and people are walking around opening and closing their mouths with nothing coming in, nothing going out. (*She blushes and laughs, jumping down in embarrassment.*) And that sounds crazy, I know.

ARTHUR. No. Some nights working in a canning factory in Denmark I'd stand up on the loading bay beside the hoist and

I'd look down at three in the morning on the workers below, nobody speaking, the limbs moving automatically, the curious stillness behind all the bustle. And I'd start thinking it was the conveyor belt and the loading machine that were alive, that they were thinking more cans for the arms, and at seven in the morning the machines would stop and the arms of the men would move back and forth till somebody remembered to press a switch. So maybe I'm crazy too, but that's why I came home.

The GIRL approaches him. She lifts her arms, then folds them behind her back. He does the same. They repeat the action again.

ARTHUR (*hesitantly*). How . . . old . . . ?

GIRL. Eighteen. (*Pause.*) And you?

ARTHUR (*after a moment*). Thirty-five.

She walks behind the platform in embarrassment and leans on it.

GIRL (*softly*). You don't think I'm a slut?

He smiles and shakes his head. Gradually her head comes to lean against his shoulder.

GIRL. You're not a queer, are you?

He laughs.

ARTHUR. No (*Laughs again*). Why do you ask?

GIRL. Don't know. I suppose . . . well, you haven't tried anything. (*Quickly.*) Not that I want you to, like . . . but often lads can be pushy, just want to get you out by yourself and then get away.

ARTHUR. So did I once. So did every man.

The GIRL comes back around to face him.

GIRL. You won't take the wrong idea about me.

ARTHUR. I'll only take whatever idea you want.

GIRL (*leaning her face towards him*). Will you . . . ?

They embrace and kiss. There is a subtle interplay of lights to suggest time passing. Lights return to normal as the GIRL turns around so that she is still in ARTHUR's arms but facing away from him. They are both silent as if in their private thoughts.

ARTHUR. It was the strangest thing.

GIRL (*looks up*). What?

ARTHUR. The church. Near the flats. There was such an overspill of people living there that they put up a temporary one. The tin one they called it – a sort of huge prefab. Inside as a child you'd hear the rain splattering against the corrugated tin roof. I'd forgotten that sound till one winter in a Dutch factory ... sleeping in those long iron dormitories, the Turks, the Moluccans, the first few of the Irish. I'd wake at night and remember ... like it would always be there, part of me ... to return to. (*Stops.*) First night I got home I went walking, buildings boarded up, new names over shops. I came to the lane where the church had been. There was a crackling sound, then I smelt the smoke. They were clearing the site. There were just the girders of the church left and everything else still smouldering, waiting to be shifted. Hadn't been there or any other church since I was fifteen. But it was in my mind as something that would never change.

Listening to him the GIRL *suddenly shivers and steps away.*

ARTHUR (*concerned*). What's wrong?

GIRL (*retreating behind the barrel*). I don't know. You know that feeling like this has happened before. Suddenly ... it scared me.

ARTHUR. Shush ... it will be dawn soon. Did you ever wait up for the dawn.

The GIRL *shakes her head.*

ARTHUR (*approaching her*). So strange, you're exhausted, you can't go on, and then ... felt it on so many nights working in factories ... the first hint of light and you can feel it through your body, energy, from nowhere, strength you didn't know you had from deep within you ... Then the light comes and it floods you. Hey ...

GIRL. What?

ARTHUR. Never thought I'd ... feel new again, like now ...

GIRL (*moving away, this time behind the platform which she leans on*). Arthur, I don't want to hear ... you scare me, I don't always understand you ... you don't talk like real people.

ARTHUR. Real people?

Silently the PORTER *and the* FRIEND *emerge on stage. The*

PORTER *stands at the front left while the* FRIEND *who has donned a mask stands with her back to the audience.*

GIRL. You know what I mean . . . safe. (*She points.*) See that house, with the light still on.

ARTHUR (*looking*). Yeah.

GIRL. That's his light, will burn till I go in. Never this late before. He'll be worried . . . listening for me. It's funny . . . when I was young and he was working. (*A pause as she looks down at her hands.*) He talked like you . . . like he wasn't scared of looking over his shoulder . . . like . . .

The PORTER *suddenly turns, his face white with anger, his hands clenched.* ARTHUR *retreats to edge of stage.*

PORTER. And now you're taking up with this fellow, this knacker.

GIRL. He's not, Dad.

PORTER. Well, whatever he is, he's too old for you. Can't you see child, he's no job, he's got nothing. Good Christ, I worked hard enough all these years to try and get you something, to try and lift you up. Where's he going, where can he bring you? Some corporation flat. You're only a child yet. You're throwing your life away for him.

GIRL. It's not serious Dad, I've only met him twice. I'm not even sure about him. It's just that he's . . . different. There's something . . .

PORTER. Different! May be different to you but I've seen his like all my life. Every week there'd be another one of them in the factory and within the month they'd be gone. Fly-boys. Drifters. Only certainty was that they'd be gone. How could he build a life for you like I've tried to build for your mother? Tell me that, how? A knacker in a leather jacket, with one hand longer than the other and the rattle of his bike waking the street at every hour of the night. What's so special about him then?

GIRL (*crying out suddenly*). He's not dead! He's not beaten! He's . . .

PORTER (*quietly*). Like I am, is it? Beaten?

There is a pause while the mood changes. Then the GIRL *speaks quietly.*

GIRL. Do you remember Dad? Bull Island? (PORTER *smiles ruefully*.) The thrill of hiding up there in the sand dunes waiting for you to find me, peering out at you climbing up. Remember?

PORTER. I'd park the car on the strand and you'd be gone before my back was turned. Always running. A proper little rascal.

The GIRL *suddenly runs over to the far side of the stage with childish strides. She hides behind the barrel as he comes looking for her. She runs out, avoiding him and then, looking over her shoulder, stands for a moment with hands clenched, giggling. He circles her and when she tries to run he catches her and throws her up in his arms. She shouts for him to let her go and he lowers her onto the floor where she puts her feet on his shoes so that when he pulls her up again she is dancing with him like a child with her father. A note of sadness enters his voice.*

PORTER. That was a good car that. I kept it well.

GIRL. You'll have a car again Dad. Only a matter of time.

The PORTER *lets her go, looking down at his hands in a gesture of futility.*

GIRL. You looked after us well, Dad. You still do.

PORTER. Feel so useless love. Wish I was dead sometimes. You'd have the insurance then at least.

GIRL (*crying out as she runs to him*). Daddy, don't say that. Don't wish it. You're the best.

PORTER (*lifting his hands to examine them, then pulls the platform back up and pushes it into place fiercely as he speaks*). I've good hands. Can make things with these. Give me wood and I'll make it. Tables, chairs, shelves. I never thought I'd be idle with these. A skill for life they said. Always find something.

GIRL. It doesn't matter, Daddy. You've done so much, all your life. It's time to rest now.

PORTER. The women cried the day we left. Out in the open at the gates of the factory. The television were there. All the fuss, the papers. Then they left us alone. With just our thoughts.

Lights fade on him and the GIRL *and rise on* ARTHUR *who is now standing beside the barrel and on the* FRIEND *who has turned with the mask still over her face.* ARTHUR *turns slowly till he is facing her in silhouette.*

ARTHUR. Ma. I know you can't hear, but I talk to you still. You have to talk to someone.

FRIEND. I know son. I talked to you often enough those years you were abroad.

ARTHUR. I was never one for writing, Ma.

FRIEND. Never expected you to, son. You had your own life.

ARTHUR. She's so much younger than me, Ma. All the lads I knew, they're all gone. The girls with prams, so suddenly old.

FRIEND (*softly*). Fifteen years son. A sorrowful decade and a half.

ARTHUR. We had our joyful one.

FRIEND (*ironic as she slowly lowers the mask*). How often did I see you on your knees telling your beads?

ARTHUR (*laughs*). As often as I saw you.

FRIEND. Still, we had our good times.

ARTHUR. Mornings I'd climb down the steps from these flats and people would shout, Arthur Cleary! Arthur Cleary! Come in! Come in!

FRIEND. Me laughing from the balcony at your mates trying to dance like Zorba the Greek.

ARTHUR *puts his hands out onto two imaginary shoulders and moves his body in the motions of a Greek dance.*

ARTHUR. Closing time Fridays walking up from town, playing football in the traffic. Remember I'd bring you a baby power and we'd sit round drinking bottles of Guinness from brown paper bags.

FRIEND. At three in the morning, they'd still be arriving. Is that Arthur Cleary's? Have we found the place?

ARTHUR. This is the place, but now I can't find them. Ma, I can't find you. I can't find my old self. Feel so old . . . except when she's beside me.

There is a pause to suggest time passing.

ARTHUR. Mrs Burke told me, Ma, how you lived out those last years on white bread and tea.

FRIEND. They barred me from the pub son, when the new

owners did it up. Barred when I was the first woman who refused to be corralled inside the snug years before. Singing, they said I was. What's a pub for only singing?

ARTHUR. You broke your hip trying to cross the road when a security van broke the lights.

FRIEND. Shagging Culchie drivers.

ARTHUR. I wasn't running from you Ma. You know that, don't you? (*She doesn't answer.*) It was just . . . the time. So easy to drift between jobs and places, it just seemed right to wander off for a while and then wander back. Only I never did. Oh, I often imagined it, arriving back, no warning, nothing, just being there at dawn with a bottle of brandy and the stubble of three days travel. (*Quietly.*) Only it wasn't like that, was it?

FRIEND. You've never been to the grave son. Though I was never there myself before I went to keep him company in it.

ARTHUR. Had a drink for you Ma, instead. Knew you'd prefer that. Among the disco lights and the canned music. And sang *Who Fears to Speak of Easter Week* for you. The owner almost shat himself. I think he thought I was cracked.

FRIEND. When did we ever give a shite what any of them thought of us, son?

ARTHUR. When did we ever Ma? (*Pause.*) Why am I talking to you, Ma? The dead cannot talk.

FRIEND. They can, son. But only among themselves.

Spotlight fades on FRIEND *on final word as* ARTHUR *looks back, suddenly frightened as the lights fade and rise on the* GIRL *who is standing in the centre of the stage holding the motorbike helmet in her hands.* ARTHUR *approaches her cautiously and after looking at him for a moment she silently hands him the helmet back. He looks at it for a moment and then turns away and walks slowly off to the far left of stage where he puts the helmet down and stares into space. The* GIRL *backs away and then silently approaches the* PORTER *and mimes saying goodbye, her hand resting for a moment on his shoulder, her lips lightly touching the back of his neck. The lights die on them and return to the* FRIEND *who has run on-stage and sits on the box. The* GIRL *approaches her.*

FRIEND. Did you say goodbye to him, like we agreed?

GIRL. I did. (*She sits on the box as well.*) He was waiting for me along the quays, staring at the water like he always did. Didn't think I'd have the courage. 'Arthur, I'm sorry,' I said . . . 'it's just too big a gap, it's not right.' He never spoke, Sharon, his face looked old, suddenly, like all the air had drained from it.

FRIEND. I know it's hard. You were fairly gone on him but it's for the best. You'll see. Be like old times again.

The FRIEND *rises and the* GIRL *follows her.*

GIRL. All the way home, felt like throwing myself from the bus. I came in, Sharon, saw my father, just sitting staring at the box. And I remembered a man who feared no other, a brown wage packet left on an oilskinned table. If he could only cry, I could stay with him, but his kind were never taught how to show grief. I need to learn to breathe. Sharon, I need Arthur and I don't know how to ask, to teach me . . . to wake up and not be afraid of what the day will bring. (*Pause.*) I've packed a bag, Sharon. If he'll take me in I'll go to him, or I'll go somewhere else, anywhere, but I don't fit here anymore. (*Pause.*) Will you be glad for me?

FRIEND. What's wrong with here?

GIRL. You hate it, you always say you do.

FRIEND. But I'll settle for it. I'm not running half-cocked after anybody. Real life isn't like that. This isn't a bleeding movie Kathy, real people don't do this. You're even starting to talk like that header.

GIRL. I can't breathe here, Sharon.

FRIEND. Have you ever tried opening and closing your mouth? For God's sake, Kathy, your man's a fossil and he doesn't need to breathe. You're just walking out, leaving me.

GIRL. Not you, I'll see you the same, just . . .

FRIEND. How could it be the same . . . you, me and him? Been calling for you since I was five . . . for school, dances, mitching out, covering up for you. And you say it will be the same. We were never good enough for you, isn't that right?

GIRL. Sharon, please.

FRIEND. You'll beg for one of these houses one day. You'll settle for a squawling brat and yellow pack bread and a thrill off the fridge, if you're lucky. Just like the rest of us.

GIRL. I'm going, Sharon.

FRIEND. Go on then and good luck, kid. 'Cause I won't know you when you're running back in a week's time with your tail between your legs. Do you hear?

The FRIEND *storms off-stage and the* GIRL *is left alone as the* PORTER *walks silently past. The recorded voice is heard.*

GIRL's *voice.*

I had a room with fresh linen
And parents to watch over me
A brown dog slept at my feet
I left them for Arthur Cleary.

When the lights rise they suggest dawn. ARTHUR *is still standing at the edge of the stage. He has a bunch of keys in his hand. The* GIRL *approaches and stands a few feet away from him, speaking to his back.*

GIRL. Been walking all night, round and round these flats. (*Pause.*) I left, Arthur. Am I crazy or what?

Neither speak for a moment.

ARTHUR. I don't know. And I don't care, except you're here.

He throws her the keys and, as she comes forward they embrace. The lights go down and the sinister music from the first FRONTIER GUARD *Border scene returns. When a weak light returns it is shining above* ARTHUR's *head as he stands against the wooden platform with the* PORTER *shining his torch up and down the bars from behind. The* FRONTIER GUARD *approaches and shines his torch at* ARTHUR's *face.*

FRONTIER GUARD. Passport please.

ARTHUR *recovers.*

ARTHUR. Oh, sorry.

He hands him a passport which the FRONTIER GUARD *opens and examines.*

FRONTIER GUARD. Ah Irish. Irish. Boom-boom! eh! (*He laughs.*)

ARTHUR. Yeah. Boom-bleeding-boom.

FRONTIER GUARD *hands him back the passport.*

ARTHUR. Eh? Where am I now? Which side of the border am I on?

FRONTIER GUARD. What does it matter to you Irish? Either side you are a long way from home.

ARTHUR (*shrugs his head towards the light behind him*). What's he looking at the wheels for?

FRONTIER GUARD. Looking for? (*laughs.*) It is the rules, Irish. We will go on soon. (*He turns to leave him.*)

ARTHUR (*suddenly puzzled*). Wait, have you . . . eh, have you checked my passport before?

FRONTIER GUARD *returns, shining torch at* ARTHUR.

FRONTIER GUARD. Before? We only check once.

ARTHUR. Well then, do I know you from somewhere?

FRONTIER GUARD. Maybe you take this train before, Irish?

ARTHUR. No, somewhere else. Somewhere different.

FRONTIER GUARD. You know a brothel called BB's in Stuttgart?

ARTHUR. No.

FRONTIER GUARD. Neither do I! (*He laughs heartily.*) Funny, eh?

ARTHUR. I do know you. Wait.

He looks closely at the man who shrugs his shoulders and walks behind the platform. Suddenly the PORTER *and himself begin to sing in a Dublin accent.*

FRONTIER GUARD & PORTER. Ah poor old Dicey Riley, she has taken to the sup, sup, sup!

FRONTIER GUARD *comes back around and stares at* ARTHUR. *He holds his hand out and speaks in his Deignan voice.*

FRONTIER GUARD. Hey, wait a minute (*He shakes his hand.*) I know you.

Reverting back to the FRONTIER GUARD *he walks back behind platform, leaving* ARTHUR *confused and frightened.*

FRONTIER GUARD & PORTER (*out of sight*). Poor oul Dicey Riley, she will never give it up!

Lights go back, there is a banging and as they rise the PORTER *scarpers, with child-like steps across the stage to exit at far side. The* FRONTIER GUARD *emerges with a leather book in his hand, (which he has been banging on the wooden supports of the stage) and shouts.*

FRONTIER GUARD. Frankie! Young Frankie Doyle! I saw you there, I'm no fool you know. Come back here, tell your mother I want to see her.

ARTHUR *has turned to stand on left side of platform with his hands around the* GIRL. *The* FRIEND *emerges on right side of stage.*

FRONTIER GUARD (*politely to the* FRIEND *as he turns*). Ah, Mrs Burke. Fine weather.

FRIEND. The better for not being in your clutches, Mr Deignan.

FRONTIER GUARD. Always here to help Mrs Burke.

FRIEND. Go and shite.

She exits.

FRONTIER GUARD (*smiles after her*). Charming. (*Turns back to imaginary door and shouts.*) I know you're in there Mrs Doyle! I'm not a fool you know. If you can't pay them you shouldn't take out loans. (*He consults his ledger.*) Mrs Doyle, didn't I see young Frankie from the car driving up to the flats. Three weeks Mrs Doyle, three weeks. God would have made the world three times. You think that husband of yours could have made three pounds even. Easy knowing the creator of heaven and earth didn't come from this block of flats.

Suddenly the FRONTIER GUARD *sees* ARTHUR *and the* GIRL.

FRONTIER GUARD. Eh, what are you at then? (ARTHUR *and the* GIRL *ignore him.*) Headtheball, I'm talking to you!

ARTHUR (*quietly, still looking at door*). I live here.

FRONTIER GUARD. Since when? Old Mrs Cleary used to live there.

ARTHUR (*turning*). I was born here.

FRONTIER GUARD. Tell me another. I've had me eye on that place since the oul bat died. A troublesome oul biddy she was too. This law and that law. (*He snorts.*)

ARTHUR (*quietly, still not looking at him*). Nice to know my mother had such a concerned friend.

FRONTIER GUARD (*snaps fingers*). Wait a minute. I have you. Arthur! Arthur Cleary! Sure, wasn't I a year behind you in school? Deignan, Larry Deignan. My mother had the shop on the corner. Sure, I used to look up to you. Only the mother, you know, wasn't too keen. (*Pause.*) So, the famous son, eh, the wanderer.

ARTHUR. Will you stop?

The FRONTIER GUARD *approaches.*

FRONTIER GUARD. No offence meant, Arthur. I thought you were just squatters. You get some dodgy types around here. (*Puts out his hand.*)

ARTHUR (*ignoring his hand*). So I see.

FRONTIER GUARD. Don't know what brought you back. Great to see you all the same. Do you remember . . . the day you had to be dug out of old McCarthy the teacher, the day you were expelled from school? God, you were a legend then. You remember me, Arthur? Don't you? And the mother? The little shop on the corner. Here, I'll give you my card. I could be of use to you settling in.

ARTHUR (*ignores his hand, he finds the keys*). I remember the firelighter.

FRONTIER GUARD (*bewildered*). The what?

ARTHUR. The young tinker lad my mother gave a threepenny bit to once. He went looking for sweets in your mother's shop. She gave him a firefighter and a penny change. He thought it was coconut and stuffed it in his mouth. You must remember him now, you were laughing about it long enough. Never able to speak again. I used to see him begging near the Four Courts. Your mother always said, it will teach his sort a lesson. (*He gives a slight laugh.*) Yeah, I remember her well.

FRONTIER GUARD *moves in close as if about to strike* ARTHUR, *then gives a little laugh.*

FRONTIER GUARD. Always the jokes Arthur, eh? I'll leave you my card. It will be a pleasure hearing from you.

He presses it into ARTHUR's *hand and exits.* ARTHUR *looks at it, then tears it up and exits into where the flat would be. The* GIRL, *who has been leaning on the platform during this, now comes forward and carefully picking up the pieces of the card, stares at them before exiting with them carefully held in her hand.*

ACT TWO

A motorbike engine is heard for a moment in the darkness before the engine is switched off, and the soundtrack takes on a rural nature as the lights come up. There is a shout before ARTHUR *enters first from the back of the stage at a trot as though after coming down a slope and turns to catch the* GIRL *who rushes on after him.*

ARTHUR. No problem to you. I told you so.

GIRL. No problem for you in those boots. The feet are stung off me. There's nettles up there like bamboos.

ARTHUR. We'll soon be rid of those.

He kneels and plucking imaginary leaves from ground, begins to rub her lower legs.

ARTHUR. Dock leaves. Your only men. (*The* GIRL *is looking around her.*) Well, was I right? Knocksedan. Isn't it great?

GIRL. Tell me about it again.

He stops rubbing and looks up at her.

ARTHUR. Sure can't you see it with your own eyes?

GIRL. It's not the same. It's only weeds and bushes and rocks, but when you describe it it's special, it's your world.

ARTHUR (*looking around him*). It's as much yours as mine. That's what's special about it . . . it's just here, it's anybody's.

GIRL. It's not here Arthur. Not the way you knew it. With other people . . . well places seem to pass before them like scenes in a film, but with you it's all kept inside – everywhere's special.

ARTHUR. It's just a place.

GIRL. All you have are places . . . and the dole.

ARTHUR. We manage.

GIRL (*going to sit on barrel*). You're a sap, Arthur Cleary and I'm worse for going along with you. Tell me about this one. Come on. Who did you come here with?

ARTHUR *comes over for her to climb on his back. They stand staring out at the audience.*

ARTHUR. Anyone who would come. Or just alone.

GIRL. Girls?

ARTHUR. Girls who'd go sick from the factories to swim here in the river with me. Two hours getting them to take their dresses off for five minutes in the water. (*Grins.*) But it was worth it. That mound there. (*He points.*) Man-made. Older than Christ. Some evenings I'd climb up there in the dusk and it was as though you could almost hear it saying to you. I know you. I know everything you will ever feel. I have felt it all before.

GIRL. More likely it was saying. Stop standing on my skull, you're giving me a headache. Hills don't talk Arthur. (*She looks around her again.*) Was this always here?

ARTHUR. Of course.

GIRL. Never saw it or knew it. All these hidden bits of the city . . . (*Her voice changes.*) Six weeks today Arthur.

ARTHUR. You should go back, see him.

GIRL. Tell him what . . . now I know Knocksedan and the Pigeon House and Howth Head at night and the lanes off Thomas Street. Jesus Arthur, you couldn't explain that to real people . . . it's not real life, that's what Sharon said.

ARTHUR. What's real life; a clean job, pretending you own some mortgaged house on an estate, death from cancer at forty?

GIRL. That's what Sharon said I'd settle for. This is so good it frightens me . . . (*She taps him on the head as though it was wooden.*) Arthur are you listening to me?

ARTHUR. I am in my granny. I'm wondering are the logs still down there that you could cross the river by. We'll climb down and have a gander.

GIRL. Jesus, more nettles, more briars.

ARTHUR *lowers her down his back.*

ARTHUR. Sure a little prick will do you no harm.

GIRL. Oh, are you coming as well?

She runs as he grabs at her in mock anger and chases her towards the edge of the platform which she mounts and, picking up his helmet, she places it back to front on his head. She turns him round and, with a little kick, sends him out into the middle of the stage. Sinister music begins as she retreats and both the FRONTIER GUARD *and the* PORTER *emerge onto the stage.* ARTHUR *gropes his way forward until his foot hits against the box. He stops and takes the helmet off as the* FRONTIER GUARD *and the* PORTER *form themselves into a queue behind him, slouching down with the look of broken men with long patience.* ARTHUR *is standing facing the barrel, staring around him as if confused at how he got there. The queue moves in a sequence of short mimed jerks, during which* ARTHUR *glances behind him to see the* PORTER. *There is silence for a moment as* ARTHUR *turns to look at the* PORTER. *Then he turns again to stare at him. During the ensuing conversation the* FRONTIER GUARD *keeps staring between them.*

ARTHUR. Johnny isn't it . . . Johnny Carroll.

PORTER *looks suspicious and then recognises him.*

PORTER. Arthur Cleary? I thought you were off in Germany?

ARTHUR. I was, but I'm back. (*Looks up.*) You'd have thought they would have painted the dole office in my absence. But, come here, I thought you were well in for life up there in McGuirks.

PORTER. I was. Till I was laid off. But that's four years ago. Sure that place is just a crater now. All that row of factories is the same. You can see them from the train with the roofs caved in. There's nothing here now Arthur. Not like long ago.

ARTHUR. Do you remember, where was it . . . that timber yard off Francis Street? We both started together at nine o'clock. A right hole. We left it at eleven. Told your man to fuck himself.

PORTER. And we were fixed up over in that carton factory in the Combe by lunchtime. Those were the days. There was always a start somewhere. Seems like another world now, walking from one job to the next. If people get in anywhere these days they stick like plasticine.

ARTHUR (*thinks*). Mind you, the carton factory was a hole too. (*Snaps fingers.*) What a weird bunch worked there. Remember – Dockets?

PORTER (*mock voice*). Have you a docket for that, son? Have you a docket? (*Normal voice.*) And the little guy in the white coat. You could barely see his head over the machines.

ARTHUR (*hand over his mouth*). 'Stop walking in that hole' (*Looks around.*) Who said that? If I catch the lad who said that he's fired.

PORTER. Remember Boots?

ARTHUR. Boots! For God's sake. I'd forgotten him. Refused to wear anything else, just the one pair day or night. We used to claim he slept in them.

PORTER. You had a song about him, remember? The Elvis voice, up on the pallet of cartons, doing all the movements with the brush. Remember Boots even caught you?

ARTHUR. How did it go?

PORTER. Jaysus, it's a long time.

ARTHUR. Wait: (*Mock Elvis accent.*)
'My granny would like to roll and roll'

He points at the PORTER *waiting for response.*

PORTER. 'But I'm too tired to dig her up,'

TOGETHER.

My goldfish woud love a bowl
'Cause he hates crapping in a cup, .
My wife's abandoned me,
But I don't care two hoots
'Cause all I really want to do
Is stomp around in black rubber wellington boots.

The two of them have mimed a dance during verse to the increasing bemusement of the FRONTIER GUARD. *Now with their hands impersonating guitars they move in for the kill, moving closer and closer together with each word until the* FRONTIER GUARD *is squashed between them, almost bent double with his hands still in his pockets.*

TOGETHER. 'Boots! Boots! Boots! Boots!'

FRONTIER GUARD (*ironically, looking at* ARTHUR). The King, eh?

PORTER. The real McCoy. Arthur Cleary.

ARTHUR. That's where we first met Eamonn, 'member –

PORTER. The original rocker. (*He throws shapes.*)

ARTHUR. Suede shoes, the lapels on the jacket, the whole works. Where's he now?

PORTER (*quietly*). He's fucking dead Arthur. He blew his own brains out last year. We're all fucking dead Arthur, or as good as, in this kip.

ARTHUR. We've a few pints to sink before they lower us down yet. Do you remember the time . . .

PORTER (*surly*). No. It's gone.

FRONTIER GUARD *nudges* ARTHUR *with his shoulder.*

FRONTIER GUARD. Will you hurry fucking up. Some of us have jobs to go to.

ARTHUR (*noticing* FRONTIER GUARD *and speaking to him*). Do I know you, mate?

FRONTIER GUARD. You don't know nothing.

ARTHUR (*puzzled*). From somewhere . . . that face. (*He moves forward to the barrel.*) Half two?

He steps back, deflated, and picks up the helmet. The two men circle him.

PORTER (*turning with a shrug of his shoulders*). Welcome home Arthur!

As the two of them leave the stage the FRIEND has come around from the back of the stage carrying a mask in each hand. The FRIEND will speak for both masks, changing her voice slightly for each. First mask peers down as if from a balcony.

FIRST MASK (*raised*). Come 'ere.

SECOND MASK (*lowered*). What?

FIRST MASK. Come 'ere.

SECOND MASK (*raised*). What?

GIRL appears and walks across the stage, miming the action of turning a key in a lock and vanishes off the stage again.

FIRST MASK. That's her there, Phyllis! Moved in with him bold as brass and his mother barely cold in the grave. The young ones now. Would you be up to them? Never had that class of yoke here before he came back.

SECOND MASK. Wild like the mother, Mrs Doyle. And sure what harm are they doing? Isn't it good to see somebody smiling in this place?

FIRST MASK. I don't know. A fool's paradise never lasts long. It's easy to smile without two children bawling, it's easy to smile when you don't have to sell your soul to that bastard every time an ESB bill comes in, or one of them gets sick. (*Stops and stares off to left with alarm in her voice.*) Is that Mr Deignan's car Phyllis, there stopped at the lights?

SECOND MASK. No, that's just brown. His is shite coloured.

FIRST MASK. Some days you'd be afraid to take the plug out of the sink in case his head would pop up. You know what Mrs Kennedy said to him; You're so famous round here Mr Deignan, she said, they'll have you in the Wax Works soon, only they won't need to make a model of you.

SECOND MASK. Will you relax Mrs Doyle, it's moving off. Lord you're fierce jumpy. What you need now is a toy boy.

FIRST MASK. A toy boy? I'm lucky to get a bar of KitKat and a lie in. Come 'ere to me. (*The masks are drawn closer and the voice drops.*) Do you know what he said to me the other morning, the youngest crying in the next room and him lying there with the teeth in the glass beside the bed. (*The* FRIEND *begins to lower the masks down.*) He puts a hand out suddenly and says he, (*A gruff mumble.*) Lie back Rosie, it's Saturday.

The lights go down and up on where ARTHUR *is to the far left of the stage, staring into the wings as though gazing from window. The* GIRL *is behind him lying on the platform.*

ARTHUR. He's out there again.

GIRL. Who is?

ARTHUR. Deignan.

GIRL. Forget him.

ARTHUR (*bitterly*). God, I remember him now, a little brat in short trousers, perpetual snot on his nose and even then he could buy and sell you. He used to steal sweets from the mother and flog them for half price. Then when we were fourteen . . . I remember . . . it was Johnnies. Don't know where he got them, but he told the whole school I'd bought four off him one evening and came back the next day for two.

Jaysus, they were buying them by the newtide, every penny they had ... hidden under beds, going green, never used ... and back next week for more in case he'd tell people they hadn't needed them.

The GIRL *laughs.*

ARTHUR. Before I went away I saw him one night ... Monkstown ... all the little rich kids with money and no sense. He was selling them joints, ready-rolled for half a crown. They were having to be carried home to Mammy by their friends. I took a pull ... herbal tobacco and loose shag ... he winked up at me: 'Do you want a cut Arthur, be my man here.' Christ, he looked pathetic, the elephant flares, huge tie like a red carpet. (*He pauses and his tone changes.*) I saw him yesterday in Drumcondra. Collecting rent. He's four houses there in flats. Warrens. You should have seen the number of bells on every door.

GIRL. Who gives a fuck about him? Come away Arthur.

ARTHUR. That Doyle woman is with him. Like a dog keeping its distance, terrified of a kick.

GIRL. Arthur! You're like an old woman staring out the window. You get on my nerves whenever he's around.

ARTHUR *turns.*

ARTHUR. Have we tea?

GIRL. You know we haven't. We'll do without. It's not important.

ARTHUR. Dole day tomorrow.

GIRL. I know. It's OK.

ARTHUR. Bread?

GIRL. Arthur, stop this.

ARTHUR. It was easier by myself. I didn't mind the bad days. Just take to the bed, take them in my stride. But now ...

GIRL. Don't Arthur, please.

ARTHUR. You know I'm trying, love. Every old foreman I knew. Every factory that's left. I want to look after you.

GIRL (*screams*). Stop! Can't you see. You'll become like them, you're sounding like my da. (*She rises as* ARTHUR *tries to*

speak.) I'm not fragile. I'm not some ornament made of glass.
I'm flesh and I'm blood. I don't need looking after – I need to
live. Listen, you're different Arthur and I don't mind if we
starve, just don't change, not for me.

ARTHUR. I just want to give you . . . things.

GIRL. I didn't come to you for things. I came to you for hope. I
can do without anything, except that. Shag the tea and the bread
Arthur, just make me laugh.

He sits on floor and looks up at her.

ARTHUR. The vegetarian that died . . .

GIRL. There was a big turnip at the funeral.

He claps his hands in a flourish. They both laugh.

ARTHUR. Did you hear about the blind circumciser?

GIRL. Don't tell me.

ARTHUR. He got the sack. (*He winces, then continues.*) The Kerry
suicide found hanging from the ceiling?

GIRL. What?

ARTHUR. Sean D'Olier.

GIRL. Where do you find them?

ARTHUR. Met them all on a bus last week, they were getting the
free travel. (*Pause.*) Maybe I've been away so long they're new
again. (*Pause.*) Some days I get lost. Do you know that? My feet
think they know the way and I find myself turning down a side
street that's gone. There's nothing there, just a few barrels and
some old gotchie in a hut watching over the cars parked where
the buildings used to be. Sometimes . . . it frightens me . . . you
know like in a dream . . . the sequence doesn't make sense . . .

*The GIRL climbs to her feet and interrupts him suddenly, blurting the
sentence out, half embarrassed.*

GIRL. I love you Arthur. At first I wasn't sure. First I was just
running away from everything else. But now I know. I'll follow
you anywhere, any place. I want to live in that city you carry in
your heart. You don't need this place to make it real, it's dead
here, finished. We could go away, together. We could be free
Arthur. Out in those foreign cities you've talked about, those
names . . .

ARTHUR. No. (*Shouts.*) Why do you always say this? Why can't you let me be . . . here?

GIRL. It's killing you. You're changing. Go Arthur.

ARTHUR. No. I'm . . . (*Quietly.*) I'm scared to go back. Fifteen years, love. In limbo – autobahns, trains, borders. But I was never homeless, always knew I'd come back. Here, at least, I know who I am. I don't have to register my address with the police. Can't you see that, love? (*He glances towards the window again.*) He's back.

GIRL. Who?

ARTHUR. Deignan. With her again . . . that Doyle woman.

GIRL. Sure, it's only around the corner.

ARTHUR. What is?

GIRL. You don't know Arthur, sure you don't. You don't know nothing. The post office Arthur. It's children's allowance day. He holds her book as security, gives it to her before she goes in to collect, takes it and the cash from her when she comes out. (ARTHUR *stares at her.*) You just don't understand this city, do you?

ARTHUR *is silent for a moment taking this in.*

ARTHUR. The bastard! I'll kill him!

He goes to move towards the door and the GIRL *jumps up to grab him. She tries to calm him as he curses Deignan.*

ARTHUR. Little jumped up bastard! I should have drowned him when I had the chance!

GIRL. For Christ's sake Arthur, stop! Have sense!

They tussle, at first with him trying to break free and her attempting to restrain him but gradually the struggle turns into an embrace.

GIRL. I don't want to lose you. Don't want to go back to that . . . hopelessness.

He strokes her hair, soothing her.

ARTHUR. There's nothing to fear love. I've had his measure all my life.

GIRL (*softly*). Not any more, Arthur. He's more dangerous than you think. You don't know him. How he works.

ARTHUR. All my life I've known him and his sort.

GIRL. For my sake, fear him.

ARTHUR. You're always afraid.

GIRL. Afraid for you. For the rest, I would spit in their faces.
It's so good here with you it frightens me. I keep saying that, I
keep thinking nothing this good can last.

ARTHUR (*stroking her hair*). When I found you I found home
again. No matter what you say. No matter if I get lost at
times. With you Kathy, it feels like it was. There's nothing
more I want now, nowhere else to go. At times it's like this
whole city's in terror of something that will never happen.
Let's forget them all. We have this flat and each other, there's
nobody can break that apart.

GIRL (*turning to look up at him with urgency in her voice*). Arthur,
listen to me, they're all watching you and you don't realise it.
The pushers, they hate the way you look at them. Even the
kids round here, Arthur, they haven't a clue who you are. I
see them dismantling that bike with their eyes, breaking it
down into needles and fixes. To them all, you're just an
outsider. And now Deignan. You remind him of things. His
kind own this city now, Arthur. He'll want to own you as well.
Don't you know that?

ARTHUR (*laughing as he climbs up on the platform*). I own this city
and you and the thousands of us who live in warrens of estates
and these blocks of crumbling flats. It's ours Kathy, and it
doesn't matter what titles they give themselves or what
rackrents they collect, it doesn't even matter if they tear down
every street so we can't recognise it. They still can't take it
away from us. Because when they're rotting in the soil there'll
still be thousands of us, swarming out into the thoroughfares
every evening. (*He climbs down to take her in his arms.*) Come on,
no more squabbling. This room is getting us down. (*He runs his
hand down to her chin and gently cups it.*) Lift up your head Kathy.
We'll leave the bike here for a change, walk down through our
town together, yours and mine. I want to show you off.

She looks up at him and they kiss.

GIRL. You never heard a word I said, did you?

ARTHUR (*smiles*). Silly talk from a silly time. (*He begins to walk
across the stage with her legs resting on his.*) Dole day tomorrow

love. Bread, tea, pints of Guinness and, you'll see, work will come soon. Summer's coming. I could always knock out a living in the summer months, no matter what. Just wait. That's when it will all come back. Trust me.

Suddenly the FRIEND *rushes on stage and barges against* ARTHUR'*s back, separating them.* ARTHUR *looks back startled as the* FRIEND *vanishes. The* GIRL *has drifted from the stage. As we hear a shout off the stage from the* PORTER, ARTHUR *walks back to raise the platform again and begins to wipe his hands on a piece of cloth as if fixing his bike. The* PORTER *races on stage and runs to the far end. The* FRONTIER GUARD *follows him more slowly.*

FRONTIER GUARD (*calling to the* PORTER). Don't bother your bollix Sean, you'll only be wasting your time there. (*He catches his breath and points.*) Six hallways, two back entrances and twenty-four front doors. You might as well be pissing against the wind. We'll just wait here and watch.

PORTER *leans on the back wall and stares up.*

PORTER (*breathless*). You wouldn't mind only they'll flog the stuff for a tenth of the price. (*Catches his breath.*) It's demoralising this. I don't know, years ago you used to get to chase a much better class of criminal. I'm too old for this carry on.

The FRONTIER GUARD *has walked over to the centre of the stage and spotted* ARTHUR. *He approaches him.*

FRONTIER GUARD. Columbus was right Pascal. The world is round and the same faces keep spinning back. You go and check the hallways.

PORTER. What's the point? You said yourself . . .

FRONTIER GUARD. Do it!

PORTER (*resigned*). Right.

He exits and the FRONTIER GUARD *approaches* ARTHUR *who has been ignoring them.*

FRONTIER GUARD. Thought I'd seen the back of you, Cleary.

ARTHUR. Would be a foolish man to show his back to you, Mr Lynch.

FRONTIER GUARD. Detective Lynch to you. Always the

bitter word. Like the mother. Sorry to hear about her, Arthur. (*He pats Arthur's shoulder.* ARTHUR *nods, accepting the condolence.*) She was a good woman, always made me the cup of tea when I had to come and take you in. But sure, you were only children. God knows youse thought youse were the toughest men in the world, but you were like babes compared to the lads on the go now. Like babes in the wood, eh Cleary?

ARTHUR. So you say, Mr Lynch.

FRONTIER GUARD (*putting his arm on Arthur's shoulder*). You wouldn't be nervous now to be seen out here talking to me Cleary?

ARTHUR. You know me, Mr Lynch, I'd talk to the dog in the street.

FRONTIER GUARD (*looking up at the mass of windows above*). But nobody else knows you, Cleary. You should be nervous. They're watching us from up there. They're wondering.

ARTHUR. Shag them.

FRONTIER GUARD. It's them shagging you I'd be more worried about. (*He walks back to* ARTHUR *and changes tone.*) I think you've a problem, Cleary.

ARTHUR. I'm listening.

FRONTIER GUARD. A problem of perspective. Where do you stand now? This isn't the messing you and your friends got up to. This isn't a crate of beer fecked off a lorry, or a fist fight in a lousy cinema. There is a woman back there lying in a pool of her own blood – they went for her handbag and took half her arm. There is an old man down there at the traffic lights with a piece of glass stuck in his eye where the bastards broke the window of his car. That was never your scene Arthur. I know you since you were mitching from school. Are you with them, Cleary, or are you with me?

ARTHUR *turns to look at him for first time.*

ARTHUR. You always took your work fierce personal, Mr Lynch. You don't give a shite if that man loses his sight. I remember you chasing me after that fight outside the Savoy. Two nights you spent sitting in the wasteground across there, waiting for me to come home for a meal. It's still your private game isn't it, you alone against them. You're a bit old for this, Mr Lynch. Have they no desk jobs?

The FRONTIER GUARD *spits.*

FRONTIER GUARD. Ah fuck their desks and their computers.
You don't fight these bastards on a screen. I'm not ready for
grass yet. Listen, Arthur, you'll need me yet. I've ears you
know and you've got an acute shortage of friends in this
neighbourhood.

ARTHUR. I'll take my chances.

FRONTIER GUARD. Come on Arthur, pick a side. I could use
a pair of eyes Arthur, and you could use a friend.

ARTHUR. You were always good at using.

FRONTIER GUARD. You saw a girl come in here. Don't tell
us you didn't.

ARTHUR. Your little friend might need help by now, or do you
not fancy the tricky corners any more.

FRONTIER GUARD (*shouts*). Pascal get out here.
(*Threateningly to* ARTHUR.) I asked you a question.

ARTHUR. What girl?

PORTER *returns, slightly out of breath. We understand that he does
not know* ARTHUR *and presumes there is a standard questioning of a
suspect taking place.*

FRONTIER GUARD. Don't be a fool, Arthur.

PORTER (*circling* ARTHUR). Have you the tax up to date on
that?

ARTHUR. Yes.

PORTER. Insurance?

ARTHUR. Yeah.

PORTER (*miming speaking into a radio with back to the audience*).
What's the registration number?

ARTHUR. PSI 850.

FRONTIER GUARD. Clearly! You were messing with that
bike like you're always doing. Now don't tell me you didn't
see a girl. (*No response, shouts.*) I'm talking to you, sonny!

ARTHUR (*looking up*). Daddy?

FRONTIER GUARD. Don't get fresh with me. Just don't. The

time for that is past. I don't know what you're doing back
here, but I know it's illegal. It has to be, you look fucking
happy.

PORTER (*still circling*). Have you the duty paid?

ARTHUR. Yeah.

FRONTIER GUARD. One of these times I'm taking you
down for a nostalgic visit to the station. How'd you fancy a
surgical glove up the arse?

ARTHUR (*quietly*). Cost me fifty guilders in any other
country.

FRONTIER GUARD. You've made your choice Cleary. Now
you can sink or swim in it. Do you get my drift?

ARTHUR. Yes. Mr Lynch. I know you're really saying
welcome home son.

Lights go down again on centre of stage and rise on the GIRL *who
walks on from the right.*

GIRL. Grief is a knot
That is choking my throat
Rage is a whirlwind
Imploding through my skull

If only I had known
Your life to be in danger
I would have clawed
My way between you and them

I would have bitten
Into their skin with my teeth
I would have stubbed
Out their eyes with my nails

If only I had shouted
When you walked from the flat
Or ran to the balcony
Still naked to call you back

The FRONTIER GUARD *has retreated behind the raised
platform with a mask over his face. The* PORTER *approaches him
from the left and mimes handing something to him as music begins to
intrude on the verses. He receives in return a bag of white powder.
The* FRIEND *has approached from the left. The following muffled
dialogue takes place in the background while the girl is still reciting.*

FRONTIER GUARD. What do you want?

FRIEND. I need some stuff.

FRONTIER GUARD. Where's the money? Where's the money?

FRIEND. I'll get it tomorrow.

> FRONTIER GUARD *gestures with his hand and then vanishes.*
> *The* GIRL *finishes reciting and remains to the left of the stage. The*
> FRIEND *is pulling at the platform and shouting over the loud music.*

FRIEND. I'll get you the money! I'll get you the money! I'll get you the money tomorrow.

> *She pushes the platform and as it falls the entire stages goes black. The*
> *frontier post music begins and the* PORTER, *now lying under the*
> *platform that* ARTHUR *is standing on, begins to shine the light up*
> *and down through the bars. The* FRONTIER GUARD *enters and*
> *shines torch directly into* ARTHUR's *face.*

FRONTIER GUARD. Passport please.

> ARTHUR *turns.*

ARTHUR. Sorry.

> *He hands him the passport which the* FRONTIER GUARD *opens*
> *and examines.*

FRONTIER GUARD. Ah Irish. Irish. Boom-boom! eh! (*He laughs.*)

ARTHUR. I know that joke. You've made that before. It's ... it's like a dream ... recurring. I know you. Where is this place, what side of the border am I on?

FRONTIER GUARD. What does it matter to you, Irish. Either side is a long way from your home.

ARTHUR (*shrugs his head towards window*). What's he looking at the wheels for?

FRONTIER GUARD. Looking for? It's the rules, Irish, the rules.

> *He hands back the passport and turns to stare out towards the right of*
> *the stage.*

ARTHUR. Wait! (FRONTIER GUARD *stops with his back turned.*) How long have we been here? (*No reply.*) I keep thinking this . . . happened before. I can't remember things like I used to. Have I shown you my passport already? (*Waits but no reply.*) Turn around. I know your face. I have seen you before. Why are we so long here? Tell me! (*Raises voice*) What's keeping us here?

FRONTIER GUARD (*turning sharply and blinding* ARTHUR *with the torch*). You are keeping us here.

FRONTIER GUARD *turns away again.*

ARTHUR. What do you mean? That doesn't make sense. (*Shouts.*) What country have I come from? I can't remember! I can't! Which one?

FRONTIER GUARD. One you cannot return to.

ARTHUR. Why? What have I done? Had I an accident? Why can't I remember anything? How do I know your face? (FRONTIER GUARD *begins to move.*) No wait! I'm talking to you!

FRONTIER GUARD *steps out of light and walks to left of stage.* ARTHUR *stares after him, then turns to shout under the platform.*

ARTHUR. Hey! You! Where is this place?

The PORTER, *without acknowledging his presence, switches torch off and crawling out, moves to left of stage where the* FRIEND *is now standing.*

Where . . .?

The FRONTIER GUARD *walks up to the* GIRL *as if to a widow at a wake.*

FRONTIER GUARD. You know, he was a legend . . .

ARTHUR *is left alone standing on top of the platform.*

ARTHUR. It was clear until I started thinking about it. Like I've been here forever waiting for this train to start . . .

FRONTIER GUARD. I used to look up to him in school. You know, I could have been a help to him settling in.

He walks away from her.

ARTHUR. Can't . . . it's all fading. Wait. A laneway . . . that's right, flowers between the stones . . . barbed wire . . . bits of glass . . .

GIRL (*cries*). Arthur!

ARTHUR. And a girl! That's right, no name, can't remember, too painful . . . I loved her, she was younger, Dublin . . .

FRIEND. Wild, like his mother that lad.

ARTHUR. But why was I running . . . suddenly scared?

FRIEND. The door was open day and night, children sleeping on the floor whenever their mothers were in hospital. As poor as anyone here herself but she always gave.

ARTHUR clutches the belt he is wearing then lifts his hands up in shock.

ARTHUR. My belt, it's begun to rot. Like it were transformed back into flesh.

FRIEND. Never begrudged him, but the life was gone from her. How long? I must remember. A laneway, then what? A journey through empty streets.

FRIEND. The lad should have watched his step.

The FRIEND retreats and the PORTER approaches the GIRL.

ARTHUR. Night time . . . walking for hours. From the laneway. Why? I was going somewhere, but couldn't leave.

PORTER. The real McCoy, Arthur Cleary.

ARTHUR. Cars abandoned, bronze statues in O'Connell Street staring down.

PORTER. Always drifting from one job to the next.

ARTHUR. Where has everyone gone? Only one voice like a whisper from a sidestreet . . . calling me back . . .

GIRL (*cries*). Arthur!

The PORTER retreats from her.

ARTHUR. Not letting me go. Had to find her . . . The night went black, the moon dim like the end of a tunnel. I'm swimming towards it, but . . . always pulled back . . . by her voice, calling. And then . . . here . . . why? Why?

GIRL (*screams*). Arthur!

She shudders as if coming out of a dream and looks over to where ARTHUR is standing on the platform.

GIRL. You weren't there when I woke. I was frightened.

She walks towards him and he embraces her, soothing her as he strokes her hair and they sit on the edge of the platform.

ARTHUR (*soothing*). Frightened? Of what?

GIRL. Arthur ... (*Pause.*) Tell me about it all again, where you fed the swans on the steps on a Sunday. All the places. The sounds of the names are lovely, like ... like legends, dreams. I can see it when you talk.

ARTHUR (*teasing softly*). Capel Street, Rialto, Phibsborough ...

GIRL. No Arthur, say them. They're far away, safe.

ARTHUR (*quietly, soothing*). Altona. Blankensse, with little cobbled steps and terrace cafés built on jetties onto the Albe that would rock in the wake of the boats passing. Wedel where the ships would play their national anthems as they left the mouth of the river.

GIRL. Wedel.

ARTHUR. And the dormitories. Always the same. That time my ribs were cracked in the strike of foreign pickers and I lay for a week in the third bunk up, staring at the streets of Dublin tattooed along the veins of my wrist. The stink of Turkish cigarettes, photos of kids, pin-ups, and always at night the same talk of returning, even if you couldn't follow the languages, you knew what they were talking about.

GIRL. And then you came back. You never told me why Arthur.

ARTHUR. (*pause*). Can't really explain it. Just happened one night, halted at a border post. Lines of tracks, containers stacked on sidings. I'd pulled the window down to watch a guard shining his light under the train when suddenly I was overcome with longing for something ... I don't know ... something I'd lost ... (*Pause.*) I keep thinking I've found it and it slips away again.

GIRL. A city's like a person, Arthur, it can never stay the same.

ARTHUR. In that limbo between states I wanted it back, everything ... waking in the bay windows of flats with a raw throat from drink, walking to the fifteen acres for a game of ball, or back along the quays always bumping into someone. Even when you were broke you felt you belonged. Never felt that way anywhere else. (*He pauses, thinking.*) Always looking for it. Some Sundays in Hamburg I'd walk past the boats tied up at Landensbruck and down the mile between Reeperbahn and St. Pauli, the stink of decaying food in back lanes, the illuminations so tacky in the daylight, and the few bored whores sitting in windows smoking or trying to hustle from doorways. The Turks, the Slavs, the Irish, the white niggers, wandering between the lines of video cabins with their deutschmarks. It was the only part of Hamburg that made me feel at home. (*He gives a half laugh.*) You'd think it would be the last, the sex shops, the murals, but it was the drunks crumpled up like stalks on the pavement, the lines of vomit and urine, the beggars. All the signs of home you never saw in public over there.

GIRL. Arthur, we could try . . . there's England . . .

He pauses as if trying to understand it himself as well as tell her.

ARTHUR (*quietly*). Could have been that way for ever, drifting from city to city. Only something happened at that border post. I saw my reflection in the window . . . so suddenly old, so stale with experience. I felt this panic I couldn't explain . . . that if I stayed in the carriage I would be damned to wander forever across that continent. The guard had stamped my passport and made the usual joke. I was alone. I turned the door handle and jumped, began to run as the official with the torch shouted after me. I never looked back, just dodged past shunting wagons and containers till I reached the gates and was out into the countryside. There was woodland, through the foliage I could see lights of trucks from an autobahn. I kept running until I came to what I thought was a ruined house. When I got closer I realised it was a war monument, the shell of a building where people had been shot. I smoked cigarettes all night leaning against the plaque, clutching that battered green passport in my hands. Next morning I hitched to the nearest port, caught a ferry to Holland, a plane from there. Island's Eye, Lambay, wheeling over Swords so huge below me it was hard to believe I was home.

On the word 'home' there is a loud banging as the FRONTIER GUARD *slaps his money-lender's book against the wooden support on the right of the stage.* ARTHUR *and the* GIRL *part and rise. They stand as if in a doorway, facing away from the* FRONTIER GUARD.

FRONTIER GUARD (*in Deignan voice*). Mrs Doyle, this is
ridiculous. I am not blind or stupid. I know you are in there.
You've had enough warnings already. I'll smash this door
down if I have to! Do you hear?

The FRONTIER GUARD *sees* ARTHUR *and stares at him.*

FRONTIER GUARD. Still here, Arthur. (*No reply.*) Hear you
haven't been too lucky on the job front. It's a tough one.

ARTHUR (*turning*). Summer's coming, Deignan.

FRONTIER GUARD. So is Christmas. Listen to me, Arthur,
don't like to see a school pal down on his luck. I've a lot of
business in this block, but it's troublesome, a lot of hassle.
Time is money, you know what I mean. I'm too busy to chase
it. I could use somebody, someone I could trust, to keep an
eye on things for me.

ARTHUR. Summer's coming, I'll be busy.

FRONTIER GUARD. Doing what? Mugging tourists?
Cleaning kitchens at two pounds an hour? Listen. I'm not
talking anything heavy Arthur, and the money'd be good.
Right, you've a few messers like the Doyles, but the rest are
no problem. I mean . . . they're grateful. Genuine. Ask
yourself what bank wants to know people here? If it wasn't for
me Arthur . . . they'd be nothing bought . . . no furniture, no
clothes at communion time, no presents at Christmas, ESB
cutting people off. We're talking about people nobody else
gives a shite about, we're talking about providing a service . . .

ARTHUR (*cutting in firmly*). Thanks anyway.

FRONTIER GUARD (*sharper*). Think about it Cleary. You'll be
a long time rotting in that flat. It's the best offer you're likely
to get.

ARTHUR. I'll manage.

FRONTIER GUARD. OK, suit yourself.

*He turns to walk off and has gone a few paces before he turns back. His
tone changes slightly.*

FRONTIER GUARD. Well, just do this for me so. (*Opening
book.*) When you see Mrs Doyle, you tell her from me . . .

ARTHUR. Do your own dirty work, Deignan.

FRONTIER GUARD (*sinister tone*). I don't think you realise the situation here, Cleary. This is now, it's not your mother running up and down here telling people they're entitled to this and that. You think you're somebody Cleary, because you swaggered around here once. I'm not asking you, I'm telling . . .

ARTHUR *moves forward as the* GIRL *grabs his shoulder to try and hold him back.*

GIRL. No Arthur, no . . .

ARTHUR (*shouts*). The scum of the fucking earth. You weren't born, Deignan, your mother hatched you out in the back of that filthy shop! You and that spa of a brother of yours!

FRONTIER GUARD. It wasn't your money made my family rich, with your twist of tea and your Vincent de Paul vouchers!

ARTHUR *grabs the folder from the* FRONTIER GUARD's *hands. He releases the clip, turns, and throws the papers up in the air, scattering the pages down into the audience as if over a balcony into a courtyard.*

GIRL. Oh Jesus! No! Oh God!

FRONTIER GUARD (*shaken but in a low voice*). You pick up every one of those, Cleary.

GIRL (*terrified*). I'll go, I will . . .

She moves to brush past ARTHUR *who stops her with his hand and reaches out with his right to grip* FRONTIER GUARD'S *shirt and pull him towards him.*

ARTHUR (*quietly but with menace*). Don't ever address me again, Deignan. Don't ever come near me, don't even be on the same landing as me. Ever.

FRONTIER GUARD *squares up to* ARTHUR *as if about to strike him, but suddenly flinches when* ARTHUR *blows into his face.* ARTHUR *releases him dismissively.*

FRONTIER GUARD. You're a posthumous man Cleary. Do you hear me? I don't strike the dead, it's not worth the effort.

FRONTIER GUARD *backs off stage. The* GIRL *is gazing down into audience at the pages.*

GIRL (*softly as she reaches her arms out as though trying to catch the papers*). Blowing, like death warrants, death warrants.

The GIRL *moves to stand against the backdrop of the stage. As she speaks she tears at the cloth with her hands and it comes away leaving a blood red background. Music begins.*

GIRL's *voice (recorded):*

You went down steps
Because the lift was broken
You paused outside
And strolled out of my life

Across a courtyard
Where housewives were talking
Lying between sheets
I could hear the engine start

As she has been reciting, the masked figures of the FRIEND, *the* PORTER *and the* FRONTIER GUARD *have begun to close in on* ARTHUR *from the back of the stage with raised sticks in their hands. The* PORTER *is laughing, a hollow, mocking sound.*

GIRL.
I drifted into sleep
To see a horse come riderless
Over fields trailing
A bridle smeared with blood

Towards a white house
Where a woman stood screaming
As I shuddered awake
I realised her voice was mine.

All light has died except for one flashing white light shining from the front of the audience. ARTHUR *runs to his right where the* FRONTIER GUARD *kicks the barrel towards him.* ARTHUR *catches it, falling backwards and throws it himself so that he lands with the barrel like a pillow behind him. Over the intense music the* PORTER *strikes the barrel a number of times as the others raise their sticks.* ARTHUR *shudders each time the barrel is struck and then hangs limply against it as the scene dissolves into a sudden black out. The stage clears of characters and a single torch light, held by the* PORTER *(unseen) from just off the bottom left of the stage, catches* ARTHUR *sitting on the edge of the platform. The* FRONTIER GUARD *enters behind him, held by the* FRIEND *(unseen), and is picked up by a torch beam shone from just off bottom right of stage as he sits down beside* ARTHUR.

FRONTIER GUARD (*speaking, as if just going through the motions*).
Passport please.

ARTHUR *turns.*

ARTHUR. Sorry.

He doesn't hand over passport but FRONTIER GUARD *still speaks.*

FRONTIER GUARD. Ah Irish. Boom-boom! eh! (*He laughs.*)

ARTHUR. I know that joke. You've made that before. I . . . I
know you. Where's this place, which side . . . (*His voice trails off
in sudden fear.*)

FRONTIER GUARD. (*interrupting*). What difference does it
make. Either side is a long way from home.

ARTHUR. (*speaking as though going through the motions of a dream*).
What's he . . . ?

FRONTIER GUARD. Looking for? It's the rules, Irish.

ARTHUR. Have I shown you my passport already? Have I been
here before?

FRONTIER GUARD (*slight pause*). Yes.

ARTHUR (*quieter*). Then why are we stopped?

FRONTIER GUARD. It is the border, Irish.

ARTHUR. Which border? Where am I?

FRONTIER GUARD. Don't you know by now?

ARTHUR (*thinks, then quietly*). This is it isn't it . . . as far as you
take me.

FRONTIER GUARD. You catch on faster than most.

ARTHUR. How long . . . do we wait here?

FRONTIER GUARD. Till you decide to go.

ARTHUR. It's funny . . . so much I can remember now. (*He
pauses.*) Her name, the feel of her skin. She was younger, you
know, far younger than me.

FRONTIER GUARD. She was then.

ARTHUR. What do you mean?

FRONTIER GUARD. So many trains run through here, day and
night, in all directions, all times, coming and going.

ARTHUR (*looking down at platform*). Who's on that one? Where's it going?

FRONTIER GUARD. Europe . . . The future . . . Her children.

ARTHUR. Not mine.

FRONTIER GUARD (*smiles*). Life goes on, you pick the pieces up. Would you have had her put on black and spin out her life in mourning?

ARTHUR. Do they know of me? These children?

FRONTIER GUARD. She taught them your name like a secret tongue.

ARTHUR. It goes on so . . . without me.

FRONTIER GUARD. She cried, Cleary, walking the quays, praying for the courage to hurl herself in. She held you here for years, begging you to haunt her. Then she learnt to let you go, so you could pass on, not remain trapped in her grief.

ARTHUR. Then why am I still here?

FRONTIER GUARD. You must let her go, not plague her dreams.

ARTHUR. How?

FRONTIER GUARD. I'm only the railway guard, Irish.

There is silence for a moment.

FRONTIER GUARD. Forget them, Irish, forget her. This is between you . . .

ARTHUR *slowly turns to the waiting guard.*

ARTHUR. And who? (*There is no reply.*) What's out there in front of me? (*The* FRONTIER GUARD *shrugs his shoulders.*) I have your face now. You've been with me all along haven't you?

There is no reply. ARTHUR *waits a moment before continuing:*

What do I have to do?

FRONTIER GUARD. Remember everything, every moment, longing, whisper, every touch you've ever known.

ARTHUR. And then?

FRONTIER GUARD. Let go.

The torch light on the FRONTIER GUARD *goes out suddenly.*

ARTHUR. Into nothing? Is there any . . .?

He waits for assurance. The FRONTIER GUARD *offers none.*

ARTHUR. I was always clinging on. Never able to change. (*Silence.*) It's not easy. I'm scared. (*Half laugh.*) All so suddenly precious. Every moment like a film running through my skull. Never wanted it back so badly.

He looks slowly around him, wipes his lips nervously and then stares down at his hands for a moment, before raising them slightly.

ARTHUR. Let go.

The torch light on him, dies on the word 'go'. The stage is left in total darkness and briefly over the faint music we hear the sound of train wheels growing in volume for a few moments before fading away.

The End

Marina Carr was born in Dublin in 1964. She was brought up in
Tullamore, County Offaly before going to University College,
Dublin, to read English and Philosophy, graduating in 1987. She
then lived in New York for one year, teaching and writing. On
her return to Dublin, she enrolled at U.C.D. to do a Masters
degree on Samuel Beckett – a thesis which has been left aside
for a while. Her first play, *Ullaloo*, had a rehearsed reading with
Derek Chapman, Olwen Fonere and Tom Hickey at the 1989
Dublin Theatre Festival. It will be presented on the Abbey
Theatre's Peacock stage early in 1991.

Low in the Dark is Marina Carr's second play. It was performed by
'Crooked Sixpence' Theatre Company in the Project Arts Centre,
Dublin in 1989, and was directed by Philip Hardy. A third play,
The Deers Surrender, was written for, and performed by, the Gaiety
School of Acting in Andrews Lane Theatre, Dublin, in June
1990. Marina is currently working on a film script and a radio
play for the BBC, and a new play for the theatre.

Characters

BENDER, is in her fifties. Attractive but ageing.
BINDER, is BENDER's daughter. In her mid-twenties, a spoilt brat, whimsical.
BAXTER, is in his mid-thirties. He is CURTAINS' lover.
BONE, is in his late-twenties. He is BINDER's lover.
CURTAINS, can be any age as she is covered from head to toe in Curtains. Not an inch of her face or body is seen throughout the play.

The set

Stage left: Bizarre bathroom; bath, toilet and shower. A brush with hat and tails on it.
Stage right: The men's space; tyres, rims, unfinished walls and blocks strewn about.
The floor is chequered in cream and black.

Low in the Dark was first performed by 'Crooked Sixpence'
Theatre Company at the Project Arts Centre, Dublin, on
24 October 1989 with the following cast:

CURTAINS   Brid Mhic Fhearai
BENDER   Joan Brosnan Walsh
BINDER   Sarah Jane Scaife
BAXTER   Peter Holmes
BONE   Dermod Moore

Directed by Philip Hardy
Costumes by Leonor Mc Donagh
Set design by Liz Culliname
Lighting by Brian O'Rourke
Music by Bunnan Beo Ensemble
Stage manager, Lorraine Whyte

ACT ONE

Scene One

Sound track on, lights on middle stage space.
CURTAINS *walks down the middle space, looks right, looks left then looks straight ahead.*

CURTAINS. Before they ever met the man and woman had a dream. It was the same dream. The woman dreamt she came up from the south to meet the man from the north. It was the same dream. The man dreamt he came down from the north to meet the woman from the south. It was the same dream with this difference ...

BINDER (*gets up from the toilet where she has been sitting*). Open those bloody curtains!

CURTAINS, *caught mid-story, gives herself a vigorous dusting with a carpet beater and walks off.*

Why does she never open her curtains? Even an inch!

BENDER (*from the bath*). Even half a one!

BINDER (*yelling after her*). Open those bloody curtains!

BENDER I'd love to rip them off her! There is a life to be lived, I'd say as I'd rip them off, or didn't you hear? And then I'd tell her, It's not every woman can say that she's been loved!

BINDER. Go on! Give us a go in the bath.

BENDER (*pushes her away*). Go away!

BINDER. You look old today!

BENDER (*nonplussed*). I'll be older tomorrow.

BINDER. There's grey in your hair!

BENDER. Yours is falling out.

BINDER. You've put on weight!

BENDER. That's the baby.

BINDER. Another one?

BENDER. And why not?

BINDER. It's not fair.

BENDER. To who?

BINDER. To anyone . . . to you, to him!

BENDER. It might be a her.

BINDER. Never, babies are always boys.

BENDER. Even when they're girls.

BINDER. And it's not fair to me! I'll have to sit here and wait and listen to you screaming!

BENDER. A good scream would do you the power of good!

BINDER. I've nothing to scream about.

BENDER. That's your tragedy.

BINDER (*looking at herself in the mirror*). Do you like my hair?

BENDER. I love your hair?

BINDER. And. . .

BENDER. And your lips.

BINDER. Yeah, I love them too, will I put on more lipstick?

BENDER. Sure why not, give me some too. (*Both put on lipstick.*) Here! Put him in the shower. (*She's just had a baby, baby crying sounds.*)

BINDER. Why didn't you tell me? (*Holds up the baby.*)

BENDER. You accuse me of screaming too much, so I had a silent birth this time.

BINDER. Did it hurt?

BENDER. After the first million you get used to it.

BINDER. Can I feed him?

BENDER. Go ahead!

BINDER (*breast-feeding and examining the baby*). It's a she!

BENDER. What'll we call him?

BINDER. Alexander.

BENDER. We have an Alexander!

BINDER. There's no harm in another one.

BENDER. Please yourself.

BINDER. She sucks like a man.

BENDER. She'll have luck so! (*Finishes her drink, lights another cigarette.*) I wish her luck . . . I wish her all the luck in the world, give me another drink!

BINDER. You drink too much!

BENDER. I don't drink half enough! I deserve one after that ordeal . . . remember, not even a scream.

BINDER. That was very underhand of you.

BENDER. A drink for her sake and put him in the shower and give him a doll!

BINDER. They're for the girl-babies.

BENDER. Well then give him a train and give his mother a drink!

BINDER. I'm her mother!

BENDER. Who's mother?

BINDER. It's my baby, so leave off!

BENDER. Yours? I just had him!

BINDER. It's a her!

BENDER. Silently!

BINDER. You're hallucinating again. I had him.

BENDER. Binder don't start or I'll send you back.

BINDER. You can't! Remember you tried, I'm too big.

BENDER. I'll try again.

BINDER. He's my baby, and what's more I won't call him Alexander, horrible name!

BENDER. It was your idea.

BINDER (*to the baby*). I'll call you Jonathon, won't I?

BENDER. We already have four Jonathons, anyway it's a girl, look I'll give you the next one.

BINDER. You always say that . . . anyway there won't be a next one!

BENDER. There's plenty where she came from...as soon as I get my figure back I'll have another and then another, because I am fertile!

BINDER. I had a dream last night your uterus fell out.

BENDER. I dreamt your ovaries exploded!

BINDER. At least I have ovaries and eggs, lots of eggs, much more than you because I'm young. I'm in my prime.

BENDER. I've had my fair share of eggs. Now give her to me.

BINDER. Take her then! (*Throws the baby.*) But don't expect me to hit her when she starts screaming!

BENDER (*to the baby*). We don't expect anything from her do we?

BINDER. He's a very ugly baby!

BENDER. There's no such thing as an ugly baby. (*To the baby.*) Is there? You're the image of your father, aren't you?

BINDER. Who's his father?

BENDER. None of your business! Isn't it enough that he has a father...somewhere...here now put him away gently. (*Kisses the baby and gives it to Binder.*)

BINDER (*examining the baby*). I still think it's a she. (*Throws it in the shower.*)

BENDER. I'd better write to him. Get out the pen and paper!

CURTAINS *enters, goes straight for the Venetian blinds and examines them.*

BINDER. Hello, how are you?

BENDER. Oh there you are!

CURTAINS. I love your blinds, they really keep the light out.

BINDER. And the shower curtain?

CURTAINS (*examines the shower curtain*). Yes it's magnificent! Truly magnificent.

BENDER. I bought it in a sale. Eh where did you get your curtains?

CURTAINS (*outraged*). Don't be so impudent!

BINDER. We told you all about our blinds and our curtains!

CURTAINS (*smugly*). Did I ask you about them! No I didn't!

BENDER. Yeah, well you're always in here touching them up, looking for information about them. I even lent you one of the blinds and it came back filthy!

BINDER. I had to scrub it!

CURTAINS. What about the stories I tell you about the man and the woman?

BINDER. I don't need your stories! I have my own man.

BENDER. So have I.

BINDER. You have not! You've no one, only me!

CURTAINS. So you don't want my stories anymore? (*Goes to walk off.*)

BENDER. No wait! We didn't say that.

CURTAINS. I can always talk to myself you know. I don't need this abuse.

BENDER. Calm down will you . . . was the man very handsome?

CURTAINS (*sitting in state on the toilet*). Yes.

BINDER. And strong?

CURTAINS. Yes.

BENDER. And the woman?

BINDER. She was lovely.

CURTAINS. Yes she was. And the woman said to the man, 'I believe you're born to haunt me'.

BENDER. The woman was right.

BINDER. The woman was wrong.

CURTAINS. The woman was right.

BENDER. And what did the man reply?

CURTAINS. He said nothing.

BINDER. Ah, why didn't he say something?

BENDER. I bet he said something, you're just too mean to tell us!

CURTAINS (*up and away*). Goodbye.

BENDER. No wait! (*Curtains has gone.*) She always leaves us like this.

BINDER. Can I get in the bath?

BENDER (*pushing her out of it*). No! We've to write that letter, are you ready?

BINDER (*bored*). Ready.

BENDER. My dearest. . .My dearest? My dearest man, I am writing to tell you that you have another son. . .

BINDER. Daughter!

BENDER. That you have another child. It was a difficult birth but. . .

BINDER. It wasn't!

BENDER. It was a terrible birth, but I survived it. I think I would survive anything. It looks like you. Do you remember the night I Conceived?

BINDER (*stops transcribing*). Do you?

BENDER. Of course.

BINDER. Really?

BENDER. Yes.

BINDER. How did you know?

BENDER. I cried. Women always cry when they conceive.

BINDER. No they don't!

BENDER. Well they should. . .where was I?

BINDER (*reads*). Do you remember. . .

BENDER. Grand. How is your music going?

BINDER. Are you sure he's a musician?

BENDER. Of course I'm sure.

BINDER. Supposing he's not?

BENDER. OK, OK cross that out. . .how is your. . .

BINDER. Work?

BENDER. That's too vague.

BINDER. But they usually work.

BENDER. OK, how is your work going? I wish you would come home...all my love.

BINDER. And the address?

BENDER. Just leave it there. He'll know it's for him when he comes.

BINDER (*throwing the letter on the floor*). He'll never come, they never do.

BENDER. They always come in the end.

BINDER. Yeah when you're past wanting them.

BENDER. Do I detect a note of bitterness?

BINDER. Yes, I'm very bitter today.

BENDER. Why?

BINDER. Because I'm afraid I'll end up like you!

BENDER. Now I'm bitter!

BINDER. You've every right to be. Look at you!

BENDER. I'm always open to suggestion, but, aaaaah! Oh! Help me! Help! Aaah! Someone help me! It's coming! It's coming!

BINDER *rushes to put on a hat and tails and grabs a bunch of flowers. Dramatic music comes on.* BINDER *runs to the bath.* BENDER *is in the throes of childbirth.*

BENDER. I thought you were never coming!

BINDER. My love, look! (*Shows the flowers.*) For you. (*Throws them on her.*)

BENDER (*throws them back at her*). Get away from me! Aaah! Aaaah!

BINDER. Is dinner ready darling?

BENDER. GAAAS!

BINDER. Where are my slippers?

BENDER. Epiduuraaal!

BINDER. You've been very thoughtless these last few days.

BENDER. EPIDUURRRAL!

BINDER. Are you in pain?

BENDER. EPIDURAL! AAAH! AAAAH!

BINDER. It'll be over soon.

BENDER. It'll never be over! I'm going to die!

BINDER (*pats* BENDER's *head nervously*). You're not going to die! It's coming out.

BENDER. Is it? AAAH!

BINDER. Push! Push! Nearly there! It's a...push! It's a son! (*Holds it up.*) We have a son! (*Walks off with the baby.*)

BENDER (*struggling out of the bath*). I have another son. (*Exits.*)

Scene Two

BAXTER *and* BONE *come on stage right.* BONE *has his arm around* BAXTER *as if they are a married couple.* BAXTER *wears high heels, a woman's hat, a dress, and a necklace around his neck. He looks pregnant.*

BAXTER (*woman's voice*). You're marvellous darling, you really are.

BONE (*pointing to the wall*). So you like it?

BAXTER (*examining the wall*). It's exactly what we needed...exactly.

BONE (*thrilled*). Do you think?

BAXTER. How high will you build it?

BONE. Well how high would you like it?

BAXTER. I don't mind as long as it's higher than everyone else's. (BONE *has begun building.*) Can I help?

BONE. I think you should do your knitting.

BAXTER. I want to help with the wall!

BONE. Knit darling, knit!

BAXTER *sits in a chair reluctantly and begins knitting.*

Pause. Brief tableau of the knitting and building.

BONE. How is the knitting?

BAXTER (*still playing the role of a woman*). Grand, grand.

BONE. And the baby?

BAXTER (*puts a hand on his stomach*). Quiet today.

BONE (*still building*). And how are you?

BAXTER. A bit tired but otherwise. . .

BONE. Are you happy?

No reply from BAXTER *except to knit faster.*

With me?

The real BAXTER *erupts out of the role-play.*

BAXTER (*in a deep, man's voice*). I heard you!

BONE. Well are you?

BAXTER (*back to a feminine voice*). Yes.

BONE. Are you sure?

BAXTER. Yes.

BONE. Really?

BAXTER (*deadpan*). I am very happy with you. I cooked you
your favourite.

BONE (*delighted*). Did you? A whole tray of them?

BAXTER. Two trays! Twenty-four buns all for you.

BONE. Ah you'll have one.

BAXTER (*in his real voice*). I will not!

BONE. I'm sorry I shouldn't have said that.

BAXTER. You know I hate those things! (*Back to the woman's
voice.*) I only cook them for you.

BONE. You're spending too much money.

BAXTER (*knitting*). You're not earning enough!

BONE (*innocently*). Am I not?

BAXTER. I think you should get another job.

BONE. Two jobs?

BAXTER. If you did you could have buns everyday, and I could knit you a decent scarf. (*The scarf is about twenty feet long.*)

BONE. But I'd never see you!

BAXTER (*real voice*). Exactly.

BONE. Watch it!

BAXTER (*niggling female again*). Do you think there is any point in us going on?

BONE. Of course there is.

BAXTER. Just asking.

BONE. I hate it when you say things like that! You're trying to upset me.

BAXTER. I'm not!

BONE. You are! (*Points to the wall.*) I do everything to please you!

BAXTER (*real BAXTER, throws down the knitting*). I'm fed up of this! It's pointless!

BONE (*determined to finish the scenario, as before, points to the wall*). I do everything to please you!

He waits for the response from BAXTER. *None is forthcoming. He forces the knitting into* BAXTER's *hand, annoyed.*

Yes you do darling!

BAXTER. Yes you do darling.

BONE. And I love you for it!

BAXTER. And I love you for it.

BONE. Now would you like some tea?

BAXTER. Now would you like some tea?

BONE *knocks off* BAXTER's *hat.*

You always end it like this!

BONE. You always force me to! If you'd just say what you're supposed to say.

BAXTER (*taking off women's clothes and shoes*). Women don't talk like that!

BONE. That one did! (*Unsure.*) How do women talk?

BAXTER (*putting on his own shoes*). I don't know! They just talk, they never stop and there's no sense in anything they say, ever! Anyway I'm off!

BONE. You're always leaving me here.

BAXTER. You could go somewhere yourself you know.

BONE. Where?

BAXTER. Anywhere...just move around, I suppose.

BONE. Here?

BAXTER. Here's as good as anywhere, it's just matter in motion, place is unimportant.

BONE. Well, will we have some tea and buns before you head off?

BAXTER. Alright...but just tea for me.

BONE. A little apple tart and cream?

BAXTER (*delighted*). Apple tart and cream! What would I do without you? Hah?

BONE. I don't know...I suppose...eh...I've eh, met another woman.

BAXTER. Another woman?

BONE (*apologetic*). Yes...it'll...it'll eh, probably be over soon...yeah.

BAXTER. Has it started yet?

BONE. No.

BAXTER. Then how can it be over?

BONE. Well eh...after you start eh...it usually finishes after a while.

BAXTER. That's no excuse.

BONE. I know, I know...but when she talks...

BAXTER (*cynical*). I know when she talks.

BONE. And the lipstick on...

BAXTER. The soft hair...

BONE. The smell on the pillow...

BAXTER. The shoes...

BONE. The earring left behind...

BAXTER. Did she leave an earring?

BONE. Yes. (*Produces one from his pocket.*) And a sock. (*Takes a pink sock from the other pocket.*)

BAXTER. Can I? (BONE *gives him the sock.*) Lovely colour.

BONE. I washed it for her.

BAXTER. Did you?

BONE. And hung it out to dry, and took it in, and ironed it.

BAXTER. You don't iron socks...

BONE (*taking back the sock.*) This one you do.

BAXTER. Or shoes or underwear and what about me?

BONE (*examining the sock*). What about you?

BAXTER. You've upset everything, you know that!

BONE. Yes.

BAXTER. And who's going to pick up the pieces when she's gone?

BONE. Maybe this time she won't go.

BAXTER. She'll go! You'll pick a fight with her and she'll go! And then we'll run up and down mountains till the anger is gone. And when the anger is gone we'll drink until you have forgotten her. And when you've forgotten her, we'll play a few games and then you'll start all over. Can I see the sock again?

BONE. Will you give it back?

BAXTER. Yeah.

BONE. Sure?

BAXTER. Yeah!

BONE *gives* BAXTER *the sock and watches him examine it.*

BONE. Can I have it back now?

BAXTER (*still examining*). Take it easy will you?

BONE. Next thing you'll want her earring and then you'll
   disappear!

BAXTER. Can I eh, can I try it on?

BONE. It won't fit, I tried it already.

BAXTER. Small foot?

BONE. Tiny.

BAXTER (*trying on the sock*). Describe her?

BONE. Ah Baxter don't! You'll stretch it!

BAXTER. I let you try on the blue slip!

BONE. But it fitted!

BAXTER. With a stretch (*Examining the sock on his foot.*) What's
   she like?

BONE. She's long blond hair on her arms and long dark hair
   on her head and she's a handbag full of things.

BAXTER. What things?

BONE. Women's things, I suppose.

BAXTER. Did you not look?

BONE. I didn't get a chance.

BAXTER. Does she knit?

BONE. I didn't ask her yet.

BAXTER. Suppose she doesn't.

BONE. We'll cross that bridge when we come to it. (*He points
   at the sock.*) Look you're ruining it! (*He takes it off* BAXTER's
   foot.) I'll have to wash it again now, your big ugly foot mark
   all over it!

BAXTER. There was a time you were very glad to have this
   big ugly foot for company!

BONE. I'm sorry.

BAXTER. You're always sorry! (BONE *gives him the sock.*)
   How does she walk?

BONE. I haven't quite mastered it yet, but it's something like this. (*Does a female walk*, BAXTER *copies him*.) She takes short little steps and her feet turn in a little.

BAXTER. Cute. Do her eyes turn in?

BONE. No, she has level eyes.

BAXTER. I love a slight squint. Remember the Blue Slip? (*Both turn in their eyes*.) One of her eyes turned ever so slightly.

BONE. Gave her a dotty look.

BAXTER. Very attractive, that dotty look. Does she use her wrists?

BONE. Yeah, she goes like this a lot. (*Twiddles his right wrist*, BAXTER *does likewise*.)

BAXTER. Like this?

BONE. Something like that, and when she walks, (*He starts walking again*, BAXTER *follows him*.) she tosses her head. (*He tosses his head*, BAXTER *mimics*.) And when she takes off her shoes, she takes them off from behind, like she puts her leg some way behind her and puts her head to the side and her hand down. (*He demonstrates*, BAXTER *copies*.)

BAXTER. The Necklace used to take hers off like that. And when she was putting on her bra she used to fasten it in the front first and then turn it around and put in her arms. (*He demonstrates*.)

BONE. A lot of women do that.

BAXTER. They do not! Most of them fasten it from behind. (*He stretches his arms behind to indicate*.)

BONE (*trying to do it*). God I don't know how they manage it. Does the curtain woman wear a bra?

BAXTER. I think so.

BONE. What do you mean you think so?

BAXTER. Sometimes I almost feel it but I've never seen it.

BONE. Surely you know what a bra feels like?

BAXTER. Of course I know what a bra feels like! But there are many different types of bras. There's the platex, the cross-your-heart, the Saint Bernard, there's the two-in-one, the three-in-one...

BONE. The all-in-one, there's the light-support, the medium-support, the extra-support...

BAXTER. And there's them tops like tee-shirts only they're bras, and yet they couldn't be classified as the bra. Do you know the kind I'm talking about?

BONE. I wasn't born yesterday. Is that the kind the curtain woman wears?

BAXTER. More or less.

BONE. Which?

BAXTER. Less.

BONE. So what you're saying is you don't know. You mustn't care about her very much or else you'd know what type of bra she wore!

BAXTER. She's a 38B OK!

BONE. Pink Sock's a 32A.

BAXTER. We all have our limitations.

BONE. Well at least she has a handbag and her knickers are silk!

BAXTER. Curtains doesn't wear any.

BONE. You're not serious?

BAXTER. She says they're a sign of weakness.

CURTAINS *enters, followed by* BENDER *and* BINDER.

BENDER. And then what did the man say to the woman?

BINDER. He said shut up and lie down for a while.

BENDER. He did not! Curtains what did he say?

CURTAINS. He said, 'you're the crack in my pane of glass'. Hello Baxter.

BAXTER. Hello Curtains.

BONE. Hello Binder.

BINDER. Hello Bone.

BENDER. Hello Bender. Hello Bender.

The pace accelerates.

BONE. Binder this is Baxter. (*No one looks at anyone.*)

BINDER. Baxter this is Bone.

BAXTER. Binder this is Bone.

BONE. Baxter this is Binder.

BINDER. Bone this is Baxter.

BAXTER. Bone this is Binder.

BENDER. Bender this is Bender.

CURTAINS. Then the man got up one morning and looked out of his window. 'It's time' he said to himself, 'that I started riding'. So he got up on his bicycle...

BONE. Can I?

CURTAINS. Certainly you can.

BONE. So he got up on his bicycle and he rode all over the Earth, he cycled over the sea...he cycled over the sea... (*Forgets.*)

BENDER. For it was a sturdy bicycle. One evening as he was flying over the highways, he saw the woman in his path.

BONE. 'Get out of my road', he yelled!

BINDER. But she would not, he said it again, louder this time...

CURTAINS. Everybody.

ALL. 'Get out of my road', he yelled!

BINDER. Still the woman would not move.

BAXTER. 'I've two choices', the man said to himself, 'I can knock her down or I can stop'. In fact he did both.

CURTAINS. Which proves?

BONE. Which proves that the bicycle is streets ahead of the human mind.

CURTAINS. 'You!', she said, 'if you have courage get off your bicycle and come with me! I've...'

BENDER. 'I've nothing to give', the man said. 'Don't worry', the woman replied, 'I've learned how to steal'.

CURTAINS. So the man and woman walked. They walked a million miles. Then the woman turned to the man and said...

BAXTER. 'Hello.'

CURTAINS. And the man answered...

BINDER. 'Hello yourself.'

CURTAINS. The woman said, 'How are you?' And the man replied...

BINDER. 'I'm fine, how are you?'

CURTAINS. The woman did not reply.

BONE. So the man said again, 'How are you?'

BAXTER. Still the woman did not reply.

BENDER. She did so!

BAXTER. She did not!

BONE. Curtains, did she?

CURTAINS. I suppose.

BENDER. She said to the man...

Pause, all look at CURTAINS.

CURTAINS (*starts to go off-stage*). 'I need change, I need to make strange, I need to kill an albatross, I need to lie with the golden ass.' (*At this point she is off-stage.* BAXTER *follows her.*)

BENDER (*heading towards the bath*). And then the man said to the woman...

She drifts into the bath, her voice trails off, she talks to herself.

BINDER. Bone.

BONE. Binder.

BINDER. Will we?

BONE. No! I've to build. (*He throws the sock at her.*) You know I hate women who leave their things after them!

BINDER (*picks up the sock*). You washed it!

BONE. I did not! When can I see you again?

BINDER. I'm here now.

BONE. Now is no use.

BINDER. I made you some buns.

BONES. How many trays?

BINDER. Three.

BONE. I wanted two! There's your bloody earring as well! (*He throws it at her.*)

BINDER. How is the wall?

BONE. Grand.

BINDER. Will I see you tomorrow?

BONE. You might. Can I have the sock back?

> BINDER *gives him the sock.* BONE *kisses her and goes off.*
> BINDER *heads back to the bathroom.*

BENDER (*from the bath*). What did he say to you?

BINDER. He told me my lipstick was lovely.

BENDER. Give me some. (BINDER *gives it to her. She puts it on.*) Did he kiss you?

BINDER. Yes he did.

BENDER. The cheek of him! Where?

BINDER. Everywhere!

BENDER. And you let him?

BINDER. Yes.

BENDER. I don't believe what I'm hearing.

BINDER. There's no harm in it.

BENDER. There's plenty of harm! You're disgusting! He's only using you.

BINDER. I love being used.

BENDER. I think you should finish with him for your own sake.

BINDER. Just because you've no one . . .

BENDER. Hah! I've had every man I've ever wanted! All I have to do is this! (*She clicks her fingers.*) And they run.

BINDER. In which direction?

BENDER. You need a good trouncing!

BINDER. I'll trounce you back!

BENDER. It's no joke having a child the likes of you!

BINDER. I never asked to be born!

BENDER. Oh yes you did! Screaming out of the womb you came, ripping everything in your path asunder and you haven't stopped since!

BINDER. You should have aborted me.

BENDER. Too late now.

BINDER. Yes.

BENDER. No use crying over spilt milk.

BINDER. Hmm.

BINDER *starts reading a porn mag. There is the sound of babies crying.*

BENDER. I suppose we'd better feed them.

BINDER. I fed them already.

BENDER. All of them?

BINDER. Yeah.

BENDER. The Pope too? (*No answer from* BINDER.) I don't know what I'd do without you.

BINDER. Don't start! I can't stand it when you get all emotional.

BENDER. I don't like you reading those magazines. They'll give you the wrong idea about men.

CURTAINS *enters, goes straight to the Venetian blinds and starts opening and closing them.*

BINDER. Look will you leave those alone.

BENDER. Come into the bath beside me...you seem very excited.

CURTAINS. I've something to tell you both.

Pause, BINDER *and* BENDER *look at her.*

BINDER. Well?

CURTAINS. I bought a new slip.

The following is accelerated.

BENDER. What colour?

BINDER. What size?

BENDER. Silk?

BINDER. Cotton?

BENDER. How much?

BINDER. Where?

BENDER. When?

BINDER. How?

BENDER. Why?

CURTAINS. Stop!

She rummages around under her curtains and produces strings of beaded wood, Indian-style curtains. Four or five strands. All three examine it.

BINDER. It's amazing.

BENDER (*jealous*). Ah I had one of those.

BINDER. You never had.

BENDER. Sure they wear out in no time.

CURTAINS. So you like it?

BENDER. I'd like to see all of it. Open the curtains and do a twirl.

CURTAINS. You want jam on it.

BENDER. So you bought it. I got mine as a present. A present from an Indian called Chipachi.

CURTAINS. Well where is it now?

BINDER. He took it with him when he left her.

BENDER. He did not! I threw it at him. I said get out and take your slip with you. (*To* CURTAINS.) Come on into the bath beside me, here, there's room.

BINDER (*as* CURTAINS *gets into the bath*). You never let me in the bath.

BENDER. I loved your story today.

BINDER. It was beautiful.

CURTAINS. I hope you're learning from it.

BENDER. Oh we are.

CURTAINS. Then the man looked at the woman...

BENDER. How did he look at her?

CURTAINS. A long, slow look he gave her. 'Woman', he said, 'I threw my bicycle in the ditch for you, and this is how you repay me!'

BENDER. The cheek of her! If I was that man I'd have left her there and then! Some bubble bath? (*No reaction from* CURTAINS.) We all need a good scrub. He gave it to me for...

BINDER. I gave it to you.

BENDER. He gave it to me for the smell. 'I love the smell of you', he said, 'after a bath'.

CURTAINS. 'Big deal', the woman said, 'I got out of the sewer for you'.

BINDER. Bet that shut him up!

CURTAINS. Not at all! He started to look at the woman again...

BENDER. Razor?

CURTAINS. The woman let him look and let him look and said nothing.

BENDER (*still holding the razor*). Me neither.

BINDER. The hairier the better.

BENDER. But not on the face.

CURTAINS. Finally, the man said, 'your silence is driving me crazy'.

BINDER. For some reason they don't like them on the face.

BENDER. Well pull it out when he's not looking.

CURTAINS. Then the woman turned to the man and said, 'How many lovers have you had?' 'One', the man answered.

BENDER. And if he sets the pupil on the shaven patch, give him the gentle eye.

BINDER. You know that flutter that kills them! (*Does one.*)

CURTAINS. 'One', the man answered.

BENDER. The danger has passed.

BINDER. Really? Only one?

CURTAINS. 'One,' the man answered, 'one and all the rest'.

BENDER. Let him torture himself a little for having doubted you, then just when he's beginning to doubt himself, say, you're such a beautiful man darling. . .

BINDER. What did he mean by 'one and all the rest'?

CURTAINS. 'Ah yes, one', the woman replied.

BENDER. Beautiful man always throws them! Think it's the juxtaposition. Let him come to terms with it, there's time.

BINDER. There's plenty of time.

BENDER. Then say it again, you're such a beautiful man darling.

BINDER & BENDER. So hairy.

CURTAINS (*getting out of the bath*). 'Ah yes, one,' the woman said, 'one is all one ever has, the rest come too early or too late'. (*She exits.*)

BENDER. What's she talking about? (*She drinks pensively, then sings.*) Dandelion wine will make you remember. (*Pause.*) Do you remember?

BINDER (*reading*). Yes I remember.

BENDER. Put on the hat and tails.

BINDER. Ah Bender!

BENDER. Do you remember?

BINDER (*puts on the hat and tails, bad humour*). Yes I remember!

BENDER. Let me finish! . . .the first time we heard that song?

BINDER (*impatient*). Yes I remember!

BENDER. Tell me about it.

BINDER (*with arms folded, she rattles it off*). You wore a pink dress, very low cleavage, there were too many lights and too few drinks.

BENDER. And then?

BINDER. We drank.

BENDER. And...

BINDER, We left.

BENDER. Go on.

BINDER (*singsong*). I ripped the clothes off you, the few you wore.

BENDER. I was always decent! (BINDER *begins taking off the hat and tails*.) Put those back on!

BINDER. I've done it a hundred times!

BENDER. Please Binder...just once more, for me.

BINDER (*puts them back on*). Well make it quick!

BENDER. And put some feeling into it this time!

BINDER (*with feeling*). We walked through the trees and the moon...the moon was there... (*Ordinary voice.*) Well come on! (BENDER *struggles out of the bath*.)

BENDER. Slow down will you! The moon?

BINDER (*annoyed*). What about the moon?

BENDER. Where was it?

BINDER. Below us.

BENDER (*coy*). Never!

BINDER. Yes it was. We were looking at it through the lake.

Music on at this stage.

BENDER. Now I remember. (*Both look down.*) Isn't it?...isn't it?...isn't it just?

BINDER. Yes it is.

BENDER. And the stars?

BINDER. The stars are there too, they'll be there long after this planet has turned to dust.

BENDER (*breaking their arm link*). He never said that!

BINDER. Well I'm saying it.

BENDER. Keep to the rules! Go on.

BINDER *puts an arm around* BENDER, *they walk.*

BINDER. Did you know that Fionn MacCumhail hunted on
these very mountains?

BENDER. No I didn't.

BINDER. That this lake is called Pallas Lake, named for Pallas
Athene who swam here once.

BENDER. No, I never knew.

BINDER. Do you know anything? Do you?

BENDER (*breaks the embrace*). No! That comes later, much later
and his tone was never that harsh!

BINDER. What comes next then?

BENDER. St Brigid's Well.

BINDER (*arm around* BENDER *again*). And over here is St
Brigid's frog-spawned well. And up here is the fairy fort, we
used to play around it as children.

BENDER. You live in a beautiful place.

BINDER. That's true...it's beautiful...yes it is.

BENDER. Will we talk about us?

BINDER. What about us? We're alive, we're together, we're
rotting.

BENDER. You make it all seem so pointless.

BINDER. Well is it not?

BENDER. No, we're young.

BINDER. That's true.

BENDER. We've our whole lives ahead of us.

BINDER. Can't argue with that.

BENDER. We're happy.

BINDER. Are we?

BENDER. Do you still love me?

BINDER. Of course.

BENDER. Say it!

BINDER. I love you.

BENDER. Have you said it to others?

BINDER. Hundreds, and I'll go on saying it. I'll say it a million times. I'll say it even when I don't mean it. I'll yell it to the space between the branches, I'll whisper it as they nail the lid on.

BENDER. That's exactly how he said it.

BINDER (*taking off hat*). Must've been a rare tulip.

BENDER. None rarer, none rarer. (*They exit.*)

Scene Three

BONE *enters, lays a brick, sits in a deck-chair and starts knitting.* BAXTER *arrives with a necklace around his neck and nail polish in his hand.*

BAXTER. How is the knitting?

BONE. Grand, grand.

BAXTER (*offers nail polish*). Will you?

BONE (*offers knitting*). If you will.

BAXTER. It's my turn.

BONE. I did the necklace yesterday.

BAXTER. I did the knitting last night.

BONE. You did not. I was with the Pink Sock last night.

BAXTER. I sat in that chair for hours, must've knitted a yard at least.

BONE. It's my turn.

BAXTER. It's not!

BONE. How is Curtains?

BAXTER. Closed, and the Pink Sock?

BONE. Puce...she never opens the curtains?

BAXTER. Never.

BONE. You're lying.

BAXTER. She never opens them.

BONE. Does she make apple tart?

BAXTER. Yes.

BONE. And cream?

BAXTER. Sometimes cream.

BONE. When she feels like it.

BAXTER. It's worth waiting for.

BONE. Has she said anything you'll remember after she's gone?

BAXTER. Well has the Pink Sock?

BONE. She's too busy baking.

BAXTER. Curtains says nothin'.

BONE. Not even a phrase?

BAXTER (*offering the nail polish again*). Look will you do this or won't you?

BONE. Always the necklace!

BAXTER. Always the knitting!

BONE (*pointing to the nail polish*). She's gone!

BAXTER (*pointing to the knitting*). She'll never arrive! (*Begins to open the nail polish.*) I'll do her myself.

BONE. OK! OK! Give it to me.

BAXTER *gives him the polish.* BONE *sits down, takes off a shoe and begins painting his toe nails in a female pose.* BAXTER *takes off the red necklace and puts it in his pocket.*

BAXTER. OK are you ready?

BONE. Ready.

BAXTER (*does a little walk, then turns*). Well.

BONE (*woman's voice*). Hello Darling. (*They kiss.*) How was your day?

BAXTER. Fine and yours?

BONE. Very busy.

BAXTER. You're painting your nails again.

BONE. Yes, it's wearing off. Are you hungry?

BAXTER. No, I can wait.

BONE. Well I should cook you something soon because I'm going out at eight o' clock.

BAXTER. I thought you were staying in this evening.

BONE. Well I've changed my mind.

BAXTER. That's not what she said! She said I'm sorry, but I made this arrangement that slipped my mind until a few minutes ago.

BONE (*real* BONE). She was very forgetful.

BAXTER. Can you not cancel it?

BONE (*back in the role*). Do you really want me to?

BAXTER. Yes.

BONE. OK, I'll stay in. Happy?

BAXTER. Yes, are you?

BONE. Yes. (*Hands him nail polish, ordinary voice.*) Here!

BAXTER. No wait! It's not finished yet!

BONE. Hurry up.

BAXTER. You're spoiling it all! Can we start again?

BONE. No!

BAXTER. I love your dress.

BONE (*back in his role*). Do you?

BAXTER (*exploding*). It's not 'do you'! It's 'I wear it for you'! I love your dress!

BONE. I wear it for you.

BAXTER (*pleased*). Do you?

BONE. Yes.

BAXTER. Red's your colour.

BONE. Red's my colour.

BAXTER. And sometimes rust.

BONE. And sometimes rust.

BAXTER. I bought you a present.

BONE. Oh. (BAXTER *puts the necklace around* BONE'*s neck.*) It's lovely.

A long look ensues.

BAXTER. OK, It's my turn now.

BONE *takes off the necklace and gives it to him.*

BAXTER. Wait! (*He takes the necklace, puts the lid on the polish and puts the necklace around his neck.*)

BONE. Do you want me to do Curtains?

BAXTER. No.

BONE. OK the Pink Sock! (*Hands* BAXTER *the pink sock.*)

BAXTER (*puts the sock on his hand like a glove*). I don't know what she says.

BONE. Make it up. Come on.

BAXTER (*woman's voice*). Do you like my lipstick?

BONE. Yes I do.

BAXTER. And my sock?

BONE. Yes.

BAXTER. I want a baby.

BONE. So do I.

BAXTER. Will you buy me a present?

BONE. Of course I will.

BAXTER. I want a bath.

BONE. You want to trap me.

BAXTER. I do not.

BONE. Yes you do, you women are all the same.

BAXTER. I'm different.

BONE. I want to be free. I think we should finish.

BAXTER (*gets up from the chair*). OK, goodbye.

BONE. Come back here! Where do you think you're going?

BAXTER (*sitting again*). You said you want to finish with me.

BONE. And I do.

BAXTER (*gets up again*). All the best so.

BONE. No, that's not what she'd say! She'd say, 'Don't leave me', She'd say, 'I need you Bone'.

BAXTER. I need you Bone.

BONE. You don't.

BAXTER. Alright, I don't.

BONE. No! You do.

BAXTER. I do.

BONE. You don't

BAXTER. I don't.

BONE. You do!

BAXTER. I don't!

BONE. You do!

BAXTER. No, you need me!

BONE. Me? I don't need anybody.

BAXTER. Neither do I.

BONE. I wish you'd stop talking about your mother.

BAXTER. I wish you'd stop talking about yourself.

BONE. You're very aggressive.

BAXTER. I am not.

BONE. You are.

BAXTER (*moves towards him, shouts*). I am not!

BONE. OK you're not.

BAXTER. Will you marry me?

BONE. Why?

BAXTER. Because, that's the why.

BONE. That's no reason to marry.

BAXTER. Then because we can hate one another legally.

BONE. I love the Pink Sock!

BAXTER (*normal voice*). Really? (*Takes off the sock.*)

BONE. Yes.

BAXTER. Then you're lucky. (*Gives him back the sock.*)

BONE. Am I?

BAXTER. Will we build for a while?

BONE. OK. (*They build.*)

  CURTAINS *comes on followed by* BENDER *and* BINDER.

BENDER. I'd love to meet that man.

CURTAINS (*angrily*). You'll never meet him. He belonged to the woman!

BINDER. Go on. Continue the story.

CURTAINS. I don't feel like it now.

BENDER. Was it something I said?

BINDER. Please Curtains...and the man said to the woman...

CURTAINS. He didn't say anything!

BENDER. Yes he did! He said...

CURTAINS. Who's telling this story?

BINDER. She's sorry.

BONE (*stops building*). Is it time for the story?

CURTAINS (*looking at* BAXTER *who remains building*). As soon as Baxter is ready!

BAXTER. I heard it last night. (*He walks off.*)

CURTAINS. So the man and woman walked, not speaking unless spoken to, which was never as neither spoke. Going along the path in this amiable fashion they came upon a woman singing in a ditch. 'Sing us your song', the man said. The woman sang.

In Salamanca I mislaid my daughter,
In Carthage they killed my son,
In Derry I lost my lover,
In this ditch I've lost my mind.
'You've ruined our day', the man said. 'Don't be so cruel',
the woman said and turning to the woman in the ditch, she
asked, 'Is there anything we can do except help you?' The
woman did not reply. So the man and woman hit her and
moved on.

CURTAINS *goes off, followed by* BENDER.

Scene Four

BONE *and* BINDER remain on stage. BONE *has the twenty foot
scarf around his neck.* BINDER *is knitting the scarf which* BONE *is
wearing. They begin walking around the space,* BINDER *following*
BONE.

BONE. Can I carry your handbag?

BINDER. Another bun?

BONE. Three please. (*Turns to receive buns out of her handbag.*) How
is the knitting?

BINDER. Grand, grand.

BONE. And the baby?

BINDER. What baby?

BONE. And how are you?

BINDER. Pissed off.

BONE. Are you happy?

BINDER. Can I have a bun?

BONE. With me?

BINDER. Well can I have a bite?

BONE. Of course. (*Gives her a bite of the bun. Gives her a kiss.*)

BINDER (*both still walking,* BONE *ahead*). I want a baby!

BONE. Do you like the wall?

BINDER. Will I put on more lipstick?

BONE. I built it for you.

BINDER. Women always cry when they conceive.

BONE. I do everything to please you.

BINDER (*stops walking, knits furiously*). I'd love to get a man pregnant!

BONE. Slow down will you, you're knitting too fast.

BINDER. He'd arrive home shaking. 'Well, what's up?' says I . . .

BONE *begins walking around* BINDER *in a wide circle, wrapping the scarf around her.*

BONE. Darling you know when you make buns? . . .

BINDER. I'm pregnant, he says . . .

BONE. The temperature has to be just right . . .

BINDER. 'Are you?' says I, giving him a level look . . .

BONE. Has to be 150 degrees . . .

BINDER. 'Yes', he whispers, 'Must've got caught' . . .

BONE. And you have to pre-heat the oven . . .

BINDER. And who's the mother I'd say, kind of harsh . . .

BONE. For fifteen minutes exactly . . .

BINDER. Need you ask, he'd say and the tears would start . . .

BONE. Otherwise they don't taste the way they should.

BINDER. OK! OK I'd say, I'll stand by you for what it's worth, but I'm not promising anything, now dry your eyes. Another bun?

BONE. I haven't finished these yet.

BINDER. How is the wall?

BONE. It's coming on great.

BINDER. And the lawn?

BONE. Mowed it yesterday, mowed it today and I'll mow it tomorrow.

BINDER. You're marvellous darling.

BONE. No, you are.

BINDER. I'm very fertile.

BONE. How is the knitting?

BINDER. Millions of eggs going to waste!

BONE. And how is the baby?

BINDER. Quiet today, how is the Black and Decker?

BONE. Drilling away, and how are you?

BINDER. A bit tired but otherwise...

BONE. Will you come and live with me?

BINDER. I want to marry you!

BONE. Same thing.

BINDER. It's not. I want a house with a bath and a man in it and a baby, all together, all forever, all for me.

BONE. I want a permanent relationship for a month or two, and sure who's to say the third month would be the death of us? Are you happy?

BINDER. No I'm not!

BONE. I want a woman who knows how to love. I want lazer beams coming out of her eyes when I enter the room. I want her to knit like one possessed. I want her to cook softly.

BINDER. I want a man who'll wash my underwear, one who'll brush my hair, one who'll talk before, during and after. I want a man who'll make other men look mean.

BONE. Can I carry your handbag?

BINDER. Another bun?

They exit.

Scene Five

CURTAINS *runs on followed by* BENDER *who is beating her with a carpet-beater. She gives her three or four good belts. Suppressed howls from* CURTAINS *for the first three, a howl for the fourth.* BENDER *is enjoying it. Perhaps* CURTAINS *is too.*

CURTAINS. Thanks very much.

BENDER. Wait, I'm not finished yet.

CURTAINS. Ah, I think I'm clean enough.

BENDER. No, there's a bit of dust here!

She gives her a sudden belt on the spot. CURTAINS *howls.*

CURTAINS. That's fine thank you.

She puts out a hand for the carpet-beater. BENDER *belts her hand, the hand disappears behind her curtains.*

BENDER (*still belting her*). If you'd just take them off! I could belt you till tomorrow and there'd still be dirt flying! (*This speech is punctuated by belts at regular intervals.*)

CURTAINS. No harm in a bit of dirt. (*Winces with each belt.*)

BENDER *stands back to admire her efforts. She flicks bits of dust off* CURTAINS *here and there.*

BENDER. Just one more on this section!

She takes a run at her, belts her with all her might. CURTAINS *falls,* BENDER *is panting.*

Clean as a new pin! Wait!

She gives CURTAINS *one more belt while she's down.*

CURTAINS (*on the floor*). I feel great now.

BENDER. Oh we nearly forgot about the face, Curtains.

CURTAINS. You're right.

She turns her head towards BENDER *and receives a swipe.*

Great, just great.

She gets up, takes the carpet-beater, puts it behind the curtains, then sits on the toilet.

So the man and woman walked some more. . .

BENDER (*now in the bath*). Did they?

BINDER *enters.* BENDER *motions her to ssh.* BINDER *sits.*

CURTAINS. And they came to a hill where three men were nailing three women to three crosses. 'What have we here', the man said. 'I want vinegar', the one on the middle cross yelled,

'Get me vinegar!' 'Would wine do?', the woman asked. 'Has to be vinegar!', the one on the cross screamed. The one on the right roared, 'WE'LL BE BACK! WE'LL BE BACK!' And the one on the left said, 'Put silk on a man and he's still a goat, put silk on a goat and she's still a woman!'

BENDER. Oh my God, immaculately receive me.

BINDER. Conceive me spectacular.

ALL. In the name of the mother, the daughter and the holy spirit. (*Pause.*) Ah! (*Pause.*) MEN!

BENDER. That was eh, really moving.

CURTAINS. I put everything into those stories.

BENDER. Well it was lovely to see you.

CURTAINS. It was. (*She doesn't budge.*)

BINDER *goes to the shower, throws three babies on* BENDER *and sits with two, both breast feeding.*

CURTAINS *gets up and goes over to the shower. She grabs an armful of babies, and orchestrates the feeding of the babies. Soundtrack of babies gurgling and crying comes over.*

CURTAINS. One day the woman turned to the man and said, 'It's time you had a baby'.

BINDER (*to* BENDER). It's time you stopped having them!

BENDER (*looking at the three babies on her*). And who have we here?

BINDER. The three Jonathons.

BENDER. My darlings, all my little darlings, and what ages are these three?

BINDER. You had them!

BENDER. Jealous?

CURTAINS *distributes babies by the armful to* BENDER *and* BINDER, *and also grabs babies back at random from them.*

CURTAINS. 'Have one yourself', the man said to the woman.

BINDER. I think you should go on the pill.

BENDER. After this one I'll go on it.

BINDER. That's what you said the last time. Think you're a fucking artist or something!

BENDER. I am an artist, a bloody genius in fact! Show me the art that is life! You can travel the whole world and nowhere, nowhere will you find it except in the big stretch marked belly of a woman. Now Jonathon you'll have to wait while Jonathon and Jonathon drink first.

CURTAINS. 'Babies are for women', the man said to the woman. 'I think we have a crisis on our hands', the woman said . . .

BENDER (*throws baby at* CURTAINS). He's all done!

CURTAINS *throws a yellow baby at* BENDER, *and throws a pink one at* BINDER.

BENDER (*to* BINDER). You're cold towards me today. I gave you everything!

BINDER. You gave me life, that's all.

BINDER. I've received less and been grateful for it. Give me the pink one!

BINDER. What's wrong with the yellow one?

CURTAINS. Today she prefers pink.

The yellow baby is swapped for the pink baby. All three of them are involved in the throwing and the catching.

BINDER. The yellow one's whinging!

BENDER. It wasn't from the wind he got it, just like the father, a right auld whiner!

CURTAINS. He'll grow up disturbed, kill you when he's twenty-one.

BINDER. Wish I had.

BENDER. I never prevented you from learning calculus, did I? Give me the yellow one! (*Another swop.*)

CURTAINS. Sit down there on that stone till I tell you something, the woman said to the man. The man did as he was told.

BENDER (*to the yellow baby*). My baby, my poor little unloved, unwanted helpless thing. I wish to God your fathers would come home.

BINDER. I knit, he builds, he builds, he knocks it down and he builds again.

CURTAINS. The woman is born full and dies empty. The man is born empty and dies full. He dies full unless he miscarries.

BENDER. God I'm stuck, just like that black hobo on east 51st one evening. 'Lady,' he said, 'lady I'm stuck here a long time!' 'So am I,' I answered, 'so am I'.

BINDER. Caught him rooting in my handbag twice. I said, 'why are you ransacking my handbag?'

CURTAINS. He dies full unless he miscarries.

BENDER. But I gave him a dollar and he gave me a light, then he invited me to stay with him on the cardboard...

BINDER. And the lawn, the lawn is beautiful...

CURTAINS. The man began to panic, 'Where's my bicycle?' he said, 'I want my bicycle!'

BENDER. The pair of us could still be there, a trash can for a pillow...

BINDER. And his Black and Decker! He'd drill the eyes out of my head if I'd let him.

CURTAINS. 'Your bicycle can't help you now,' the woman said, 'you have to come with me'.

BENDER. His lice-ridden head on my breast, maybe I would have been happy there, maybe.

CURTAINS. 'Come with me', the woman said to the man! (*She dumps the remaining babies on top of* BENDER *who is in the bath*.) 'Come with me and I will change you beyond recognition!' (*Exit*.)

BENDER. Where's the Pope?

BINDER. On your mountain!

BENDER. That's the Doctor!

BINDER. Show? (BENDER *holds up a baby*.) That's him.

BENDER. I know my children! This is the Doctor! Here on my right breast is the Black Sheep! (*Points to the yellow one*.) On my left the President! Now, where's the Pope? (*Accusingly*.) You have him!

BINDER. I haven't!

BENDER (*panics*). Well where is he? (*She throws babies out of the bath.*)

BINDER. Calm down, he's probably in the shower.

BENDER. I want the Pope! Get me the Pope!

BINDER (*flings the Pope at her*). He's not Pope yet!

BENDER. Woe betide you when he is! Neglecting him like that! (*She gives reverential and preferential treatment to the Pope.*)

BINDER. You fed him already! (*Exits.*)

BENDER. I'll feed him again. I want him fat and shiny. Holy Father, (*Bows to the baby.*) You'll pull your auld mother up by the hair of her chinny chin chin, won't you? We'll have tea in the palace and I'll learn Italian and the pair of us side by side, launching crusades, banning divorce, denying evolution, destroying the pill, canonizing witches. Oh, a great time we'll have, you singing the Latin with a tower of a hat on you, the big stick in your rubied fist and them all craw-thumping around the hem of your frock and whispering for miracles. And me sitting there as proud as punch in the middle of the incense and the choir. Oh a great time we'll have, the pair of us, we will surely.

She's in the shower among the babies. She closes the shower curtains.

Scene Six

CURTAINS *comes on with* BAXTER *underneath her curtains. She begins moving, slowly at first, swaying back and forward. Her breathing becomes audible, the swaying increases in tempo, the breathing increases. The swaying becomes jerky. She is now gasping, and the swaying reaches its height. All the curtains are shaking. Climax. Breathing subsides. The swaying subsides to silence. Hold for a few seconds.*

BAXTER *appears from behind the curtains, naked from the belly up.* (*He mustn't be seen until this point.*) *He puts on his necklace and waits expectantly. She hands him out a slice of apple tart.* BAXTER *looks at it then looks at her.*

BAXTER. Any eh…any cream?

CURTAINS (*shakes, a squirt of cream*). Do you think I'm sexy?

BAXTER. Of course.

CURTAINS. Sexier than the Necklace?

BAXTER. I'm not in the business of comparing.

CURTAINS. Well I am. There's a landscape that lovers inhabit or so I'm told.

BAXTER. Yes, you only realise you've been there when you've left. The fever is too high. You're not on this earth and you've no desire to be, and you've...

CURTAINS. Rubbish! You know nothing about love.

BAXTER. I know one thing about love. If it's there you don't have to talk about it.

CURTAINS. You're with a talker.

BAXTER. Then talk to yourself.

CURTAINS. So the man and woman came upon a man with a good leg and a bad leg and a halter around his neck. 'Why do you wear that halter around your neck?', the woman asked.

BAXTER *remains impassive.* BONE *and* BINDER *drift on stage.*

CURTAINS. Binder, you know this story.

BINDER. 'I'm looking for the horse who wore it', the cripple replied. 'Then you're sick', the man said...

BONE. 'So sick I'd be for finishing you off right now.' The woman said, 'I think that's an excellent idea'.

CURTAINS. 'No wait!' the cripple said. 'I have to find her, I need to see her, I want to explain, for the horse is gone, the horse is gone and the halter remains.' 'Very well', the woman said, maiming his good leg. He thanked her and hobbled on. As they were walking along the man and woman fell in love...

BENDER (*from behind the shower curtain, a roar*). What?

CURTAINS (*shouts*). They fell in love!

BENDER (*running from the shower*). Go back! Go back! This is the part I've been waiting for.

CURTAINS. I've just started on this story.

BENDER (*disbelieving*). Has she Binder?

BINDER. Yes.

BENDER. Wait! Wait! I want to settle myself for this. Lipstick Binder!

BINDER *produces lipstick, puts some on and hands it to* BENDER *who puts some on.* CURTAIN'*s hand emerges from curtains. She puts some on.*

BONE (*taking out aftershave*). Some aftershave Baxter? (*He puts some on,* BAXTER *puts some on.*)

CURTAINS. Is everybody comfortable?

BENDER (*bursting with excitement*). Hurry up! Hurry up!

CURTAINS. So the man and woman fell in love. . .

BENDER. Did they?

CURTAINS. They fell deeply even. The man put it down to the accident of birth, the boredom of the path and the finality of death. (*The men nod.*) The woman put it down to the perfume, the lipstick and the finality of the tit. (*The women nod.*) 'My love,' the man said to the woman, 'let's make hay before we're snowed in altogether'. 'Certainly we'll make hay a stor mo chroi [Love of my heart], the woman replied. For the woman loved the man and the man loved the woman.

BENDER. Wonderful.

BONE. Go on! go on!

BAXTER. Sssh.

BINDER. Listen, will ye.

CURTAINS. So. . .

ALL. So?

CURTAINS. So they made hay and they made hay and they made hay, and one morning they woke and the harvest was done.

BENDER. It was not! They made hay and more hay! Didn't they Binder?

BINDER. Yes they did! They made hay and more hay!

CURTAINS. They didn't! The harvest was done!

BONE. I don't believe you!

BAXTER. You're making it up!

CURTAINS (*with finality*). The harvest was done! 'Let's walk some more', the man said with a hint of contempt in his voice. The woman began to cry.

BENDER. That's not fair! Why did he have to make her cry?

BAXTER. He didn't make her! Her bladder was too near her eyes, that's all!

BINDER. He did so make her! She was fine the night before, wasn't she Curtains?

CURTAINS. She was ecstatic.

BONE. And what about the man? Maybe he couldn't help the contempt!

BAXTER. He only asked her to walk!

BENDER. I know that note of contempt. I know it so well. It lurks in the saying, not in what's being said.

BONE. I think you're over-reacting.

BENDER (*points the finger*). That's it! The very note I'm talking about! The note that says 'There's no magic here'.

CURTAINS. So the man and woman walked some more. They walked the world seeking a topic of conversation.

BENDER. What did I tell you?

CURTAINS. At the end of his tether, the man spoke of the hills of the north...

BINDER. The woman spoke of the hills of the south...

BAXTER. The man spoke of Sile na Gig who haunted him.

BENDER. The woman spoke of an adulterer who roared in a pigsty for his severed flesh, to have it returned in a bowl of soup from the conjugal kitchen.

BONE. He hinted at desperation sung in ditches.

BINDER. She hinted at desperation not sung at all.

BAXTER. He mentioned mysteries that might claw at your bones.

CURTAINS. They agreed to be silent. They were ashamed,

for the man and woman had become like two people
anywhere, walking low in the dark through a dead universe.
There seemed no reason to go on. There seemed no reason
to stop.

End of Act One

ACT TWO

Scene One

Lights up. CURTAINS *is standing centre stage, impassive.* BONE *and* BINDER *walk on, both pregnant.* BONE *is following* BINDER, *who now wears the scarf.* BONE *knits. Both nod at* CURTAINS. CURTAINS *nods back.*

BINDER. How is the knitting?

BONE. Grand, grand. How is the baby?

BINDER. Acting up. Another bun?

BONE. Men always cry when they conceive.

BINDER. And the wall?

BONE. I suppose it's an emotional time for them.

BINDER. And how are you?

They exit.

BAXTER (*from behind the curtains*). Any apple tart?

There is a lot of movement underneath the curtains.

CURTAINS. So the man and woman continued walking...

BAXTER. Cream? (*A pause.*) Thank you.

CURTAINS. And the man said to himself, 'I've two choices...'

BAXTER. Did they never get tired?

CURTAINS. 'I've two choices, I can run or I can hide', the man said...

BAXTER. I hate your stories.

CURTAINS. Curtain up your mouth!

BAXTER. Un' curtain, yours!

CURTAINS. If you think you're getting in the window tonight, forget it!

BAXTER. There are other windows.

CURTAINS. Then go and find one.

BAXTER. The Necklace never spoke like you.

CURTAINS. Well she should have.

> BONE *and* BINDER *enter still knitting, still pregnant,* BONE
> *still following* BINDER.

BONE. Please Binder, can I carry your handbag?

BINDER. First the knitting, now the handbag!

BONE. Just for a few minutes.

BINDER. OK. (*Gives him the bag.*) Don't root in it this time,
you mess everything.

BONE. I promise I won't. (*He's already rooting in it. He produces
tampons and goes to put two in his pocket.*)

BAXTER (*from behind the curtains*). Lovely day.

BINDER. I hope this weather keeps up.

BAXTER. How are you doing Bone?

BONE. Grand and yourself?

BINDER (*catching* BONE *with tampons*). Bone!

BAXTER. Could be worse.

BINDER. Bone, they're women's things!

BONE. Are they? (*He puts a pill in his mouth.*)

BINDER. And so is the pill! Anyway it's pointless taking it
now, you're already pregnant!

BONE. I took every precaution.

BAXTER. I want a baby!

BINDER. Did you?

BONE. It was your carelessness and now you take it out on
me.

BINDER (*touches her stomach.*) And what about your
carelessness?

BONE. You begged me for a baby!

BINDER. I begged you for one baby, not two!

BAXTER. Bone, how did you manage it?

BINDER. Can I have my handbag back?

CURTAINS. The woman said to the man, 'Let's go away
somewhere'. 'We're already away somewhere', the man
replied...

BONE. I made some buns for you.

BINDER. I made some for you.

BONE. Will we eat our own then?

BINDER. Will we swop? (*They swop.*)

BONE. How is the baby?

BINDER. Fine, how is the baby?

BONE. Quiet today, and the knitting? (*He's knitting.*)

BINDER. Grand, grand and how are you?

CURTAINS. So the man and the woman fought...

BONE. Did they?

BENDER (*comes on and gets into the bath*). They did not!

CURTAINS. They did so! They fought in the morning before
they got up. They fought all day as they walked and they
fought in the evening before they slept!

BENDER. Liar! They made hay and were happy.

BINDER. Yes, that's what they did.

CURTAINS. One evening the man turned to the woman after
they had fought and before they slept. 'I suppose a good ride
is out of the question', the man said.

BAXTER (*from behind the curtains.*) Men don't talk like that!
(*Gets out of the curtains.*)

BENDER. Oh yes they do!

CURTAINS. 'You mean you want to make love', the woman
replied...

BONE. Make love! I call a ride a spade!

BINDER. Then you'll be digging forever!

CURTAINS. The man paused. 'If we can still call it love, then yes I want to make love...'

BENDER. 'I don't feel like it', the woman said.

CURTAINS. 'Soon we'll be sleeping in separate ditches', the man said. The woman said nothing.

BINDER. She didn't have to. She let her body talk.

CURTAINS. 'You're starting on this power between your legs stuff again', the man said.

BENDER. 'It's the only power you've left me with, I might as well use it. Goodnight.'

BAXTER. 'I could always force you', the man said.

CURTAINS. 'Yes, you could always force me', the woman replied.

BONE. 'But I never would', the man said.

CURTAINS. 'Oh you're so good to me', the woman said and slept.

CURTAINS *walks off*. BINDER *drifts into the bathroom and goes up to the window.*

BONE. I feel like an animal.

BAXTER. Don't mind her.

Exit BONE *and* BAXTER.

Scene Two

BENDER *is in the bath, smoking.* BINDER *has her head stuck out of the window.*

BINDER (*out of the window*). Hey you!

BENDER *gets out of the bath immediately.*

Variation on the fall? With me?... Not up to it? You're not up to much, are you?

BENDER (*pushing* BINDER *aside*). Don't be so rough with him! (*She leans out of the window, feminine, gentle, baby voice.*) Hello... fine, and you? Tired? Me too... would you like a bath? A hot one? With loads of bubbles and we could have a little chat and maybe some wine?...Do you like red or white?

BINDER. Or Blood?

BENDER (*pushes* BINDER *onto the floor*). You shut up! (*Soft voice again.*) Red? Me too.

BINDER. She prefers white, anyway there's no wine up here, not a drop!

BENDER. Sorry...what's your name anyway? Salvatore... foreign...yes I know it means saviour, and your last name? Di Bella...The beautiful Saviour...that's lovely, that's really lovely...Mine? (*To* BINDER.) He wants to know my name.

BINDER. Wait till he hears it.

BENDER. My name? Well now when you translate it...it means...

BINDER (*pushing* BENDER *aside*). Her name is Bender and when you translate it, it still means Bender!

BENDER. Stop it!

BINDER. Because she is a bender! All her life she's done nothing but bend! She bends over, she bends back, she bends up, down, under and beside. She is Bender! And me? I'm...

BENDER (*knocks* BINDER *down with a clout*). Don't mind her! I don't know what she's saying!

BINDER. Now you go away and leave us alone! We have no room for your misery. (*She gets into the bath.*)

BENDER. I'm sorry... he's gone...I wonder where he'll go.

BINDER. Isn't it enough that he's going somewhere!

BENDER. The sooner you have that baby the better!

BINDER. The sooner you stop having them! I'm fed up looking after them!

BENDER. I'll go on the pill!

BINDER. You said that before!

BENDER. This time I will... (*Puts the hat on* BINDER's *head*.) And you, great impregnator, scattering your seed all over the

Earth, of late; making tremendous efforts to screw the moon, would you not gestate with me a while?

BINDER. It's out of the question!

BENDER. That's not what he said! You love to say horrible things to me when you've the hat on!

BINDER (*throws the hat at her*). Do it yourself so.

BENDER (*picks up the hat, slams it on her head and takes on a male pose*). Listen, I have my work. (*Takes off the hat.*) What about me? (*Hat back on.*) Don't I spend all the time I can with you? (*Hat off.*) It's not enough, I miss you. (*Hat on.*) I miss you too. (*Hat off.*) That's a lie. (*Hat on.*) It's not. (*Hat off.*) It is. (*Hat on.*) It's not. (*Hat off.*) It is. (*Hat on.*) It's not. (*Hat on and off at accelerated speed.*) Tis, not, tis, not, tisnot, tisnot, etc. (*Eventually she throws the hat off.*) Ah go to hell!

BINDER *is out of the bath by this stage. She has put some music on, some romantic love song and is dancing away with the hat.*

BINDER. Come on Bender, dance with me.

BENDER. I don't feel like dancing.

BINDER *continues dancing*, BENDER *goes to the window.*

BENDER. I wish Salvatore Di Bella would come back, we'd be happy together, I know it.

BINDER (*puts on the hat, Italian accent*). Eh Bellissimo, com estai? Sono Salvatore Di Bella, I am the greatest lover in the world, come with me and we will do many things together, we will swim in the Caspian sea, (BENDER *begins to laugh.*) And drink the Vino, Blood or white?

BENDER. Blood.

BINDER. Ah me too, the blood I love, and after we drink and swim and eat, then mi amore, (*Puts arms around* BENDER, *they dance a slow dance.*) then we will talk of many things, but light, and we will not stop to think, never, because mi Amore, when you stop to think, then is triste, molto triste, because the universe, she is an incurable wound, blistering on the belly of the void, she is one vast unbearable grief.

The dance and music stop. They exit.

Scene Three

BONE *enters, hugely pregnant, wearing one high-heel shoe and one man's shoe. He looks at the wall, looks at the knitting then makes a decision.*

BONE. A brick! (*He lays a brick.*) A stitch! (*He knits a stitch.*) A brick (*he lays another brick.*) A stitch! (*Another stitch.*) A brick! A stitch!

He sits in a chair in admiration, hand on belly. He looks at the knitting then looks at the wall.

That's how it's done.

BAXTER *has arrived.*

BAXTER. How is the baby?

BONE. Splashing around.

BAXTER. Can I listen? (*He kneels and puts his ear to* BONE's *belly.*)

BONE. Still alive?

BAXTER. Of course.

BONE. I have dreadful nightmares about it.

BAXTER. That's normal. (*Still on the floor, he looks up at* BONE.) Bone I asked you not to wear high heels when you're pregnant.

BONE. I'm only wearing one.

BAXTER. Even so, you'll get varicose veins, then you'll say I neglected you.

BONE. Well you are. We used to have great times together, way back before the necklace.

BAXTER. Yes, way back before the knitting...you used to sew, beautiful needlework. I could sit and watch you all night.

BONE. And you ate only meringue...you had taste then.

BAXTER. And you wouldn't so much as look at a bun. God! We had such dignity.

BONE. Blue was your colour.

BAXTER. Ah yes, the Blue Slip, she was light, she was happy.

BONE (*hand on his stomach*). It was all easier then, I was younger, freer and cheesecake was the thing.

BAXTER. If I'd only stopped for a little think, never dreamed a necklace or apple tart could bring a man so low.

BONE (*patting his stomach*). Soon there'll be hope, new life.

BAXTER. I hope it's a girl-baby.

BONE. So do I.

BAXTER. I'll buy her a necklace to haunt some fool or other.

BONE. And we'll teach her to sing and dance.

BAXTER. How to put lipstick on.

BONE. How to flutter the eyelids.

BAXTER. How to say no, when she means yes.

BONE. And yes, when she means no.

BAXTER. And we'll tell her fairy tales of happy ever after.

BONE. So she won't strangle herself in the cradle...suppose it's a boy-baby.

BAXTER. Never, babies are always girls.

BONE. Not always.

BAXTER. Bone, I don't think we'd survive another man-child.

BONE. I'll do my best.

BAXTER. I want a girl-baby and that's final!

BONE. You don't know what I go through!

BAXTER. And what about me? No one's forcing you to have it!

BONE. It should be the most natural thing in the world to have a baby!

BAXTER. A girl-baby, yes.

BONE. Your snide remarks won't get us anywhere.

BAXTER. You think it's easy for me watching you? Swelling day by day, while I canter 'round barren as a mule!

BONE. You could cross the great water yourself you know.

BAXTER. I crossed it once...nearly killed me.

Pause.

BAXTER *takes two buns out of his pocket, shyly.*

I made you some buns.

BONE (*moved*). You think that much of me?

BAXTER (*still holding the buns*). I suppose.

BONE. Not shop bought?

BAXTER. No.

BONE. Am I getting through to you at last?

BAXTER. I wouldn't go that far...look take them will you?

BONE (*taking the buns*). I...I...I don't know what to say.

BAXTER. Silence might be better.

BONE. But surely this is an occasion which calls for a phrase.

BAXTER (*pleased*). Maybe.

BONE. Or a word even...can you think of one?

BAXTER. No. (*Watches* BONE *eating a bun with pleasure.*) Can you?

BONE. No.

BAXTER (*impatiently*). Take your time.

BONE (*still thinking*). Still no.

BAXTER. Bear in mind my weakness for the spoken word.

BONE (*still thinking*). I'm really sorry Baxter, it just won't come.

BAXTER (*disappointed*). It's OK. OK.

Pause.

BONE *eats a bun still searching for a word*, BAXTER *is deflated.*

BONE. Would a meaningful look maybe compensate?

BAXTER. Depends on the look.

BONE. OK, walk a bit and then turn, you'll find I might surprise you.

BONE *assumes a tragic look.* BAXTER *walks and then turns with a big smile. He sees* BONE's *look, his smile decreases to a sad expression. He shuffles around, head down, hands in pockets.*

BONE. What's wrong Baxter?

BAXTER (*hurt*). You look like I've poisoned you.

BONE. Well have you?

BAXTER. If that's what you think! (*Goes to walk off.*)

BONE. Baxter I'm sorry, that was really cheap of me after all the trouble you went to. Give me one more try?

BAXTER. Alright then.

BAXTER *turns and walks.* BONE *assumes a grin from ear to ear,* BAXTER *turns, his face impassive, he looks at* BONE, *a long look, gradually a smirk, which eventually broadens into a dazzling smile.*

BONE (*grin frozen on his face*). Well?

BAXTER (*still smiling*). You see you can do it if you want to.

BONE. There's hope for me yet.

BAXTER. I'll stand by you through thick and thin for that look.

BONE. Will I look at you again?

BAXTER. Let's not over do it, the heart's not up to such powerful feeling.

BONE. Oh, the baby, she just kicked.

BAXTER. Are you alright?

BONE. It's normal isn't it?

BAXTER. It is not? C'mon I'm taking you to the Doctor! (*Both exit.*)

Scene Four

BENDER *and* BINDER *come on reading* 'True Romance' *magazine.*

BENDER (*reading*). 'Doug moved closer to Sofia, his hot breath on the nape of her tiny neck. He held her tightly in his tanned, hairy, muscular arms. Sofia shrieked! "Doug," she said, "I can't". "Of course you can", he murmured, his tongue in her ear. "No! Doug! please, I have leukemia", Sofia gasped. "Well I haven't!", Doug answered, his fingers travelling down her spine and lower. "Oh Doug," Sofia whispered, "I wish I didn't have to die, I wish..."

CURTAINS (*coming on*). So the man and woman walked some more and...

BENDER. Shut up!

CURTAINS. So the man and woman...

BENDER *and* BINDER. Shut up!

CURTAINS. Will I show you my new slip?

BENDER. Saw it already, anyway it's not new anymore. It'll soon be in flitters.

CURTAINS. It will not! Eh can I look at your blinds.

BENDER. If you tell me where you got those curtains, you can have the blind.

BINDER. And the shower curtain.

CURTAINS. I bought them in a sale. (*Whips down the shower curtain and begins attaching it to her curtains.*)

BENDER. You did not!

CURTAINS. I did.

BENDER. I've never seen curtains like those in a sale.

CURTAINS. Then I made them.

BINDER. You told me you couldn't sew.

CURTAINS. I lied.

BENDER. You're lying now! (*Whips the shower curtain off her.*) And don't dare look at it again.

CURTAINS (*sits on the toilet*). So the man and woman walked...

BENDER. Excuse me!

She pulls CURTAINS *off the toilet, lifts the lid, spits in the toilet, closes the lid and gets into the bath.*

CURTAINS (*sitting on the toilet again*). So the man and...

BINDER. Excuse me! (*Pulls* CURTAINS *off the toilet, spits, closes lid.*)

CURTAINS (*on the toilet again*). So the man and woman...

> BENDER *gets up like a shot.* CURTAINS *leaps up,* BENDER *spits in the toilet.* CURTAINS *watches her then races to the bath and spits in the bath.* BENDER *spits in the toilet.* CURTAINS *spits in the bath, four spits each, tit for tat style.*
>
> CURTAINS *is back on the toilet.* BENDER *is back in the bath. Both mouths are working furiously to collect spit. They look at one another. Both get up slowly,* BENDER *standing in the bath. They stalk one another, sumo wrestler-style, face to face, then a synchronized spit.* CURTAINS *runs off.* BENDER *remains in the bath, standing, looking after her.*
>
> BINDER *has been reading a newspaper throughout, the deaths column.*

BINDER. Didn't you know Adams? (*No reply.*) He's dead...says here he died peacefully, in brackets.

BENDER. He would.

BINDER. Another fella here died peacefully too.

BENDER. Who can die peacefully?

BINDER. And this one. (*Reads.*) 'Mary Rose Lee, 97, beloved of Jimmy,' suddenly, in brackets.

BENDER. No one dies suddenly at 97! She's probably been dead for years only Jimmy didn't notice. Sure how would he? He's probably 99, blind, deaf, toothless, crawling around, waiting himself to be struck suddenly or peacefully. Or maybe he's dead too, only they don't notice because of the upset over Mary Rose. And a couple of months from now they'll put another notice in the paper, 'Jimmy Lee, died,' suddenly, in brackets. And poor Jimmy has been dead a long time, even longer than Mary Rose and God knows how long she was dead before they copped on. Sure they might never even have been alive.

BINDER. I want to live forever.

BENDER. You've a lot to learn.

BINDER. Or if I die, I want to die for someone or something.

BENDER. No one dies for anyone anymore, they're all just dropping off peacefully or suddenly, or slashing their wrists in private or shooting one another in the back. Where's the noble death gone to? That great noble death, that great noble life.

BINDER. Like Cuchulainn and Ferdia?

BENDER. Yes. (*Puts on hat.*) Tonight my friend, my beloved brother, I anoint your wounds, I cook for you the wild pheasant of the forest, I make your bed soft to lie on, sleep well my friend, sleep well and may your dreams prepare you.

BINDER. You make him sound like a woman.

BENDER. Great men always sound like women. They feel as sharply as we do, they contradict themselves left, right and centre and they cry a lot too.

BINDER. I've never seen a man crying.

BENDER. Then you're mixing with the wrong sort.

BINDER. How do you make them cry?

BENDER. There's no set rules. Some of them'll cry for a reason and some of them'll just cry anyway.

BINDER. Very strange. (*Puts hat on* BENDER'*s head.*) C'mon it's my turn.

BENDER. I don't feel up to it.

BINDER. I always do it for you.

BENDER (*resigned*). Which one?

BINDER (*hands her a red scarf*). The black musician.

BENDER (*ties the scarf around the hat*). Can I do it in the bath? (BINDER *looks at her.*) OK OK.

She gets out of the bath. BINDER *puts on lipstick, and checks herself in the mirror. She walks in to middle space and stands there demurely. Music starts playing, reggae.* BENDER *walks over, the magnificent Negro walk.*

BENDER (*into* BINDER'*s ear*). Hi Baby cake, you wanna jive with me a while?

BINDER. Sorry?

BENDER. You wanna dance?

She doesn't wait for a reply, she takes BINDER's *hand and they move a few steps. Dance.* BENDER *the confident rhythm of the negro,* BINDER *self-consciously.*

BENDER. Well you ain't no New Yorker honey.

BINDER. Irish.

BENDER. Say what?

BINDER. From Ireland.

BENDER. I'd never have guessed, My grandmother's Irish.

BINDER (*suspiciously*). Is she?

The phone rings in the bathroom. Both stop dancing then, a mad rush to the phone.

BENDER. It's my turn to answer it!

BINDER. It's mine. (BINDER *makes a dive for it, seductive voice.*) Hello.

BENDER *is struggling to get it off her, both roll around on the floor, struggling with the receiver.* BENDER *eventually gets it off* BINDER, *holds her by the hair and lies on her at the same time.*

BENDER (*seductively*). Hello. (*To* BINDER.) It's a man!

BINDER (*gives her a punch*). I know it's a man!

BENDER. Yes...yes..

BINDER. Let me listen!

BENDER. I know, I know, overdue? Yes, yes...

BINDER. What's he saying?

BENDER (*fighting her off and seductive at the same time*). Did we not pay it?

BINDER (*a roar*). I can't hear him!

BENDER (*moves to let* BINDER *hear*). Don't worry about it, We'll pay it, ...when?

BINDER. Keep him talking!

BENDER. Well, when would you like us to pay it?... soon...what do you mean by soon?...today?...(*To* BINDER.) He's going!

BINDER (*grabs the phone off* BENDER). What time

today?...Before 5.30, eh, sorry we can't make it before
5.30...tomorrow...OK...(*To* BENDER.) He's going!
(BENDER *takes the phone from* BINDER.)

BENDER. What time tomorrow?...Anytime...that's very
considerate of you...Are you sure?...sorry, excuse me,
sorry I can't hear you all of a sudden, (*Winks at* BINDER.)
Yes, could you repeat what you just said, yes, yes, yes, OK.
(*Shouts.*) Wait!...well...how are you anyway? (*Pause.*) He's
gone!

BINDER. I told you not to get personal, they hate it when you
get personal!

BENDER. I couldn't help it!

BINDER. We could have kept him there half an hour at least!

BENDER (*still on top of* BINDER). I didn't mean it alright!

BINDER. You meant it! You knew he preferred me so you
had to move in! hadn't you?

BENDER. Preferred you! The croaky little voice of you with
your ostrich eyes and your pancake diddies!

BINDER (*whispers*). Menopause, men o pause,
men...o...pause!

BENDER. Stop it! (*Starts hitting her.*)

BINDER. Menopause, hot flush, empty womb.

BENDER (*chasing her*). Stop it! Stop it!

BINDER. The womb will be empty and the tomb will be full!

BENDER. Stop it!

They are off by this stage.

Scene Five

BAXTER *and* BONE *run on.* BONE *is hugely pregnant,*
BAXTER *is exercising him.*

BAXTER (*running on the spot*). Right! Down on the floor!

BONE. Ah Baxter! (*Gets down on the floor.*)

BAXTER. Come on Bone, just a few more.

BONE. I'm tired.

BAXTER. Come on, you don't want to get all flabby. Just three more. (BAXTER *flexes* BONE's *legs four times*.) That's grand.

BONE (*still on the floor, from behind his hump*). I'm seriously contemplating an abortion.

BAXTER. Are you crazy?

BONE. I have a right to choose.

BAXTER. You have not! There's a life there inside you! A destiny, all it's own.

BONE. Stop it! You're just trying to make me feel guilty. It's painless, an overnight job. I could be back building tomorrow.

BAXTER. Bone, please don't do it, for your own sake, you'll never recover.

BONE. Rubbish! It's only a few cells, a mistake on Binder's part, that's all.

BAXTER. There are no mistakes, no accidents in this world.

BONE. Here I am, a man with a girl-baby about to come out and I'm terrified!

BAXTER. I'll help you.

BONE. What am I going to do when the waters break? Hah?

BAXTER. I'll be here.

BONE. Supposing you're not, and the big water fall comes, louder than Niagra! And, and a girl-baby bulldozing her way through me! Sure I'll probably die, you'll be sorry then!

BAXTER. Hang on! I'd nothing to do with this baby.

BONE. Well you don't want me to get rid of it and you do damn-all else except make me exercise till I drop!

BAXTER. Bone, think. Think for a minute! You might never have another one.

BONE. One is enough, believe me. If it's a boy-baby I'll shoot it!

BAXTER. It'll be a girl.

BONE. How do you know?

BAXTER. You're all over the place. With boys you're neat. I think you should have a Caesarean.

BONE. Why so?

BAXTER. Well my mother had a Caesarean, my grandmother had a Caesarean, my great grandmother had a Caesarean. If I ever have a baby I'll have a Caesarean.

BONE. You were a Caesarean baby?

BAXTER. Of course.

BONE. No wonder you're so balanced. I was a natural birth. From paradise I came, through the chink, to this galaxy of grief. I'll never forget it and I'll never forgive her for it. Purged from the womb, jostled down the long passage, the umbilical around me neck, the grunting, the groaning, the blood, the shit, the piss, and the first scream, there was the point of no return. A rough start to a rough journey I tell you. I wouldn't wish life on my worst enemy, I'll have an abortion.

BAXTER. We're all abortions, some later than others, that's all. But look on the good side Bone. Life is short, soon we'll be dead.

BONE. Not soon enough.

BAXTER. What are you going to call her?

BONE. I'm not having her.

BAXTER. Either way she'll need a name. Call her after her mother.

BONE. No. Green maybe, that's a nice name.

BAXTER. Or Red.

BONE. Red's not too bad, how about October?

BAXTER. Or December, or Sunday?

BONE. Or Thursday or Midnight?

BAXTER. Three o'clock?, four o'clock?, five o'clock?

BONE. Five o'clock? Let me think about it.

BAXTER. Six? No, six is too common, half past five maybe or quarter to six, but not six.

BONE. I know what we'll call her.

BAXTER. What?

BONE. Wall.

BAXTER. Well if you're getting personal, why not Necklace?

BONE. It's my baby.

BAXTER. OK, OK...how about Wall-Necklace?

BONE. Wall-Necklace, that's lovely, that's what we'll call her. (*Gets up.*) Well, I'd better go for my check up.

BAXTER. Do you want me to come with you?

BONE. No, Pink Sock's taking me, thanks anyway. (*Exits.*)

BAXTER. No problem.

He looks around for something to do. He lays a block then puts a hand on his stomach, feeling for a baby. Disappointment. He puts a hand on the necklace.

We parted...amicably. I said take whatever you want.
Are you sure?
Yes.
You took everything. Everything except the two easy chairs, the carving knife and the bed. You weren't about to take that to your new abode. Not the evening you left, nor the next evening, but an evening long after, I walked through the streets, empty but calm, fell sideways over a stone. Not a thing between me and eternity but a sliver of moon and your memory.

Scene Six

CURTAINS *enters and goes towards* BAXTER.

CURTAINS. One time...(Baxter *puts his hands up.*) One time the man and the woman...

BAXTER. Don't talk to me about the man and the woman. (*Exits.*)

CURTAINS (*to herself*). One time the man and the woman...

She stops. The carpet-beater is in action. Music begins. She performs a little carpet, bead and curtain dance. BENDER comes on.

BENDER. Here let me help you with that!

The carpet-beater disappears. CURTAINS *turns away from* BENDER.

BENDER. I'm sorry for spitting at you.

CURTAINS. It was I who spat at you.

BENDER. I'm really sorry.

CURTAINS. No I am.

BENDER (*getting angry*). Listen! I'm really sorry for spitting at you the way I did.

CURTAINS. It's I who is sorry. I spat first!

BENDER. No way! I spat first!

CURTAINS. Well I spat harder and my aim was perfect! And I'm really sorry and it won't happen again.

BENDER (*smug*). I got you right between the two eyes. That was a dreadful thing to do.

CURTAINS. Yes it was.

BENDER. I remember a time when I would have never have treated anyone like that.

CURTAINS. So do I. Now I'd spit on anyone.

BENDER. Me too.

CURTAINS. If I tell you something, will you keep it a secret?

BENDER. Yes.

CURTAINS. One night the woman spat on the man.

BENDER. What did he do?

CURTAINS. He was asleep. And another time the woman carved her name on the man.

BENDER. Did he not wake?

CURTAINS. Of course he woke but it was too late.

BENDER. What was her name?

CURTAINS. Christ! I'm telling you that a woman carved

herself into the back of a man and all you're worried about is her name! 'I'll leave my mark on you, I'll leave my mark, even if it kills you', the woman said!

BENDER. And did it?

CURTAINS. It killed them both.

BENDER. Terribly sad.

CURTAINS. No it's not. There are worse things than dying.

BENDER. Like?

CURTAINS. There's living when you know you've never been alive.

BENDER. It seems to me you've only ever spoken out of loss.

CURTAINS. What's to be gained?

BENDER. You might as well get in the coffin.

CURTAINS. You're already in it.

BENDER. Your mass is over.

CURTAINS. You're on their shoulders.

BENDER. They're hammering your lid on!

CURTAINS. You're going down!

BENDER. After you!

CURTAINS. Your tombstone's up!

BENDER. Yours is inscribed!

CURTAINS. Yes it is! Yes it is! Yes it is! And there's moss where my eyes used to be, and I can't say if I'm clay or dust or dust or clay.

   Exit CURTAINS.

Scene Seven

BENDER *shrugs and wanders around the space. She picks up the brush with the hat and tails on it. She dances with the brush.*

BENDER (*while dancing*). You and I could have done it all. Yes, you and I. . . all is flux you said, had to look it up in the dictionary.

Pause.

Yes, all is flux, And your catch phrase, 'The only law we are certain of is the law of uncertainty, and the cold cold kiss.'

She bends to kiss the brush. BAXTER *has arrived with the necklace around his neck as usual. He watches her kissing the brush.*

BAXTER (*after a pause*). Are you my mother?

BENDER (*puts hat and tails aside*). If you're my son.

They embrace, a mechanical embrace. He kisses her, she kisses him.

BAXTER. I've grown.

BENDER. Have you a woman?

BAXTER. I had.

BENDER. None of my sons have women.

BAXTER. I think I had if I'm not mistaken.

BENDER (*getting into the bath*). Did you love her?

BAXTER. Yes.

BENDER. Not my son, my sons love only their mother!

BAXTER (*dead, almost*). I love my mother.

BENDER. (*dead, too*). I love my son.

BAXTER. Can I come in the bath?

BENDER. Certainly you can. (BAXTER *gets into the bath, not facing her.*) What's your name son?

BAXTER. Mother...

BENDER. Yes my son.

BAXTER. Mother it's Baxter.

BENDER. Baxter...(*Trying to remember.*) Baxter...were you the one who raped me?

BAXTER. No.

BENDER. Or the one who used to beat me?

BAXTER. Used you to wear red?

BENDER. Never wore red.

BAXTER. The one I hit wore red.

BENDER. Bet she deserved it.

BAXTER. No.

BENDER. Stealing a son off his mother like that. I'd hit her as well. A good clout puts manners on them when they're young. . .what's your name again?

BAXTER. Baxter.

BENDER. Baxter. . .were you the one that was crazy on train sets?

BAXTER. Hate trains!

BENDER. The one who brought me flowers?

BAXTER. I used to draw pictures for you.

BENDER. Pictures.

BAXTER. You loved them?

BENDER. Did I?

BAXTER. Hundreds of them, one after the other, for you.

BENDER. Can't remember. . .sorry. . .I miss you.

BAXTER. Do you?

BENDER. Yes.

Pause.

BAXTER. I miss you.

BENDER. Do you?

BAXTER. Yes.

BENDER (*offering breast*). Are you hungry?

BAXTER. Not any more. (*Gets out of the bath and kisses her.*) Lovely to see you.

BENDER (*going off*). Call again soon, do you hear me now, call again, next time I'll remember you. (*Exit* BENDER.)

Scene Eight

BONE *and* BINDER *storm on.* BAXTER, *who has been on his way off, stops.*

BAXTER. Binder, how do you get a man pregnant?

BINDER. Ask Bone, it was his fault.

CURTAINS (*coming on*). So the man and woman came to a fork in the road...

BONE. If Binder wasn't so careless! Never thinks of anyone but herself.

BINDER. Your nerves are at you again I see. I think you should go for a lie down.

BONE. Another bun please?

> BAXTER *hands him a bun*, BINDER *goes to hand him one*.

BAXTER. Any apple tart?

> CURTAINS *goes to give him some*, BONE *gets there first*.

CURTAINS (*a bit put out*). Cream?

BAXTER. No thanks.

BINDER (*to* BONE). Darling, I know it's not easy for you.

CURTAINS (*to* BAXTER). We could try again.

BAXTER. This is my safe period! I told you a hundred times.

BONE (*to* BINDER). You've just no conception of what it's like carrying a girl-baby.

BINDER. It's no joke carrying a boy-baby either!

BONE. Girls are harder.

BAXTER. I'm not asking for much!

CURTAINS. At the fork in the road, millions of other men and women are gathered.

BAXTER. It's your attitude I hate!

CURTAINS. Maybe you just can't conceive you know.

BAXTER. More likely there's something wrong with you.

CURTAINS. Look it happens sometimes, you're just not fertile.

BAXTER. I think you should have some tests. I want a girl-baby! It's them, Curtains! I know it is.

BINDER. I bought you a handbag.

BONE. Baxter already bought me one.

BINDER (*peeved*). Did he?

BAXTER. At least he appreciates a present when he gets one. Where's the bracelet I gave you?

CURTAINS. Binder broke it.

BINDER. I did not!

CURTAINS. She was jealous!

BINDER. It fell.

BAXTER. Bone, Binder broke the bracelet.

BONE. Did you?

BINDER. I suppose.

BAXTER. You suppose!

BINDER (*to* BONE). Well she said you were an eejit.

BONE. Well I am an eejit.

BAXTER. Yeah, he is an eejit.

CURTAINS. That's what I said.

BINDER. I'm an awful eejit. I'm sorry Baxter.

CURTAINS. Forget it!

BONE. No we won't forget it! How dare you call me an eejit?

BINDER. Yes, how dare you call him an eejit?

BAXTER. Don't speak to her in that tone of voice.

CURTAINS. Eejit!

BAXTER. Don't you dare call him an eejit!

CURTAINS. I was talking to you.

BONE. He's no eejit!

BAXTER. Of course I'm an eejit!

BINDER. I could have told you he was.

BONE. No, you're an eejit!

BAXTER. Yeah, you're some eejit!

BINDER. I am not an eejit!

BONE. She's not an eejit!

BINDER. Maybe I am an eejit!

BONE. She is an eejit!

BAXTER. No she's not!

BINDER. I must be an eejit!

BONE. She's no eejit!

BAXTER. She's a big eejit!

CURTAINS. Eejit!

BINDER. No you're the eejit!

CURTAINS. Yes I am an eejit!

BAXTER. You are not!

CURTAINS. I am!

BONE. She is!

BAXTER. Well I'm not!

BINDER. Neither am I!

CURTAINS. Eejit!

BONE. That's me!

BAXTER. No it's me!

BINDER. It's me!

CURTAINS. We're all eejits!

OTHERS. We are not!

CURTAINS. We're no eejits!

OTHERS. We are so!

ALL. EEJIT!

They scatter to the four corners of the stage and exit, except BINDER
who storms into the bath.

Scene Nine

BENDER *enters, sees* BINDER *in the bath.*

BENDER. Come on! It's my turn for the bath!

BINDER. I just got in.

BENDER. You've been there for years!

BINDER (*pointing to her belly*). How does my son look today?

BENDER. You're going to have a girl-baby!

BINDER. I am not!

BENDER. Please yourself. (*Trying to get into the bath.*) Go on, push over!

BINDER (*feeling her belly*). Oh! He just kicked.

BENDER. Well kick him back! (*Boxes BINDER's belly.*) There! Think they can take over the whole joint!

BINDER. That wasn't me baby, that was the old hag!

BENDER (*sits on the toilet and boxes her own belly*). And don't you start! (*To BINDER.*) Bet he doesn't budge for the rest of the day!

BINDER. He's crying, you've bruised him!

BENDER. He's just swimming around, anyway it's a girl-baby. Girl-babies aren't so bad. I was a girl-baby, so were you.

BINDER (*fussing over her stomach*). And look what happened to me.

BENDER. Will you stop that! You'd swear it was the Messiah you had in there.

BINDER. Maybe it is.

BENDER. You're soft because it's your first . . . what does he say to you?

BINDER. Not much.

BENDER. Did he ask you to stay with him?

BINDER. Yes he did.

BENDER. Well go on! (*No answer from BINDER, puts on a hat.*) Did he say will you stay with me? or (*Changes the position of the hat, different intonation in her voice.*) Will you stay with me?

BINDER. Can't remember.

BENDER. Yes you can! You just don't want to share it with me.

BINDER. He said will you stay with me.

BENDER (*mimes him*). Will you stay with me? The cheek of him! And what did you say?

BINDER. I forget.

BENDER (*hitting her with the hat*). What did you say? Go on! (*Hits her again.*)

BINDER. I said I can't.

BENDER. Why?

BINDER. Because of her.

BENDER. Because of me?

> BINDER *stares forward*. BENDER *taps her with the hat*.
>   And what did he say then?

BINDER. He didn't say anything then.

BENDER. He did so! You told me before he did.

BINDER. I said, she needs me!

BENDER (*hits her with the hat*.) I don't! Go on! And he said. . .

BINDER. I said she can't survive on her own! (*Gives* BENDER *a vicious look*.)

BENDER. Liar! And what did he say?

BINDER. He said, I need you too.

BENDER. And you said. . .she's the most important person in my life. . .more important than you even. . .isn't that what you said?

BINDER. It is not! We never mentioned you.

BENDER. You told me the pair of you spoke at length about me!

BINDER. I made it up!

BENDER. You did not! There were candles and wine and music, and he said, (*Puts on the hat*.) She must be an amazing woman. . .

BINDER. He never said that!

BENDER. Beautiful even! Isn't that what he said? Yes! That's how it happened. (*Puts the hat on, mimes him again*.) Will you stay with me? (*Hat off.*) Who does he think he is! I suppose he told you he loves you.

BINDER. As a matter of fact he did.

BENDER. Once they tell you they love you it's downhill all the way! Might as well get out before it turns sour.

BINDER. You talk as if my life is over.

BENDER. Well look at you, lying in my bath with a mountain on you like Kilimanjaro, your legs all knotted up, your skin gone to hell.

BINDER. Well at least the father isn't invisible!

BENDER. Give him time! Give him time.

BINDER. I'll get my figure back.

BENDER. Heard that one before. Did he buy you a present?

BINDER. He asked me what I'd like.

BENDER. And what did you say?

BINDER. I said I didn't really want anything.

BENDER. You never say that! You say, I want that dress, I want those shoes, I want this perfume . . .

BINDER. I don't want any of those things.

BENDER. That's not the point! Keep him thinking of you! Never stop wanting! And when he has given you everything you could possibly want, you say, 'Thank you Darling but I really didn't want any of those things'.

BINDER. I'm going! (*Gets out of the bath.*)

BENDER (*stands in her way*). No listen to me you, because I know something that you don't.

BINDER. Because you've done it all!

BENDER. Yes! I've done it all.

BINDER. See you.

BENDER. Come back here!

She goes to grab her. BINDER *looks at her,* BENDER *stops.* BINDER *begins to move off.*

No, we'll make a phone call.

BINDER. I'm tired of your phone calls.

BENDER. I'll let you do all the talking.

> BINDER *has gone*. BENDER *wanders around the space, with the hat and tails etc*.

> When we spoke and it wasn't often, we spoke mostly of the landscape or of food. One night I thought the silence would never end. You were listening to each wave, the different sounds, you said. You wondered when the tide was high in Ireland was it low in England. I said I didn't know, said I would find out, never did. In bed we spoke least of all. He no longer had words to describe that landscape and I had not the courage. So we lay there, side by side like two corpses, horrified at our immobility. And if we merged, must've been by some accident. No passion there for a long time now. My eyes sought the ceiling above him, while his moved towards the back door.

> *Black out, exit* BENDER.

Scene Ten

Darkness.

BAXTER. Bone! Bone where are you?

> *Lights come up*. BAXTER *has a huge swelling or hump or pregnancy on his left shoulder. He is doubled over, necklace around his neck as usual.* BONE *arrives, puts his ear to* BAXTER'*s back and listens*.

BAXTER. Well?

BONE (*listening*). Ssh!

BAXTER (*Panics*). Is she alright?

BONE. Ssh will you! (*Silence.*) Not a bother on her.

BAXTER. Give her a kiss will you, I can't reach.

> BONE *kisses* BAXTER'*s hump then he kisses his own belly*.

> Well, go on, talk to her!

BONE (*to* BAXTER'*s back*). Hello baby. (*Softly.*)

BAXTER. Louder!

BONE (*a little louder*). Hello baby.

BAXTER (*impatiently*). She can't hear you!

BONE (*shouts*). Hello Baby!

BAXTER. That's better, that's better. (*Tries to straighten up, can't.*) It's not easy I tell you.

BONE. No one ever said it was... (*Points to his own baby.*) Will you check her?

BAXTER. Right...come nearer. (BONE *puts his belly to* BAXTER'*s ear, he listens.*) She's grand, grand.

BONE. Will you rub in some olive oil?

BAXTER. That's the Pink Sock's job.

BONE. Pink Sock's gone.

BAXTER. Where?

BONE. It began, it ended, you know.

BAXTER. Yes...terribly sorry Bone.

BONE. Yes.

BAXTER *struggles with the pain of his hump. Both their movements are slow and painful now.*

BAXTER. OK, get out the olive oil.

BONE. How am I going to manage on my own with a girl-baby?

BAXTER. I'll stand by you (*Dreadful pain, groan.*)

BONE. Look, sit down will you.

BAXTER. Ah you know I can't sit down!

BONE. Well lie down.

BAXTER. I'm not a dog!

BONE. No one said you were!

BAXTER. Then stop telling me to lie down!

BONE. You lay down yesterday.

BAXTER. Did I?

BONE. And the day before.

BAXTER. My glorious past. Well today I'll kneel. (*Kneels with great difficulty.*) It'll soon be over Bone!

BONE. Easy for you to talk, you've Curtains to look after you.

BAXTER. I told you I'd stand by you.

BONE. Stand by me! You can't even sit.

BAXTER. Or lie down.

BONE. Can you not?

BAXTER. Unless someone knocks me. Check if she's still breathing will you?

BONE (*checks*). She's grand. Are you taking your iron?

BAXTER. No, are you?

BONE. No.

BAXTER. Great times ahead. (*Looks over his shoulder*, *pats his hump.*) Isn't that right?

BONE (*hand on stomach*). I'll have to be a mother and father to her now.

BAXTER. And you will too, and I'll help you anyway I can. (*Groan.*) And sure she'll have her nibs here to play with.

BONE. Hope they won't grow up masculine.

BAXTER. Not at all. Sure how would they, with me baking and you knitting.

BONE. Will you finish with Curtains?

BAXTER. Never really started.

BONE (*suddenly terrified*). Baxter! I think they're out to kill us.

BAXTER. I think they have.

Enter BENDER *and* BINDER *with the scarf around their necks.* BINDER *is knitting*, BENDER *is leading.*

BENDER (*monotone*). How is the knitting?

BINDER (*robotic*). Grand, grand, and how are you?

BENDER (*getting into the bath*, *no feeling*). A bit tired and the baby?

BINDER (*sitting on the toilet*). Fine and the baby?

Light change, all in silhouette, a spot on CURTAINS *who has just entered.*

CURTAINS. So the man and woman joined the millions of men

and women at the fork in the road. The millions of men
turned to the millions of women and said 'I'll not forget you'.
The millions of women turned and answered, 'I'll not forget
you either'. And so they parted. The men heading north and
the women heading south. Before they ever met the man and
woman had a dream. It was the same dream, with this
difference. The man dreamt he met the woman north by north
east. The woman dreamt she met the man south by south
west. Long after it was over, the man and woman realized that
not only had they never met north by north east or south by
south west, much worse, they had never met. And worse still,
they never would, they never could, they never can and they
never will.

Theme music comes on, she turns and begins walking off.

One day the man looked out of his window. 'It's time', he
said. So he got up on his bicycle and he rode all over the earth
and he cycled all over the sea. One evening as he was flying
over the highways he saw the woman in his path. 'Get out of
my road', he yelled, but she would not. 'I've two choices', the
man said, 'I can knock her down or I can stop'. He did both.
'You,' she said, 'if you have courage get off your bicycle and
come with me'.

End

Michael Harding was born in Cavan, Ireland, in 1953 and has lived and worked on both sides of the Irish border. He has published poetry and was awarded the Hennessy Literary Award for short stories in 1980. He received an Irish Arts Council bursary in 1985. His first novel, *Priest*, was published in 1986 and was shortlisted for the Book of the Year, Ireland. His latest, *The Trouble with Sarah Gullion*, published in 1988, was shortlisted for the Aer Lingus/Irish Times Literature Prize and the Hughes Fiction award.

Strawboys, his first play for the Abbey Theatre, Dublin, presented on the Abbey's Peacock stage in 1987 was a critical and box-office success and was nominated for two Harveys Awards. His second play for the Abbey, *Una Pooka*, was also staged at the Peacock and won the RTE/Bank of Ireland Award. It was published in *First Run 2* (Nick Hern Books, 1990). The BBC hope to broadcast a radio version in 1990. *Misogynist* is due to be staged at the Abbey Theatre, as part of the 1990 Dublin Theatre Festival.

Michael Harding won the first Stewart Parker New Playwright's Bursary in 1990.

Characters

A MAN, in his fifties, costumed half-way between Alice in Wonderland and an old bore in slippers and cardigan; but not comical.

A GIRL, of slight build, costumed in white, starched lace surplus (choral vestment), and nothing else.

The CHORUS. In a full production a chorus of women are to be employed. They are dressed as MONKS, and appear on a raised level, up-stage, as shadowy figures, coming and going in twos, threes or singly – kneeling; praying; entering; exiting; quietly, in the background. All the musical pieces may be sung by the CHORUS.

They enter at the end of the play as a chorus of women. The moment must be abundant with their sensual, erotic presence. The costumes are important.

Setting

The general impression should be one of props focused in an austere no-man's-land.

A space cluttered with statues and catholic inconography. There is a place where the actor can stretch himself as on a cross. A chalice, vastly oversize and ornate in a prominent position.
A large bell, capable of being rung, and many small ones and a very large video screen to be seen by the audience and the actor.

Up-stage sweeps to stairs and tall, oversize doors.

Other than this, it is an open stage and the wings may be used for entrance and exits.

Misogynist is due to be staged at the Abbey Theatre, Dublin, opening 10 October, as part of the 1990 Dublin Theatre Festival. At the time of going to press the cast was as follows:

HIM	Tom Hickey
SHE	Dervla Kirwan

Directed by	Judy Friel
Designed by	Robert Ballagh
Lighting by	Rupert Murray

A light goes up on HIM *standing centre-stage staring at the audience.*

He is nervous and speaks very fast.

HIM. Blouses.
Oh aye.
Frocks.
Yeah.
All the way.
Don't talk to me about it.
Blouses. Blouses.

When the Devil appeared to me
he came as a young man
nine years old.

He looks sideways.

Come here. Come here. I said come here. Will ye come here
for Christ sake.

SHE *edges out of the wings.*

Over here. Over here. Beside me.
That's it.
Now stand there and tell the truth.

SHE. When the Devil appeared
he came as a young man
nine years old.

HIM. Hail Mary full of grace the Lord is with thee. (*Whispers.*)
Blessed art thou among women and blessed is the fruit of thy
womb. Yes.

The bed was rickety, like, but big. Big.
And the light of the holy mother of God on the landing coming
in under the door.

I knew his relations of course.
The legions from the other side of the river.
Other side.
Who cares.
I mean who gives a fuck.
Really.

I had to chase him round the pillow for his warm hands.
Couldn't find them.
Gone they were.
Like rabbits back into the earth.

It's not far, he said, from the bottom of the bed. Teasing me.
It's not far.
An' I went for him.
Oh gosh I did.
Be jayses.

SHE. Satan.
Came as a rabbit.
Nine years old.

HIM. His head popped up again. A slap in the mouth I suppose.
There ye are now.
The dark space inside him was puzzled.
Couldn't dare ask another question.
I opened the palm of me hand and let the fingers widen.
You know,
I whispered into the dark hole of his head,
you can talk too long sometimes.
You can.
Better sometimes to say less
especially when you're in the dark.

Did ye know that ...? Eh ...? (*Laughs.*)

The Prince of Darkness has many disguises
yes.
Three hundred and sixty-four of them.
One for every day of the year,
except Christmas.
But a person like me – you take what you get.

The question is, where was the bed.
Jesus Mary and Joseph we had our bearings
arseways.

You don't sit in a wood and ask for the sea.

I could give ye half me kingdom, he said.
Half me kingdom, if you'd only dance.
Go on, dance. Dance ye fucker.
Dance.

I never touched him.

SHE *approaches* HIM.

SHE. It's all lies Tommy. All lies. (*She exits.*)

He has heard her and is troubled for a moment.

HIM. The Devil has many disguises. The Devil comes in many forms.

He kneels at the shrine of Saint Theresa and prays. •

He stands and addresses the Saint.

HIM. I've nothing against women.
Nothing.
OK.
Fuck them.
Excuse me.

In fact I'm a bit of a feminist myself.

But let's just say,
for arguments sake,
that I saw her.
Well I did.
I saw her in here.
In the . . .
well
I won't say.
I did see her.
There.
See?
Just there.
She was raising the chalice.
She was raising the chalice like this.

He demonstrates.

I mean it.
She was.
She was raising the chalice.
And mumbling under her breath.
As if she might be . . .
Well. Let's leave that.

She was raising the chalice.

Ehh . . . excuse me . . . stop that.
Stop that. Stop I said.
You shouldn't be in here.

OK
You shouldn't be in here.

So just put that thing down.
Right?
She didn't move.
Just eyed me with the corner of her eye.
Eyed me.
Put it down, I said.
And she replaced it, ever so gently on the . . . altar.

Incline unto my aid Oh God, that I should live in awe of such
a dreadful thing as I myself.

Shakespeare.

I asked her who had let her in.
Oh I was cleaning, she said.
Cleaning.
Cleaning indeed.
Cleaning.
You're lucky, I said.
I was cleaning she said.
I've a right to be here.

Let him kiss me with the kisses of his mouth.
May his name eternally be on my tongue.
Let my tongue cleave to my mouth if I forget ye
Oh daughters of Jerusalem.
Proper little madam.
Proper little madam.
And cheeky.
Cheeky into the bargain.

I asked her, her name.
I was entitled, to speak harshly to her.
I could have done worse.

I could have done a lot worse.

As it was I thought I'd just pull rank.

I will go to the altar of God, I said, the God of my gladness
and joy.
A pure heart create for us O Lord, a steadfast spirit within us.

Yes.

Don't take me for a fool

I said.
I caught you.
I caught you doing something very silly.
Yes.

He moves about now addressing some of the statues with passion.

Silly brothers, silly.
And he that shalt do the silly thing shall be
chastised.
And she that sits on the thistle shall quickly
rise.

What happens to little girls
who do silly little things.
Eh?
Speak.
Speak.
Lord.
Thy servant is listening.
Speak, eh?
What happens to silly little girls who do the
silly thing.
They get punished.

Yes.

Now I have more to be doing with my time than to pass any
more remarks about the incident. But I'd like you to
remember, little girl, that if someone else . . . a certain
someone else . . . had found you here,
doing that,
then you would be in very hot water my girl.
Very hot water indeed.

For those that wash by the rivers of Babylon
shall weep when they wash.
Remembering Zion.
That was telling her.
Bless us and save us.
Bless the lord oh my soul.
Zion bless the lord.

I wouldn't expect her to . . . kiss my boots . . .
or anything.
Oh no.
But the least I expect is a modicum of

gratefulness.
In her attitude.
Yes.
In her attitude.
And not this
bare faced
I did nothing wrong
attitude.

She was looking at me.
Don't look at me like that.

And do you know what she did then.

She asked my name.
She asked for my name.
None of her bloody business.
None of your bloody business, Miss Nosey Parker.

And
who was I.

Who was I by Christ.
By the memory of Daniel.
Who was I.
Stop looking at me like that.

Fishes of the sea and beasts of the mountain,
bless the Lord.
Stop looking at me like that.
She was looking at me.
And then she said;
Sorry.
And cast her eyes to the ground in an air of
mock submission.
Sorry.
And she stood there, and she knew that I knew
that she was only pretending.
Eyes to the ground with her air of mock
submission.
Sorry.
Fucking bitch.

Thou shalt not bear false witness against thy neighbours.

May I leave now, she asked.
Pleaded.
Thou shalt not bring calumny into thy

discourses.

Oh yes, I thought, you may leave now, you may leave now my
little temptress.

Actually that is not what I want to talk about at all.
No.
What I really wanted to talk about was . . .
fish.
Jonah and the Whale.
Three days in the fish's belly.
Why?
Why?
Or is it not patently clear why.
By the way,
but have you never known someone to open a can
of worms with one little finger.
Her little finger.
Her eyes closed.
Finger not the iniquity of thy brother, lest
thy hand be cut at the wrist.
Why Jonah.
Why a whale.
Why not.

And this is just to wind up now, right, I don't, I don't, I'm
not going to get into a knot about all this, but, but, but she
didn't actually leave.
No.
She didn't.
No.
Didn't actually leave.
Christ when I think of it.

Actually I was cleaning, she said.
Well, I think that had been established.
I knew that.
But the way she could stand there and lie.
I was waiting for you, she said.
I was waiting for you.
Just like that.
Oh I know,
I know the way these people can squirm
when they've been caught.
I know.
I haven't been in positions

all my life
without realising that.

I haven't been in the whale's belly all this time
without realising that.

For me?
For me?
I couldn't resist, she said.
She meant that you see (*Indicating chalice.*)
She meant that.
Yes.
She couldn't resist.
I just wanted to hold it.
Just once.
Just once.
Oh by Jove she sure did.
I was waiting here all day she said.
For you.
And it was there on the table.
I couldn't resist.
And she smiled.
Smiled, if you don't mind.
Smiled.

Wherefore art thou that slew the Amorites.
Where shall we go to flee thy face.
There on the table she said.
Illiterate little bitch.
If I climb the mountains thou art there.
Well I could see there was no use annoying myself at that hour
of the evening.
If I descend into the pit thou art even there
below me.
No.
No use annoying myself.
At that hour of the evening.
Best thing was to get rid of her as swiftly as
possible.

Yes, I said. Yes, well we've left that behind us now.
You're excused.
I excuse you.
You may go.
Go.
Go away.

But I've been waiting for you,
she persisted.

And now let us just remember something here.

I had just finished a very long day.
Right ...?
It was late.
Very late.
I had mountains of work to do before resting,
and,
and
I had another upset tummy.

I know I know I know;
Blessed is he who dies in harness for he shall not be bored.

What do you want, I asked
and be brief.

By the way
just by the way
did you ever notice just how cross some of
these
well heeled articulate little bitches become?
Mmmm?
Did you ever notice that.
Cross.
I mean really cross.
I notice that.
You can't have a discussion with them.
No logic. No rationality.
They get all wired up.
You notice that.
I notice that.
Rub them the wrong way and mind your nose
doesn't get chopped off.

SHE *enters, dressed as a chorister, and looks beautiful. She approaches* HIM *with solemn liturgical movements. In a firm voice, but addressed to* HIM *as a love song, she sings* Kyrie Elieson *with the monastic choir in the background providing the answers. (This and further pieces are from* Missa de Angelis *– plain chant.)*

He listens as if in prayer.

SHE *leaves.*

HIM. So anyway

she asked me
what it was like.
I suppose they're all
secretly
dying to know
what it's like.

What's what like I asked.
What's it like, she said.
She wouldn't dare actually put words on it.
It's what I do I said.
It's what I do.
Gosh, she said,
I'd love to.
I'd really love to.

You'd pity them sometimes.

Then she asked about
the Whales.
The Whales.
I said I understood these things
She said it wasn't possible
Three days.
In the belly of a fish.
Not possible she said.
Look, don't be stupid, I said.
Don't be so fucking stupid.
Look at women.
Babies.
What about them? Eh?
Now if you don't mind, I said,
if you're quite finished,
I must be getting at it.

At what, she said.
At it.
The stupid bitch.
At it.
OK.
At it.

She got the message then alright.

And then the poison really came out of her.
Out of the mouths of orphans.
Out of the mouths of babes.

It came out of her.
Do you really care for me at all, she asked.

You see? You see? You see what I mean?

Jesus such a fucking question.

Yes.
Yes.
Yes I said.
Yes of course I care for you,
being as patient as I could,
yes of course I do,
now if you don't mind
it is very late,
and you are trying my patience.

Extreme reserves of control.
That's what you need.
Extreme reserves of control.
I just keep my cool.

Tell us about your day, she said.
I beg your pardon.
Tell us about your day.
Had you a busy day?
What did you do?

Had I a busy day?
Well I could see now where it was leading
alright.
I could see now.
She didn't have to ask anything else.
She was simply
toying
with me.
Trying to provoke me.
Seeing would I throw a wobbler as they say.
Hmmm.
Well she was up against the wrong cookie here.
That's what went through my head.
Yes.
You're taking on the wrong cookie
at the wrong time
in the wrong place
my little lady
if that's your game.

If that's the game you want to play.

Right.
Right right right.
You young lady
were waiting here for me
here
all day
for me
correct or incorrect?
Correct.
Good.
You wanted to talk to me
correct?
Correct.
Good.
Now, are you aware who exactly you're speaking
to ...?
She paused.
Do you know who I am?
Ha.
She paused.
Do you know who I am?
Do you know my name?
She didn't.
I had her.
You came here specifically to see
me. Specifically.
And you can't even say who I am.
I had her.
I had her.
I thought I had her.

I heard you speaking, she said.
She had an answer for everything.

What is hidden shall be revealed, it is
written.
What is whispered in secret shall be broadcast
on the radio.
It is written.
I heard you preaching,
she said.
I heard you on the television.
I heard you from the roof-tops.

She was smart enough to have found out some of the actual
content of what I had said.
Oh yes.
She was well rehearsed alright.

And mark this,
mark you this, brothers,
does she leave it at that ...?
Does she?
No.
You were ... quite good ... she said.
You were one of the best.

There's flattery for you.
The honey lips and the silver tongue.
And yet, measured flattery.
One of the best.
Quite good.
She wouldn't say good.
Oh no.
She wouldn't say
'the best'.
She wouldn't give that much.
One of the best.
There were only five speakers in all.

A bell rings off-stage. A tiny bell. He hears it.

Two bells ring off-stage.

He picks up the small bell, then the big one.

Finally four bells are ringing.

A little incense stirs the air. We hear the Gloria in Excelcis *being sung off-stage by the chorus of sweet-voiced* MONKS.

After a few lines of the Gloria, *He leads into the sermon as the music continues in the background.*

I'm not ashamed of what I said.
Sometimes these things are necessary.
Someone has to lead.
Someone has to draw the line somewhere.
I mean we can't all just go ... beserk.

He shifts to high oratory.

Brothers,

we are living in dangerous times.
All about us are the signs of
Terror.
You know it yourself.
In political life.
In religious life.
In family life.
Every one of us can sense the creeping rot, the disintegration,
the degeneration of history.

As the great poet of our century has said, the middle
cannot last.
The middle cannot stay together.
These are times for caution.
Too much is already in flux about us.

A man blindfolded on the edge of a cliff does
not take risks in the manner of his movements.
He cannot see.
So he uses his cunning,
he uses the gifts still available to him
and the power of his legs
and his hearing
to edge himself away from the cliff
And if he knows in which direction there is
help
then he cries out
in that direction
for
eh
help.

Incline unto our aid Oh God, O Lord make haste
to help us.

And so on and so forth
about obedience,
and the necessity for authority
firm authority
at a time like this.
The need to curtail any social or liberal
excesses at a time when we are on the precipice
of
chaos.

That sort of thing.

It went down very well.
Very well.
In fact, to be truthful,
it went down terribly well.
Oh indeed.
Yes.
I'm no joke, you know.
I'm on the ascending arc as they say.
Not just there yet.
Still accelerating.
But higher than a lot of the snotty little bastards in the past
might have thought.

If I could indulge in just a tinge of petty
pride,
and I know it is indeed
petty,
but certainly,
they know who pays the piper now as they say.

I
am important.
I'm one of the keys.
And my time is
in the super sense
quality time.
I'm busy.
Busy busy busy.
That's why I have the assistant.
Yes.
I do.
I have an ass-istant.
Otherwise I wouldn't get through the day, would I.

To do the donkey work.

I expected this. I did.
That's the point.
I expected it.
I'm not overwhelmed by it.
I'm not fazed by it.
I can handle it.
And that of course is why I am not a one to be flattered.
You see?
A man who is intimidated by the heights to which he has
ascended might be susceptible to flattery.

For me,
I am who I am.
It's OK.
Par for the course.
Nothing remarkable.

On the subject of flattery
I'm untouchable.

During the speeches to follow regarding 'Tommy', he watches a video
of himself getting out of bed, having breakfast, doing menial tasks with
no sense to them, such as, moving boxes from one end of a room to
another. We often get close-ups of his face looking straight to camera
which he can freeze with a control button at suitable times.

Though the same actor is used both on stage and on the video, he refers to
the image on the video as 'Tommy'.

The assistant is always saying that to me.
Tommy.
Always saying
You were made for the job.

And the old bollox is right.
I was.
Made for it.

Look.
Look.
See?
Look at him.
Just look at him.

Tommy
you see
is a bit of a groveller.
He was made for second class trains.
Pass degrees.
He was made for toilets.
Technical things.
If there were two suits in a shop
a second-rate one
and a first-rate one,
and if the first-rate suit was half the price,
Tommy
would still come out with the second-rate suit.

It comes natural.

If there were three sisters, and two of them
were magnificent and one was ugly
Tommy
would end up in bed with the ugly one.

And he has an impeccable eye
for kitch.
You know, he knocks,
when he comes in.
Knocks.
I've never had to tell him.
It comes natural.
You wanted to see me?
he says.
I stared at him one day and said I;
Yes
I do
Tommy
I do
I wanted to see you
Tommy.
Are we alone?

And you know what he said . . .?
Yes.
He said
Yes,
just us and the Lord.
Just us . . . and . . . the Lord.
Very good living person.
Now was that trying to be amusing
or was he just genuinely
Devotional.
Tommy
I said to him one day
are you to be trusted.

I should hope so sir, he said.
I should hope so.
There's the deferential disposition that makes things great.
When the assistant has not the arrogance to even assert his
own honesty.
Not for him to decide.
You see.
Whether he is to be trusted or not.

That is my decision.
I must make up my mind.
That's the point.
And that's what those subtle few words convey.

I should hope so sir.

It's something like the old chestnut about being in the state of
grace; you can never be sure, and you can never assert that
you are. It's for the Lord to know.

Everything should work like that.

But it is very funny.
Tommy.
Are you to be trusted.
Just like that.
I should hope so sir.
You see
not for him to know.
Not for him to say.
Not for him to assert.
Convention dictates that
he hope
and I decide.

I get enormous pleasure from taking the piss out of him
like that.

He is a touch upset.

Well fuck it, we all get angry with something
now and again.
Don't we?
I mean we can't
all
be saints
all
of the time.
And I do.
I get pleasure from taking the piss out of him.
Little grovelling rat that came in second.
Oh yes.
Tommy was in the race alright.
In for the glittering prizes.
Aiming at the big stakes.
Weren't we

Tommy darling.
But you didn't make it did you.
No.
Not quite.

Now your future depends on me, and you know it, don't you,
you know it, you fucking know it, fat head.

He cools off.

And you know when I really look at it
I can't say that I see Tommy
as part of the future.
But there's no point telling him that.
He has enough worries poor man.
Let him go on serving, I say.
Let him
carry on
serving.
Waitering.
Ha ha.
Tommy
I said to him one day
I'm worried.

We're all worried, he replied.
The numbers are going down.
In spots.
In crucial spots.
Elsewhere,
the numbers
are far too high.
The juice, Tommy; the money Tommy; the philosophical
disposition, Tommy.
The post-modern irony you cock shit.
If things disimprove any further, we'll be the laughing stock of
history.

What are you doing about it?

Do you know what he ventured to suggest.
He ventured to suggest
that things would   .
work out for the best.
That we should not be too caught up with
problems in our little world.
That our little world

didn't reflect the overall situation.

God but he's pathetic.
You're a pathetic little creature
Tommy.
Pathetic.

It was her of course.
I knew that.
He knew that.
Only he was too lily-livered to say so.

Well then.
What do you make of the situation?
I venture to suggest, sir,
that the young lady is misguided.

She can hardly do much harm.

The sanctus is sung while SHE *enters in a seductive night-dress, and rings the big bell.*

He keeps well away from her.

On the video machine, a silent set of images of SHE, *dancing on a disco floor.*

He is caught for a moment between the two.

Then he rushes to a cross, not noticable as such before. He crucifies himself on the cross, shouting the following speech over the din of the fading sanctus and bell.

You're telling me she can hardly do much harm.
Can hardly do me much harm.
The Lord is my shepherd
there is nothing I shall want
and she can hardly do me much harm.
The Lord slays all my enemies and smites those
who would oppose me
and she can
hardly do me much harm.

She is reeking with venom
for Christ sake.
She is poisoned with jealousy.
She is twisted with jealousy.
And all she wants to do is to infect the world
with the bitter little juices of her . . .
the bitter little juices of her . . .

The crescendo has been reached. SHE *is gone. The screen shows a test card. The sanctus is over.*

He steps off the cross and speaks quietly.

I was going to say
the bitter little juices of her mammeries
y'know
like what Hamlet says about gall for milk or
something,
but you can't be seen to be too
Intellectual
in front of Thomas Aquinas.

Anyways, there was a kind of a lull in the room until he came
out with his next amazing contribution to historical awareness;

The reports suggest, sir, that she is by all
accounts, a very kind young lady.

Sweet Jesus give me patience with this dog's vomit.
We all know she's kind Tommy.
Ladies are kind.
Florence Nightingale was kind.
Nurses are kind.
Milkmaids are kind.
Big kind buttery women.
So she's a woman.
Big fucking deal.
Do you know nothing.
Do you know absolutely nothing.
About morality.
Culturally defined what nots.
No absolutes Tommy, no absolutes.
Relative.
History.
All that shit.
Do you know entirely nothing.

The Jews were kind.
In ways.
What the fuck has that got to do with it?

I'm sorry
Tommy said,
if I've said anything
out of place.

Why Tommy?
Why?
The question is
Why?
Why?
Answer me that Tommy.
Arse licker.
Why?
Why?

I don't know why,
says he.
No.
So that's it.
We don't know why.
Well then, let's all be idiots.
Let's all be like you Tommy.
Sublime fucking idiots who don't know why.
Who don't care why.
Who fucking cares.
That's it.
We'll have no authority any more. No obedience.
No discipline.
Just chaos.
Everybody go make up their own minds about
everything.
Everybody just listen to the radio.
Everybody just do as you please.

Oh you want that today my Lord, sorry my Lord, I don't
really feel like doing it today my Lord. You couldn't run the
lavatories on that attitude.

Tell her to go embrace my fucking arse
Tommy.

*He calms himself. As therapy he plays with a dictaphone or the video
camera which relays images to the screen.*

Hello. Hello. Hello. Hello.

You see to be really honest, this . . .
woman . . .
worries me more than I care to admit.
Oh she can go round being kind to all the people she likes.
I can tolerate that.
But it's when she starts talking that the trouble starts.

Opening her big mouth.
You see,
people are very tricky.
They can be ... persuaded.
Once she places things in a certain
context
they find nothing unacceptable in what she
says.
That's how slithery she is.
Of course, if she were to challenge me
openly. Ha.
Fairly and squarely.
Well, there'd be no contest.
I mean
I'd leave her blood on the wall.
Ha.
But you'll find she won't do that
No sir.
She knows not to stroke the tiger's whiskers too
directly.
No.
Instead she weaves her little web.
And draws people into it.
Yes.
And she's succeeding.
All the fools are mesmerized.

Do you not see what she's doing, I said.
Do you not see what she's doing, I said.
But they would not listen to me.
Fuck them.

He finishes with the camera (or dictaphone).

My brothers,
we have fought many battles,
many adversaries,
over the years.
But this little lizard in the grass is the worst of them all. In the
sweet fragrance of the grass with her kind words, gently
cloaking the fangs of poison.
This is the most deadly enemy of all.
Yes?

That sounds right.

He turns to the saint, and kneels in prayer, while in the background we hear a tinkling bell and a whispering.

You and I know
that man let loose
unbridled
is prone to terrible evil.
You and I know
that we are stained with evils unmentionable.
Uncontrollable.
Now when someone suggests that we are as pure as a drop of
water . . .
Eh . . .?
That can hardly be good news, can it . . .?
Oh I know the political little bollox would probably say it was
a question of emphasis. Cute fucker that he is.

We've got very fond of emphasis nowadays.
Emphasis.
All a question of emphasis.

A louder tinkle of a bell and SHE *enters enfolded in vestments for mass. White. In her hands a bunch of flowers. In the flowers a knife.*

She approaches HIM. *He retreats. She approaches. He is afraid of her knife.*

His face appears on screen and from the screen HE *feverishly delivers the following speech.*

It wasn't just that she walked on the lawns.
Trampled on the lawns and
plucked out all the nice flowers.
No.
More.
Much more.
She came in you know.
She came in from somewhere.
She came in.
She was there.
Here.
There.
Holding up the chalice and holding it up and
mumbling, and I heard her, honest to God, I
did, I said
stop that, stop stop stop stop stop, you shouldn't be doing this.

As the talking head on video continues, both he and SHE *continue to elaborate the cat and mouse movements.*

Put that down.
She eyed me without moving and then,
gently,
ever so kindly
she lowered the cup.
I was cleaning she said,
smiling and cleaning, cleaning, cleaning,

Cleaning . . . ?
In here . . . ?
Who the hell told you to clean in here?

The others, she said.

Noooo . . .
The others?
Oh yes, she said, the others.
Hundreds of them.
They all want me to clean.

You're cheeky, aren't you.
Cheeky, cheeky, cheeky.
What's your name I said.
She was right there.
Right there.
None of your fucking business she said.
Fucking.
She said that.
And I lowered myself.
Divine Jesus forgive me, but I lowered myself.
I shouldn't have, but I did.

He is kneeling. SHE *leaves the knife in his mouth and exits.*

He remains transfixed until the end of the speech from the head on video.

I engaged her in conversation.
It was a mistake.
I gazed and gazed and asked the unforgivable
question;
the big self revelation;
Who are you, I asked.
And she laughed.
You know who I am, she said, stop pretending.
You know who I am. And she laughed, and laughed

and dipped her finger, her little finger in the
cup and then licked it with her lips.
You know who I am, she said,
and then she went away.

End of speech from talking head on video.

Still kneeling, He recommences in a loud voice.

Come ring out our loyalty to the all powerful
and hail the rock who protects his humble
servants.
Let us go before him with fear and trembling,
for he will defend us from our adversaries,
and smite all our enemies.
He will defend us from all our adversaries and
smite all our enemies.
He will defend us from all our adversaries and
smite the fuck out of our enemies.
Amen.

*He rises, completely reassured. A fit of laughter catches him as he
continues.*

So, probably time to intercede.
Yes.
That's the name of the game.
Intercession.

*During the following, he arranges small red lights at the base of the plinth,
and white ones in the halo which is about seven feet above. He dresses in a
white robe and places himself on the plinth in a state of absorption.*

Yes.
Silly tradition really.
Often wonder where it ever started.
Oh well, traditions are important.
Not for us to reason why.
People must have their buzz as they say nowadays.
And mighty is the buzz of a little intercession.
A little channelling as they say.
A little bit of extremely specific target focused spiritualis.

So every evening I come up here,
as far back as I can remember
and light twenty-nine little lights around this plinth.
Twenty-nine little sparks of fire.
And when people look up from the street

they say
ahhhh
there he is,
he must be interceding late tonight,
and they all feel better.
So each evening,
at nightfall
I come up here, and . . . eh . . .
what you might say
. . . intercede.

Of course Tommy asked me about it one time.
Could I not use real candles . . . ?
Well thank you very much Tommy,
I told him that electricity does the trick
and why waste time with candles
and by the way
I don't go up in smoke
as I would be very likely to do
were they real candles.
Thick head.
And do you know,
He sits there and he still couldn't understand
why I didn't use real candles.
No doubt a side of him would relish the thought
of me going on fire.
But I couldn't for the life of me get him to see that it didn't
matter a shit what people thought.
It's what they saw that matters.
But if they think they are seeing candles, surely it ought to be
candles, he said. Otherwise, it could be said, that you are
conning them.

Stupid little fart.

There that's them.

A pause for intense prayer. He assumes a saintly posture.

Either it's a flame or it's not a flame.

Postures.

Idiot.

Postures.

The lights start to flash and flicker.

Jesus Christ look at that.
Just look at that.
Ingenious thing an electrician.
Where are you now Tommy?
Eh?
You couldn't do that with your candles, could you?
Eh?
All flickering at the same time.

He relishes the sight as if in a bath.

You know when she first started making headlines,
I was afraid for a while that I might have to make a comment at
some stage.
Clarify matters.
Let people know what the
'official policy' really was.
So I went to the
'professionals'
the people who churn out the ideas,
so to speak.
I put it to them.
What do I do about the little bitch,
I asked.

In a loud whisper he speaks the following, upwards, to heaven.

You know of whom I speak.

In a 'funny' voice.

Yeah yeah.

He continues in a 'funny' voice for the speech of the professional.

That's how they speak.
Well, what can we tell you, she is amusing.
Amusing.
You know,
you stand here like a fucking ninny,
with a sore neck.
just to be told she's amusing.
She's amusing.
I don't find her amusing.

Ought I to condemn her. .
Publicly.
He stared down at me as if I were a raving
lunatic.

Condemn her.
Condemn her for what?
That,
your Intelligence,
is just what I was asking you.

He steps off the plinth and extinguishes the lights during the following.

They're no good, y'know.
A lot of these people are all
intellectuals.
No guts.
All art, air, and elitism.

*There is a curtain up-stage which now rustles, giving the distinct
impression that someone is behind it.*

He shouts.

Of course I wouldn't entirely disagree with everything she says.

He stares at the cutrain, horrified, then whispers.

1, 2, 3, 4, 5, 6, 7, 8, 9 . . . 10.
Must be the wind.
Funny how just thinking about her can put you on edge.
I mean . . . why . . . should
she . . . matter to me?

I am who I am.
So what's the problem.
I'm here.
I have a life.
I can talk.
I can speak up for myself.
When it all boils down, I can do . . .

Distinct rustle of curtain.

*He rises from his cautious cat-watching pose, and abandoning all restraint,
attacks the curtain first verbally, and then physically.*

How dare you.
How bloody dare you.
come up here
and spy on me.
You're caught.
Caught.
Not good enough to undermine everything I do,
you have to come up here and eavesdrop as well.

Eavesdropper
ye slithery bitch.
Shameless little fingers.
Come out or by jingo I'll
swing this thing through you.
Out.Out.Out.Come out.Come out.

*Having battered the curtain to shreds he finds nothing more than a full
length mirror. He is unmanned and very distressed. He stares in the
mirror, entranced. He kisses the mirror.*

*Suddenly compelled to test his physique in front of the mirror, he strips
down to his underpants. He then indulges in compulsive, neurotic testing
of flab and muscle against the mirror's image.*

*There is the sound of shoes on a marble hall, a clear sign of someone
approaching the great doors. He panics.*

It's her.

He rushes about searching for a hiding place.

Where shall I go to escape mine enemy.
If I go to the highest mountain thou art there.
If I decend into the pit yet would you follow
me.
You search me and you know me.
You knot me together in my mother's womb.
I cannot flee from thy face.

It is her.
It is. It must be. I know it.

*Finally, he puts on a white robe and returns to his posture as a statue.
He is transfixed now in a beautiful vision, and still terrified. He is still.*

*The clear footfalls on the marble hall approach the door. The great doors
fling open with a flourish but no one enters, or, it is as if a ghost had
entered.*

Pause.

I know what will happen now.
I do.
Sure as hell.
She'll strut in with her high heels, singing
anybody home,
anybody ho-me.
Can I come i-in?

Christ the bloody cheek of her.

Can she come in.
As if I had any say in the matter.

He now affects a feminine voice for her lines so that he splits himself into two characters: HIM *and* HER.

HIM. Can she come in.

HER. Can I come in? (*Sing-song.*) Hallo-o. I heard noises. Is there anybody here?

HIM. She heard noises.
   Fucking marvellous.
   She has ears. What does she expect?
   Then she'll start on the cleaning again, won't she. Dusting the things. Dusting
   the . . . don't you dare.

HER. I told the girls about him you know. Oh I did. Honestly.
   Jenny and Penny. I did. Well I mean you have to tell them something.
   Or they'd be wondering.
   I don't tell them everything.
   But I did tell them some of the bits.

   Thursday.
   It was Thursday.
   Yes. Thursday.
   Thursday. It was. Wasn't it. Aye.
   Thursday.
   No maybe it was Wednesday.
   Aye right enough it was Wednesday.
   I know, for it was
   the blue tea towels.

HIM. I know it was Wednesday because it was the blue tea towels.
   Sacred heart of Jesus.

HER. He was sitting there beside me, listening to the
   three of us nattering on, you know the way we go
   on, Jenny and Penny and meself, aye, nattering on about
   perspiration.
   Perspiration.
   Yes.
   Girls.
   Maybe men don't perspire,
   but Penny certainly does.
   Oh my gawwwwwwd.

But Jenny can be funny sometimes in company
about,
y'know,
braaaaa . . .
being too tight.   .
Or other little things.
Unmentionable.
Well there we were having a gossip
and he's in the corner
on his pedestal
channelling
interceding,
squirming.
I mean is he squirming.
Rattling out the Hail Holy Queen on his teeth.
So I just told him.
I did.
Go out and make us a cup of tea pet.

And the look he gave me.
Like a knife going through ye.
Oh he went out alright.
Pounded up the stairs and off to bed in the belfry.
The belfry as I call it.

Well I had to tell them.
I mean
there's times and he's
untouchable.

HIM (*speaks heroically*). Holy Mary Mother of God pray for us
sinners
now
and at the hour
of our death.

HER. But of course when his friends are around.
The foreign ministers
as I call them.

*He moves off the pedestal, working the robe into something and getting
right into the part.*

Well he's strutting up and down in front of the
fire like a peacock.
Lashing whiskey and wine into them.
Lashing it into them.

Jesus I wouldn't be caught offering Penny a
drink, or Jenny a drink.
Ye wouldn't hear the end of it.

And the conversation?
Politics.
I just get fed up and go away.
Make them tea and éclairs.
Wheel it in on a trolly.
Like a nurse.
And go to bed.

I'll leave you boys to it, I say.
I'm off to beddy bye byes.
Oh right dear, right, bless you.
Just like that.
Oh right dear, right, bless you.
He says.
Oh right dear, right, bless you.

HIM. The cup of salvation I shall raise, I shall not
be jaundiced, I shall drink it to the dregs.
And his banner over me is victory.
Victory or love.
Fuck it,
one or the other.

HER. I should go down on me knees in front of the lot
of them some night, just for a laugh.

HIM. Just for a . . . laugh?

HER. For a laugh. He doesn't have a sense of humour though.
They told me that. Humour him they said. He doesn't have a
sense of humour.

HIM. And the graves of the dead shall open,
and terrible visions shall be seen by the men
who live in those days.
Humour.
Christ spare me her humour.

HER. I told Jenny, I did, I told her. Yes, I says, I
says to Jenny, I did, I told her I says, Jenny,
I says, I say, I says Jenny
I don't know what those boys get up to when I'm gone to bed
but I can tell ye
the furniture does be rearranged something
shocking

when I get up in the morning.
Ha ha ha.

HIM. Yes.
Yes I know her ways.
Yes.
I know as these things are known by people who
know.

His tone becomes heroic and archaic.

As the Greek might have known.
As the Gentile knew.
As the man from the Foriegn Office knew.
As any civilised man knoweth
and must be patient.
I look at her.
She looks away.

HER. God the stare of him, I mean. Like,
it's enough to give the kettle a fright.

HIM (*majestic*). Enough said.
I gaze upon her.
Even so.
And she trembles.
Is afraid to reply.
Is afraid to think.
Is afraid to be.
I understand.
Is there something wrong, dear girl?

HER. No, no, no dear, nothing.
Not a thing.
Would you like your peaches now, or will you
wait till later.

HIM. But I reply not.
No.
I am silent.
So that she will understand that it is my desire
that she goeth
the fuck
from my sight.
And will she go?
And leave me that must brood,
and reflect
to the sombre shadow of his own solitude,

wherein the silence
speaks.

Nay.
Nay.

The grand style intensifies.

So it will come to pass,
her
standing there
at some time shortly hence,
a mop in hand
dusting the little trinkets that she spies
until I cry
Hold
Don't touch that
as her frivolous hands dare to trespass
on the Altar
and seeketh out
the Holy Chalice.
Don't touch that or I'll
demolish ye.
To wit
the gentle creature will reply
God but ye can touch nothing that belongs to
him.

HER. I mean, like that model sailing ship that's down on the top
of the television.
A sailing ship I ask ye.
Sacred Heart,
didn't Jenny let it fall, and two of the little
men broke off.
Ha.

HIM. And so anon, and anon,
she doth make windings of her memories.
Her idle histories,
and photographs of the past.

*He finds old family snaps and scatters them around throughout the rest of
this speech.*

Things that have been here for years.
The bitter revenge of looking.
To sit all evening with them till it has become
dark without noticing.

To remember the way you sat upon a wall.
To tell the length of a single life in one faded
yellow minute.
And sort out all the dead from
uncles, aunts, first cousins, nephews, neices, and
the schoolfriends
to sort it out and think
can one ever sit on a wall again without
regrets.

Or go down the stairs.
I can't think downstairs.

Why (*To her.*) don't you go down and make a
sandwich or something.
Watch the telly.
Go out if you're going.
Fuck off.
I'll be down in a minute.
Yes it was like that.
She said she was about to go.
She said that.
And she stayed.
She remained.

Pause.

He is terribly upset.

Eloi. Eloi. (*Pause.*) Why hast thou forsaken us.

He rushes for the protection of his cross, his perch. When he gets there he whispers very fast.

HER. Ah gee. Ah gosh. Ah well well. Now look at
that. That was us outside the back door, in the
heat. And there's daddy. And me, and Peggy, and
Peter.
Poor Peter. Oahhhh this one, now, where is this one.
Let me see.
Oh yes, that was on the beach, and there's the
birthday cake, yes, gee, gosh, she had it in the
boot of the car all the way from God knows
where, and the whole party was held up.
Well the panic.

His voice flips and beomes loud. He moves away from the cross somewhere in the following speech.

HIM. Jesus bloody Christ you don't give up do you.
Eh?
You give a man no bloody space at all.
None.
Not even the fucking attic.
Well have it.
Have it.
Have the whole thing.

He goes wild. Moving around, tearing up photos, scattering chests of clothes everywhere, some vestments, some elegant evening dresses.

There you are.
There.
You have the whole fucking thing now.
Here,
I suppose you want this too, and this, and this, and this, and this.
Go on.
Have everything.
Have the whole bloody world for all I care.
There.

He rushes out. Banging the grand doors behind him.

A pause. Long enough for us to be aware of the emptiness. Then we hear his footsteps. He re-enters, flinging the doors open, his temper spiralling.

HER. Jesus when I think of Jenny complaining about
her philanderer. (*He puts on his robes again.*)
And she doesn't even have to worry.
That bloody buck leper of mine
she says
I have to tie him down.
At time.
Lock him up.
Couldn't trust him.
Traipsing round night clubs at his age.
Scrutinizing every bare shoulder in Corfu he was
last summer.
The animal.
Had the hotel chamber maids terrorised.
Pretending he was Benny Hill.
As if they knew who Benny Hill was.
You'd need to put him on a dog leash
when you take him for a walk on the beach.
Awful man.

An' I said to her, I did, I said to her, says I,
I said, Jenny.
Jenny.
Jenny.
Would you not be worried.
You know?
About 'health' matters.
I mean we can all catch it.
If he was carrying on.

Diseases, says she.
Carrying on, says she.
Are you codding me, says she.
Sure my Eddie is as healthy as a trout.

So he's not actually cheating on you, so, says I.

Are you codding me, says she, sure my Eddie wouldn't hurt a
fly.

It's all to do with him going bald.

God knows but Jenny talks in riddles
sometimes.

HIM (*explodes*). Yis all talk in riddles
sometimes.

HER. Penny says Jenny gets up on him. Just whips off
the trousers. Jesus, Mary and Joseph.
He loves it she says.
Mind you Penny could be only making that up.
She says her own fella is a creep.
Unzips himself in the dark and blathers at the pillow for five
minutes.
How he can manage to do it,
she says,
without hardly touching her
is a gymnastic miracle.

HIM. I'll just have to keep my cool as they say. Let her blather all
she likes.

He gazes as if at HER.

Cleaning are we?
Cleaning?

OK.
Fine.
Stay.

Stay so.
You can't leave me alone for two minutes without getting
suspicious. Sure you can't.
It's all that inane television you watch.
Maybe you need a good fright. Eh?
Is that it ...?
So what do you think I do up here all night.
Dance round the place in a pair of stockings
maybe.
Play cowboys and indians?

(*aside*). I could scare the shit out of her if I wanted to.

He finds stockings which become a balaclava.

HER. Please. Please. Pretty please, take that off. Please. Take
it off.
It makes you look ...

HIM. No. Sorry.
I don't feel like taking it off just now.
I feel like staying here with them on.
Like this.
This is what I want to do.
Right now.
How's that with you ...?
I think I ought to be allowed do as I wish in
the privacy of my own home.

He speaks in a low voice to the audience.

An extremely wise man once said, that when you come to the
end, everything stops.
Everything.
Nothing changes but everything stops.
You just continue.
Except that now you don't continue doing
something,
you continue
doing nothing,
because everything has stopped.

To HER.

So what do you make of that, sugar ...?
Doesn't much matter.
If I act the rake.
If I creep up behind you, baring my teeth to have what's my
due.

Doesn't even matter if I invade your olive groves with my little
white ghosties.
Does it.
Does it.
It doesn't matter.

He erupts.

Don't you see it's gone too far.
Too far. Much too far.
The silence.
The snivelling.
Polishing your mouth with tulips.
Polish your mouth with tulips.
There see,
it's a poem.
She sucks bulls eyes.
She blows feathers at the mirror.

And what does that mean.

He takes off the balaclava.

HER. Do I what . . .?

HIM. Do you suck bulls eyes?
Do you polish your mouth with tulips . . .? Well.

HER. Oh please, please, what are you talking about.

HIM. Your mouth. Night after night. Garlic.
And bulls eyes, watching television.
Am I making sense.

HER. No. No. No. No. No you're not. You're not making
sense. Oh I'm frightened.

HIM. Good.

He approches where SHE *might be with a knife.*

Now.
Undress yourself my Little Miss Muffet. My child.
Move.
You couldn't leave me alone could you.
Couldn't let me out of your sight.
Just because I come up here to get away from the
stench of garlic and gob stoppers.
Is that reason enough?
Or shall I make you a better one?

Take off your clothes. Everything.
Off.

He lets the robe fall away and stands in shorts, knife at the ready.

Thing is,
get her to shut up.
Get clothes off.
At knife point.
Yes.
Yes.
At any point.
Force the issue.
Grasp the nettle.

Hurry up.
I want everything off.
Everything.
Two can play at the one game you know.

HER. I wasn't playing games. Honest.

HIM. Shut up.

HER. OK OK OK OK, whatever you say.

He has given in completely to HER *role now. He is frightened, and in this speech he dresses up. The clothes should be nineteenth century, the dress being an elegant evening costume.*

Alright.
Alright.
Easy.
Easy.
I'll be good.
Please don't hurt me.
I'll be good.
I promise.
Pardon?
No I swear,
I never in my whole life
ever thought there was anything wrong with you.
Never.
No.
I didn't.
I didn't even think it.
Never.
Sure how could you need treatment.

It's me needs the treatment, isn't it. Yes . . .?
Yes . . .?

Knocking on door up-stage.

HER. It's the girls.
The girls.
Please.
Let me go.

HIM. Oh we're in a big hurry to go now, aren't we.
Now that the girls are here.
Well you can't go down looking like that, can you.
No.

Another knock.

Jesus Christ.

Another knock.

HER. But they'll know we're in.
They'll see the lights on. They'll know there's something wrong.

Knock.

There's something wrong alright.
There's something terribly wrong.

HIM. No they won't.
They won't know.
They'll never know.
You can't go down like that.
Like this.
Like that.
Like this.
Like that.
Oh God.

The knocking has been increasing, it reaches its height as the doors fling open wide.

A great blast of glorious light.

Panis Angelicus *is sung by the* MONKS *as they enter in procession. They are girls in monastic Habits.*

As the procession enters, singing, he continuously comments at it.

Yes,
Yes,
Come in,
Come in,

Come in girls.
Yes. Oh yes. Oh yes indeed.

When all are in, he screams.

In. Come in.

Finally, SHE *enters wearing a white nightdress/choral dress. He cowers before her.*

SHE. It's late.

HIM. Huh?

SHE. I said it's late.

HIM. Oh yes. Of course. It is.

SHE. Are you ready?

HIM. Yes.

SHE *binds an ornate girdle round him, with which in a few moments she may lead him out and puts a long veil over his head.*

HIM. I never thought it would come to this.
Ohhh you're so young.
Will it hurt.

SHE *nods affirmative.*

Do I look very silly.

SHE *nods negative.*

I'm a grave digger you know.
A hospital cot.
With ribbons and bells. Ha ha.

I confess. I confess.
I confess you are very young.

Yes.
I'm ready now.

SHE *begins* the Salve Regina.

He joins in.

SHE *begins to lead him by the girdle up the stairs.*

Now only he is singing.

His two hands clutch the chalice, and SHE *tinkles a tiny bell as she leads him out through the grand doors, and away down the marble hall.*

As the strains of Salve Regina *fade into the distance, the* MONKS
are lined up towards the audience. They begin to sing the Salve Regina
*again, this time singing it properly. Their robes turn out to be merely
cloaks. Underneath, their costume is similar to* SHE's *white
nightdress/choral dress.*

A long moment as they contemplate the audience.

*A warm half-light,
finally,
fades out.*

The End.

Marie Jones has been writer in residence with Charabanc
Theatre Company since its inception in 1983. Her plays for
Charabanc which include *Somewhere Over The Balcony, Girls In the
Big Picture* and *Gold in the Streets* have toured extensively to USA,
USSR, Great Britain and Ireland. She has also written *Under
Napoleon's Nose* and *It's a Waste of Time Tracy* for Replay Theatre
Company, the recently formed Belfast based Theatre in
Education Company.

Wedding's Wee'ins and Wakes her latest piece for Charabanc was
commissioned by the BBC and toured to community centres in
Belfast. Marie Jones has recently completed three television
dramas for 'Lifeschool' a BBC Education programme.

Characters

JEANETTE DUNCAN
KENNY DUNCAN, JEANETTE's husband
CATHY DUNCAN, JEANETTE and KENNY's daughter
PATSY McDONALD, JEANETTE's sister
NORMAN McDONALD, PATSY's husband

The Hamster Wheel was first staged by the Charabanc Theatre
Company at The Arts Theatre, Belfast, on 6 February 1990.
It opened at the Riverside Studios, Hammersmith, London, on
1 May 1990 with the following cast:-

JEANETTE DUNCAN   Carol Scanlan
KENNY DUNCAN   Martin Murphy
CATHY DUNCAN   Zara Turner
PATSY McDONALD   Eleanor Methven
NORMAN McDONALD   Lalor Roddy

Directed by Robert Scanlan
Designed by Liz Cullinane
Costumes by Ivor Morrow
Lighting by Nick McCall
Music by Debra Salem

During 1990, this production also toured:

Dundalk, Town Hall, 20 February
Enniskillen, Ardhowen Theatre, 22 – 24 February
Belfast, Rupert Stanley College Whiterock, 27 February
Monaghan, St Louises' Hall, 28 February
Magherefelt, Burnside Hall, 1 March
Coleraine, Riverside Theatre, 2 – 3 March
County Down, Newry Arts Centre, 7 March
Downpatrick, Down Arts Centre, 10 March
Sligo, Hawks Well Theatre, 12 – 17 March
County Donegal, Balor Theatre, Ballybofey, 21 March
Belfast, St Kevin's Complex, 22 – 24 March
Glasgow, MAYFEST – several venues, 21 – 26 May
Dublin, Project Arts Centre, 29 – 16 June
Waterford, Garterlane Arts Centre, 18 – 23 June
Limerick, Belltable Arts Centre, 25 – 30 June.

ACT ONE

Lights on JEANETTE *and* KENNY. *The wheelchair jams in the middle of the door as she is about to enter.*

JEANETTE. Oh shit . . . (*Laughs to cover up the embarrassment.*) We're stuck love, can you believe it? (*Calls.*) . . . Cathy.

CATHY *appears with a huge dripping towel with which she has been mopping up the flooded kitchen.*

CATHY (*runs in*). . . . Welcome home Daddy.

JEANETTE. If he could get home . . . we're stuck.

CATHY. Stuck?

JEANETTE. Yes stuck . . . won't go through.

CATHY. Oh right . . . am . . . what do you think then?

JEANETTE. Well, I suppose it collapses.

CATHY. Right . . . I'll put this back in the kitchen.

JEANETTE (*sees the dripping towel*). . . . What's wrong?

CATHY. The washing machine . . . don't know . . . flooded the place. (*She disposes of the towel and comes back.*)

JEANETTE *is still standing there not sure what to do.*

CATHY. Should we get m'Daddy out and collapse it and then bring it in?

JEANETTE. Aye . . . What a homecoming, eh love? . . . I'll have to get L plates for this.

KENNY *doesn't respond.*

CATHY. You back it out and then come round the front.

They struggle to get KENNY *out and both help him on to the chair.*

CATHY. How does it collapse?

JEANETTE. What?

CATHY. Is there a lever or something?

JEANETTE. It must be obvious.

CATHY. It's not obvious to me.

JEANETTE. Well . . . glad to be home love?

CATHY. Mammy, did you not ask how this collapsed?

JEANETTE (*trying to ignore* CATHY *for* KENNY's *sake*). I have a whole load of stuff taped for you, you'll not be bored anyway.

CATHY (*she can't work out how the wheelchair folds*). Could we ring somebody and ask about this?

JEANETTE. Don't be ridiculous Cathy, ring somebody? . . . (*Getting annoyed and trying not to show it.*) . . . Who? . . . I taped about ten films and all the episodes of *Blind Date*. You'll get a laugh, love.

CATHY. What about the hospital . . . should we ring and ask?

JEANETTE. The hospital . . . do you think they have nothing else to do up there?

CATHY. I've got it. (*She collapses the wheelchair.*)

JEANETTE (*she is furious but wants to change the subject*). Well we aren't half glad you're back love, the place was like a graveyard . . . isn't that right, Cathy?

CATHY. Yes . . . will we get him back into the chair?

JEANETTE. Will we get you back into the chair?

They get KENNY *back into the wheelchair with great difficulty.*

CATHY. Can I get you anything Daddy?

KENNY *nods his head.*

JEANETTE. Well, here we are then, home.

CATHY. Did you get everything you need Mammy . . . pills and things?

JEANETTE. Aye . . . (*Tries to indicate with her eyes not to talk about pills and things.*) . . . Isn't he looking smashin'?

CATHY. Aye . . . what did the Doctor say?

JEANETTE. Put the TV on for your Daddy.

CATHY *puts the TV on.*

JEANETTE. There now . . . home sweet home . . . no more boiled beefburgers and watery custard . . . the food was disgustin' love, wasn't it? . . . What would you like for your dinner the night love?

KENNY *doesn't answer.*

JEANETTE. We'll have chicken . . . you'll like that.

CATHY. I'd better see to the flood in here . . . (*She leaves.*)

JEANETTE (*to* KENNY). Alright love?

KENNY *nods.*

JEANETTE. I'll give our Cathy a hand . . . bloody machine.

CATHY *is on her hands and knees with the towel.*

JEANETTE. Jesus Christ, what happened?

CATHY. Don't know.

JEANETTE (*goes back to* KENNY). . . . The machine love . . . what do you think it is . . . ack, I'm sure it's something simple.

She goes back to CATHY.

JEANETTE. Of all bloody days.

CATHY. He seems very low.

JEANETTE. What do you expect, you talking about doctors and pills, making him feel like a flippin' cripple. I don't want you speaking in front of your Daddy like that.

CATHY. I'm being practical.

JEANETTE. No, you were makin' it sound like he was going to be in that wheelchair forever.

CATHY. Mammy, he is a big man – you can't be liftin' him in and out like that. What about getting him down to the bathroom and up to bed?

JEANETTE. We'll manage between us . . . it's only for a while. He is on the road to recovery or he wouldn't be here.

CATHY. What if I'm not in?

JEANETTE. I'll manage him down to the bathroom myself and sure if you're out we'll wait until you come back in and then get him up the stairs . . . it's not going to be forever.

CATHY. How long did they say it would take?

JEANETTE. Your Daddy is a young man . . . he has that on his side.

CATHY. How long did they say?

JEANETTE. Every stroke is different. He could be on his feet again in two weeks.

CATHY. And what if he's not?

JEANETTE. Are you putting the scud on him?

CATHY. You only have two weeks off work, so what if he's not?

JEANETTE. Keep your voice down. He'll hear you. He's depressed enough . . . (*She goes back to* KENNY.)

JEANETTE. Isn't it nice to be home love . . . ?

PATSY (*enters*). . . . Welcome home, Kenny.

JEANETTE. Isn't he looking terrific?

PATSY. Sure, he always looks terrific . . . you got the wrong one of the family . . . you and me could have went places Kenny. I'm tired telling him.

JEANETTE. Take your coat off and sit down.

PATSY. The engine's running . . . Norman is in the car. I just wanted to leave in a card . . . it's a disgustin' one . . . you'll love it, Kenny.

JEANETTE. Tell Norman to come in.

PATSY. No, sure let Kenny get settled. We'll call when he's had a chance to relax.

JEANETTE. Are you going to Keep Fit tomorrow night?

PATSY (*surprised*). . . . Aye.

JEANETTE. I'll see you there.

PATSY. Are you going?

JEANETTE. Aye.

PATSY. God save us Kenny, she only gets you home and she's running off and leaving you.

JEANETTE. Sure he doesn't want to be looking at me twenty-four hours a day . . . Our Cathy's here anyway.

PATSY. Right I'll see you then.

PATSY *exits and* CATHY *stops her* . . . CATHY *and* PATSY
speak while JEANETTE *speaks to* KENNY . . . they can't hear
each other . . . CATHY *speaks in a loud whisper to* PATSY.

CATHY (*pleadingly*). . . . Aunt Patsy, are you not staying?

PATSY. She needs time to adjust on her own.

JEANETTE. You have mountains of cards. You're a very popular
   boy.

CATHY. She is trying to behave as if there is nothing wrong with
   him.

PATSY. It hasn't hit her yet.

CATHY. He has been like that for two months.

JEANETTE. What film should we watch the night?

CATHY. Patsy, stay for a while just to break the ice. I don't know
   what to say to him; you're good at things like that.

PATSY. I'm not good with sick people . . . only well people.

JEANETTE. We could start off with the Agatha Christie and then
   maybe two episodes of *Blind Date*.

CATHY. Please Patsy, I didn't get on with him at the best of times
   . . . just for an hour or two.

PATSY. You all need to be on your own with him for a while. It's
   important.

JEANETTE. Patsy are you still there? Thought you were in a
   hurry.

CATHY. We're just talking about the washing machine.

PATSY. I'm away . . . give me a shout if you need anything. (*She
   leaves.*)

   KENNY *starts to cry* . . . JEANETTE *is about to put her arms around
   him and then decides to ignore it and keeps talking.*

JEANETTE. One of the men you work with called and left in a
   lovely card . . . Frank somebody or other. He said the boys all
   miss you for the crack on the ferry. He said as soon as you get
   back into your lorry again they're going to throw a big party
   down at the depot . . . isn't that nice of them love . . . I said it
   would only be a matter of time 'cos you can't keep a
   thoroughbred down.

CATHY *enters and sees her father crying* . . . JEANETTE *indicates for her to go while she continues to talk* . . . *she is almost in tears herself.*

JEANETTE. Those wee nurses loved you . . . I think they were jealous of me . . . can't blame them.

KENNY *indicates to* JEANETTE *that he wants something.*

JEANETTE. You want paper, love.

She looks around not knowing if she has any and then fumbles in her bag and brings out an envelope and then searches for a pen. KENNY *writes awkwardly with his left hand* . . . *then hands the note to* JEANETTE.

JEANETTE. Alright love, I'll take you down now.

She goes towards the door and stops when she realises the wheelchair won't go through.

Musical link to the next scene.

During the following scene JEANETTE *is feeding* KENNY *a bowl of soup.*

PATSY*'s house.* PATSY *is relaxing on a chair with her feet up.* NORMAN *is assembling a new exercise bicycle.* PATSY *is obviously pissed off.*

PATSY. Norman I can't hear the TV. Can you not take that thing upstairs?

NORMAN. No . . . Debrah is watching Channel 4 on our one, Colin is watching BBC 2 on his one and I want to see this side.

PATSY (*through gritted teeth*). . . . You could have taped it.

NORMAN. It's stupid taping something when you're in the house and can watch it, talk sense.

PATSY. It's bloody irritating.

NORMAN. It's not you that's doing it.

PATSY. It's me that has to listen to it.

NORMAN. Do you want me to end up like Kenny?

PATSY. Kenny jogged. It had nothing to do with being fit or not fit.

NORMAN. I'm taking no chances.

PATSY. Really . . . it's not like you.

NORMAN. Did you fall out of the wrong side of the bed?

PATSY. We're going over tomorrow night to see Kenny and Jeanette.

NORMAN. You go love . . . you're better with sick people.

PATSY. That is feeble . . . think of something better.

NORMAN. How do you think he's going to feel . . . me sitting there fit and healthy and him in a wheelchair not even able to talk?

PATSY. What is he going to think if everybody ignores him?

NORMAN. I'll go when he's had time to adjust.

PATSY. Adjust! . . . Norman, the words come out of your mouth without even thinking . . . he was driving his lorry one minute as healthy as any of us, and the next he is in a wheelchair not able to feed himself and has to be taken to the toilet . . . could you ever adjust to that?

NORMAN. What choice has he?

PATSY. None . . . but we have the choice to at least let him think we care or treat him like a social disease.

NORMAN. Alright, alright I'll go . . .

CATHY *enters*.

CATHY. Hi . . . it's only me.

PATSY. Hallo Cathy, love.

NORMAN. Want a go on this Cathy?

CATHY. Never knew you were into that.

PATSY. It's his new toy.

NORMAN. Keeps the oul blood circulating.

CATHY. My mate's Da took a heart attack on one of those.

NORMAN. Aye well . . . you need to take it easy at first.

PATSY. Sure I would be alright Cathy . . . as Norman keeps telling me, he's worth more dead than alive – oh aye, you name it, Norman's insured for it.

CATHY. That means you've no need to worry if you drop dead.

NORMAN. Well now, I wouldn't go that far.

CATHY. So you pay out money in case you get sick . . . then pay out even more money so you won't get sick.

NORMAN. Mock if you like, but I will die worth a wee fortune.

PATSY. Sure, I would rather have you poor and alive than rich and dead.

NORMAN. How is your Da?

CATHY. Depressed.

NORMAN. Desperate timing.

PATSY. I don't think he had much say in it, Norman.

NORMAN. No, I mean you're about to go off to foreign fields. That's life but, you can never be sure of anything.

CATHY. No you can't . . .

NORMAN *continues to cycle.*

PATSY (*to* CATHY). Well how are things? (*Exasperated.*) Norman, please!

NORMAN. Alright! I'll take it upstairs. (*He leaves.*)

CATHY. I'm still going.

PATSY. To Germany?

CATHY. If I don't go now she'll start depending on me and I'll never go.

PATSY. Have you told her?

CATHY. I can't . . . if I told her now she would have to face up to what's happened . . . I don't think she is ready to do that.

PATSY. She is going to need to.

CATHY. She is talking about going back to work in two weeks and expecting me to be there to look after him until she gets back . . . it's only for a while she says. If I start to do that and then tell her, it will be harder. God I don't know what to do.

PATSY. Wish I could tell you.

CATHY. Aunt Patsy, I tried for a whole year to get this scholarship, it wasn't easy . . . They know how much I wanted it . . . she was over the moon when I got it.

PATSY. Things have changed for her.

CATHY. Not for me . . . I can't afford to turn it down . . . It's such an important time to go with everything that's happened and to do *Politics* . . . Jesus it's a dream.

PATSY. I understand . . . wish I didn't for her sake and then I could tell you different . . . but I do.

CATHY. Am I a heartless bitch?

PATSY. I don't think so . . . but she might.

CATHY. I would resent staying to look after him so much. Surely it's not right to do it then.

PATSY. No, but it doesn't stop people doing it . . . or having no choice but . . .

CATHY. This is what I've worked for . . . studied for, for three years – you know that.

PATSY. You don't need to convince me, Cathy.

CATHY. I did it on my own as well . . . he never gave me much help . . . he landed home at weekends and took over and was more interested in talking about his oul trips than what I was doing.

PATSY. I don't think that meant he cared any less.

CATHY. Well he didn't show it.

PATSY. Maybe he couldn't.

CATHY. Patsy, stop trying to take his side, he wasn't interested . . . he'd rather make fun of what I was doing.

PATSY. Maybe that was all he could do.

CATHY. Well that was no help to me . . . I got through university in spite of him, not because of him.

PATSY. Cathy I don't think you should be so cruel about your father in order to convince yourself you shouldn't look after him.

CATHY. It's the truth . . . I just never said it to anybody before.

PATSY. Your Da is a big man . . . big in size and big in the mouth . . . and education can frighten the life out of people. I would say he was scared to show an interest in case the big man with the big mouth became a wee man with an even weer mouth that he was heart scared to open.

CATHY. Well then he was more concerned with his stupid macho pride than he ever was about me, and now I am expected to be a nursemaid for him.

PATSY. I'm sorry you feel that way about him . . .

CATHY. So am I . . . I don't even feel it's my duty to do it . . . suppose I should.

PATSY. Duty. Whatever that's supposed to mean.

CATHY. I'm sorry to burden you with this, you have your own problems . . .

PATSY. I don't mind love . . . sure you didn't come for advice, you came so you could hear yourself saying all the things you've thought about and couldn't say . . . it helps. I do it sometimes to the hall mirror . . . It's great, you end up saying, that's great, I knew I was right to think that all along, or Patsy you have just said a load of rubbish and you had a cheek to waste all that head room thinking about it.

CATHY. You're only having me on.

PATSY. Am I . . . you go out to my hall mirror and you'll see teeth marks on it when I've had a bad day.

CATHY. How is Norman's mother?

PATSY. He says she's starting to dote . . . as far as I'm concerned she was born that way . . . remember that film that was on about a man who poisoned loads of people with this concoction he made that didn't show up in a post-mortem . . . I'm going to get it out on video . . . God forgive me.

CATHY. Why can't he put her in a home?

PATSY. He is . . . mine.

KENNY *throws the soup around* JEANETTE.

JEANETTE. Jesus Christ!

Muscial link into the next scene.

JEANETTE *is in her dressing gown . . . she is on the telephone.*

JEANETTE. It's just going to be another week Irene I swear. Thanks.

CATHY (*enters in her dressing gown, drinking tea and sits down*). Who was that so early in the morning?

JEANETTE. Irene . . . She is covering for me in work . . . just telling her I'm going to take another week off. He is ready to come down.

CATHY. Right . . . (*She gets up.*)

JEANETTE. Why so sulky?

CATHY. It's early . . . that's all . . . and I have a bit of a hangover.

JEANETTE. Early, it's half ten . . . Where were you?

CATHY. Went out for a drink and then on to a party . . . I didn't mean to stay late but you know how these things go.

JEANETTE. I managed your Daddy up to bed myself . . . we couldn't wait any longer.

CATHY. Sorry, I just got carried away talking.

JEANETTE. It's well for you, I've been up since six getting him ready . . . but he's coming on great, that right side is getting stronger all the time.

CATHY. I hadn't noticed.

JEANETTE. Well you would if you paid more attention to him . . . don't ignore him love, it's up to us to get him well again.

CATHY. I don't see why it should be.

JEANETTE. What did you say?

CATHY. Nothin' . . .

JEANETTE. Nothin' . . . that was a pretty strong nothin'.

CATHY. I haven't woken up yet.

JEANETTE. Look, he didn't ask for this . . . remember that . . . and we are all he has . . . remember that too.

CATHY. Right . . . (*Wants to drop the subject.*)

JEANETTE. So perk up for his sake.

CATHY. I said right . . . alright?

JEANETTE. Don't snap at me.

CATHY (*calmly*). Look . . . let's go upstairs and bring him down . . . OK?

JEANETTE (*sarcastically*). . . . I'm sorry your father is such a desperate burden to you, Cathy.

CATHY. Mammy, please, it's the bloody morning, I don't need this hassle.

JEANETTE. And I don't bloody need it from you either.

CATHY. If it's getting too much for you, don't take it out on me please.

JEANETTE. Cathy if we are going to get your Daddy back to himself we'd better stop this squabblin' for his sake. He is a sick man.

CATHY. Exactly and I'm not a bloody nurse.

JEANETTE. What . . . what do you mean?

CATHY. Mammy, this is not the right time . . . I'll talk to you later.

JEANETTE. You come out with a statement like that and you want me to wait until later.

CATHY. I haven't changed my plans.

JEANETTE. What?

CATHY. I'm going next month as planned.

JEANETTE. You're what?

Door bell rings.

HARRY *enters.*

HARRY. You called Handy Harry's . . . the washing machine, love.

JEANETTE. Aye, in the kitchen.

HARRY. Lovely morning, isn't it?

JEANETTE. Aye.

HARRY. Right . . . the kitchen.

HARRY *exits.*

JEANETTE. You could put it off for a while.

CATHY. And what if he doesn't get better?

JEANETTE. Don't dare talk like that.

CATHY. What if he doesn't . . . you'll start to depend on me and then I'll never go . . . If I go now it's better for you.

JEANETTE. Oh Jesus you're very kind Cathy . . . how very considerate . . . what a considerate daughter we have.

CATHY. I don't care what you say, I am not prepared to sacrifice my future for him . . . I wish I felt different.

JEANETTE. How the hell do you think you had a frigging future . . . because he sacrificed for you . . . worked every hour that God sent so you could be happy . . . let you live here free so you could have the luxury of doing what you wanted to do, . . . what education did he get? . . . who let him sponge so he could get what he wanted?

CATHY. I'm sorry for him, but I only got what you wanted me to have . . . so why take it away from me now?

HARRY walks into the middle of the two of them and drivels on about the washing machine as he examines a piece of plastic tubing, and of course does not notice the tension.

HARRY. . . . Now I could patch this . . . know what I mean . . . it could last two days . . . could last two years . . . who's to say . . . but you come out to fix these machines and the people expect ye to know . . . Mrs, dear if I could see into the future I wouldn't be here, I'd be down in the bookies. 'How long will it last Harry?' . . . Well, I mean it's a very difficult position to be put in . . . If it lasts . . . you're the best in the world . . . if it doesn't . . . 'don't be asking that eejit Harry to fix nothin' again' . . . It's a thankless job for nobody knows the dilemmas you're in about making a decision . . . and yet they expect you to and take your word as gospel . . . tell ye somethin', it would make ye take early retirement. I know other ones that wouldn't even put themselves through the dilemmas I go through . . . it would be. . . 'Sorry Mrs, your machine's had it' but of course them's the boys that work for the bigger boys and then they move in and sell a new one you maybe didn't need . . . but who cares, they get the commission and supply you with a new one with less fixing potential than the one before . . . Oh aye they all sleep easy in their beds, not giving a damn about the poor cratur that has to hand out the guts of three hundred pounds for a new one.

JEANETTE. What are you saying?

HARRY. It's in a bad way love.

JEANETTE. Oh God don't tell me that . . . I can't do without it, do your best will you.

HARRY (*sighs*). . . . I'll promise nothin'.

He exits.

JEANETTE. So you're going then?

CATHY. Mammy, you know how much it means to me . . . the whole point of doing languages was so I wouldn't have to stay here. You know I've always wanted out of this place.

JEANETTE. How can you be so bloody selfish . . . I wish you could hear yourself.

CATHY. Do you think I'm finding it easy?

JEANETTE. I don't know . . . maybe you are.

CATHY. I haven't slept one full night since it happened, worrying, trying to decide to put it off for a year. What if I stayed and then left . . . can you imagine what that would be like?

JEANETTE. A year . . . what are you talking about a year?

CATHY. If I don't take this opportunity now I'm going to have to wait for a year . . . how the hell are you going to support me?

JEANETTE. Like we've always done.

CATHY. Talk sense . . . him not working, you not working.

JEANETTE. I'm going back to work. He is on full pay for another two months . . . and if he does have to get benefit it will only be for a while until he recovers fully. I need you until then, Cathy.

CATHY. If you gave up your job you wouldn't need me to be here.

JEANETTE. What do you mean give up my job, what will I do when he's better and I have no job?

CATHY. You're asking me to give up my plans, why not *you*?

JEANETTE. Because mine helps to pay the bloody mortgage so that you can live like a friggin' queen . . . that's why.

HARRY. How long have you had this machine, love?

JEANETTE. Ages.

HARRY. Decades love ... I'm after finding a tanner at the back of the drum.

JEANETTE. Can you fix it?

HARRY. Your pump's away.

JEANETTE. Can you not patch or somethin'?

HARRY. 'Can you not patch or something' ... what I have to listen to ... wud a wee washer not do it? ... Can you not just stick a wee screw in it? ... Or the best one ... sure it was alright this morning ... do you know what I say to that one?

JEANETTE. No.

HARRY. I say Mrs ... my Granny died one night but she was alright that mornin'.

JEANETTE. Can you fix it or not?

HARRY. She is obsolete.

JEANETTE. Ah for crying out loud.

HARRY. Don't get excited love ... I'll stick an oul bit a denso tape on her ... either that or buy a new one.

JEANETTE. I'll go for the tape.

HARRY. Wise decision ... you see nobody makes nothin' to last no more ... ridiculous ... if you don't buy every new make that comes on the market you're scuppered ... you see they have you every way. (*He leaves and goes back into the kitchen.*)

JEANETTE (*to* CATHY). In that case I think you should go now.

CATHY. Now ... this minute?

JEANETTE. I've thought about it and you are right ... God forbid that I should become dependent on you even for one day, so I think you should go now.

CATHY. Now don't be daft ... I don't mind helping you, I just wanted you to know that I intend going when I planned to.

JEANETTE. Cathy are you deaf? . . . I said I would like you to leave now . . . I think it is best for the three of us.

CATHY. But what about you?

JEANETTE. If you're not going to give a damn in a month's time why the hell should you care now?

CATHY. I do give a damn, I just wanted to give you time to prepare yourself.

JEANETTE. You have no shortage of friends you can stay with until you go.

CATHY. I don't want to leave you . . . I'm not finding this easy. Why are you turning so bitter, why can't you see it from my side?

JEANETTE. From your side . . . I'm sorry I would never understand it . . . I don't know what it would be like to be a heartless bitch that could turn her back on her own father.

CATHY. Wake up will you . . . he is an invalid . . . it could be years before he recovers, he might never recover.

JEANETTE. Don't you dare say that . . . he'll walk, he'll talk, he'll drive that lorry if it is over my dead body.

CATHY. Well that is your choice but it is not mine.

JEANETTE. You don't want him to get well, is that it?

CATHY. Ah for God sake, I am not going to listen to this.

JEANETTE. You don't like him do you . . . he was never good enough as a father . . . you were ashamed of him, weren't you?

CATHY. This is crap.

JEANETTE. I watched you when all your so-called educated friends called, you would hardly let him pass the time of day with them in case he embarrassed you.

CATHY. That's a lie.

JEANETTE. Being a lorry driver wasn't good enough as a father.

CATHY (tries to leave). . . . I'm not going to listen to this.

JEANETTE. You're ashamed of your own father and now you haven't even the heart to feel pity for him.

CATHY. I think we should go up and get him down . . . right?

JEANETTE. I don't need you or anybody else to help me . . . you go and what is more, don't think of coming back.

Knocking on ceiling.

He has heard us . . . happy now . . . now that he knows his own daughter wants nothing to do with him.

HARRY *enters.*

JEANETTE. Will it be alright?

HARRY. It could last two weeks, two months, two years, who's to know.

JEANETTE. How much do I owe you?

HARRY. Ack nothing love, sure it's only an oul bit a denso tape.

JEANETTE. Are you sure?

HARRY. Mrs, the only thing I am sure of these days is that I'm gonna die and that I'll never be a millionaire . . . all the best.

He exits . . . JEANETTE leaves with the wheelchair. CATHY exits.

Link into the next scene.

JEANETTE *comes up to the door and brings* KENNY *in . . . he is not as helpless as before. He uses her for support and manages to limp a little himself. She goes through the procedure of getting* KENNY *in and out of the wheelchair as she speaks . . .*

JEANETTE. The nurse is coming this morning Kenny . . . I want you to be half civil to her.

KENNY. I don't feel half civil . . . I don't look half civil. I don't want to see no nurse.

JEANETTE. You have to . . . she'll be delighted when she sees how well you're doing. She'll be over the moon, you couldn't talk two weeks ago . . . so just do as your told.

KENNY. I'm sick of this.

JEANETTE. It will be alright love . . . I promise.

KENNY. I sorry for being a burden, love.

JEANETTE. Don't talk a lot of oul nonsense. You were restless last night love . . . we could get single beds if you like.

KENNY. No.

JEANETTE *holds his hand . . . he looks away embarrassed at her tenderness. She drops it again.*

KENNY. Turn the TV off.

JEANETTE. It's off.

KENNY. It's not . . . turn it off.

JEANETTE. It *is* off.

KENNY. Why are you annoying me . . . turn it bloody over.

JEANETTE. Over to what . . . it's not even on. I'm going mad . . . that friggin' TV is off . . . look no picture.

KENNY. If it's over then there should be a picture.

JEANETTE. Oh I see what you mean . . . it's alright love, I get you now.

KENNY. Thank God . . . are you daft?

JEANETTE. No, you said off and over but you meant on.

KENNY. I said . . . I meant . . . I want to see *Going for Gold*.

Doorbell rings.

KENNY. Ah, shit.

JEANETTE. It's her.

KENNY. She has got two minutes before this starts.

JEANETTE. Right . . . (*She brings the* NURSE *in*.)

NURSE. How are you, Mr Duncan?

JEANETTE. He's great.

NURSE (*as she takes his blood pressure*). Have you been using your right side then? Don't let him ignore it, Mrs Duncan.

JEANETTE. Oh he doesn't . . . show the nurse, Kenny.

KENNY *refuses.*

JEANETTE. Kenny . . . show the nurse.

NURSE. Don't force him, Mrs Duncan.

JEANETTE. He can do it rightly.

NURSE. Yes . . . just try not to push things . . . how are the waterworks?

KENNY. Don't know, I never go up the Antrim Road.

JEANETTE. Kenny . . . he is full of badness.

NURSE *smiles politely*.

JEANETTE. They're smashing . . . no problem.

NURSE. No problem with incontinence then?

JEANETTE. No.

NURSE. Really?

JEANETTE. Yes.

NURSE. How is the walking?

JEANETTE. Great . . . I just help him up the stairs . . . but he is getting around rightly.

KENNY. You haven't an oul zimmer you don't want? I'm thinking of going to a . . . bus station.

JEANETTE. A what?

KENNY. For a dance.

NURSE. A disco?

KENNY. That's what I said.

NURSE. I see you're not having too much trouble with your speech . . . I will arrange for the speech therapist to call anyway . . . Much word confusion?

JEANETTE. No . . .

KENNY. How long before I can get about again?

NURSE. Difficult to say . . .

KENNY. Why are you having problems talking too?

JEANETTE. Kenny, don't be so rude.

NURSE. I get used to it. Have you seen the Occupational Therapist yet?

KENNY. I'm not making bloody stuffed dogs!

NURSE. She'll give you things to do to ensure you use the affected side.

JEANETTE. That might be good, love.

KENNY *gives her a withering look.*

NURSE. Is there anything else you want to ask?

JEANETTE. No . . . I think that is all . . . I'll see you out.

NURSE. No questions?

JEANETTE. No, honestly . . . we're getting on great.

NURSE. Goodbye Mr Duncan . . . I'll see you soon.

KENNY *gives* JEANETTE *a look and she puts the TV on just as the* Going for Gold *signature tune is heard.*

JEANETTE *talks to the* NURSE *outside.*

JEANETTE *speaks in a state of confusion in a hurried loud whisper so as* KENNY *doesn't hear.*

JEANETTE. I am going to have to leave work and you see he gets paid from work even though he's not working . . . you know the way you get paid your wages for so long and then if you're sick you have to just get the sick . . . well you see, if that runs out before he's better . . . what I'm sayin' is . . . how long will it take for him to get back to himself?

NURSE. Difficult to say . . . could take two months, two years, every stroke is different.

JEANETTE. Two years . . . but what about money . . . his job?

NURSE. I really don't know . . . I'll talk to the social worker for you, or I could send her round.

JEANETTE. Ack, there is probably no need at the minute . . . It's only if the worse came to the worse . . . just checkin' . . . that's all.

NURSE. Alright Mrs Duncan, I'll see you soon.

JEANETTE *goes back into* KENNY.

JEANETTE. She says you'll be playing football soon.

KENNY. That would take a miracle.

JEANETTE. Why love?

KENNY. I couldn't play before.

Tape of Going for Gold *signature tune plays.*

JEANETTE *comes forward and* PATSY *walks into the light.*

PATSY. Cathy phoned me.

JEANETTE. Cathy who?

PATSY. For godsakes Jeanette, will you at least talk to her.

JEANETTE. He won't even allow her over the door, so there is no point . . . if that is all you wanted to talk about you can forget it . . . come on we'll go back in to Kenny.

PATSY. Look I'm not saying she was right or wrong to make the decision, I just think you should understand that she had the right to decide for herself.

JEANETTE. I'm not prepared to listen Patsy, so you are wasting your breath.

PATSY. Alright we will forget that one . . . I think you should be trying to get some help with Kenny.

JEANETTE. Where the hell am I going to get the money?

PATSY. There are voluntary people.

JEANETTE. I'm voluntary, he's got me.

PATSY. You won't get no medals, Jeanette.

JEANETTE. I don't want a friggin' medal.

PATSY. I'm sorry . . . there must be things you can get then, to help you.

JEANETTE. Like what?

PATSY. Can't you get those hoist things that help you get out of the bath?

JEANETTE. And make him feel like an invalid.

PATSY. He is.

JEANETTE. He is temporarily out of action.

PATSY. Alright, alright, then he is temporarily out of action, then try and get something temporary.

JEANETTE. You think I can't cope.

PATSY. I think you are bloody amazing and bloody stubborn. Your husband is, temporarily or not, disabled and you should and can get help if you weren't so bloody proud.

JEANETTE. You know it all our Patsy . . . we'll see how you

cope when you have to do it ... then you come and tell me
what I'm doing wrong ...

PATSY. For Christ sake, just pick up the phone and get some
bloody help.

JEANETTE. From who?

PATSY. Right ... (*Lifts phone.*)

JEANETTE. What are you doing?

PATSY. Hallo. Hallo is that Doctor Crummie? ... No, I know
you're the receptionist ... you know what I mean ... Could I
make an appointment? ... Next week? ... No, it's not really
an emergency ... can you hold on a minute? ... (*To*
JEANETTE.) Here, this is stupid. You do it. Tell her your
husband has had a stroke ... Jeanette.

JEANETTE (*takes the phone*). It's my husband ... he has had a
stroke. No, he hasn't just had it ... he's had it for ages ...
it's just ... maybe you could help me ... I think I need am
... a hoist for him ... you know, them things that help you
get out of the bath. Could you ask him ... how ... or ....
where ... I appreciate how busy he is, it would only take a
minute to ask ... I don't want to wait for a whole week for
him to say ... he doesn't have or where I'll get one ... Age
Concern? He is only forty-five. He isn't disabled.

PATSY. He is temporarily out of action.

JEANETTE. He is temporarily out of action. He's not sick.

PATSY. Tell her it's for you, not for him.

JEANETTE. Look it's not for him it's for me. I don't need a hoist
for me, I need one for him ... so it will help me to hoist him out
of the bath. Do you understand? Then just ask the doctor will
you? ... Haven't you just said he doesn't have any
appointments? ... But I don't want an appointment. I want a
hoist ... Why are you giving me an appointment to be told no?
... Thank you. Goodbye. (*She hangs up and looks at* PATSY.)

PATSY *shrugs and tries to lighten the situation.*

JEANETTE. Any more good suggestions?

PATSY. It was a good suggestion, it just didn't happen to work
this time ...

JEANETTE. Making a bloody eejit out of me.

PATSY. I'm trying to help, for godsake.

JEANETTE. I was doing alright without a hoist, I didn't even know they existed.

PATSY. You'll get no thanks for trying to be a martyr.

JEANETTE. I'm not trying to be anything except normal . . . if people would leave me alone.

PATSY. It's not normal: your husband is disabled.

JEANETTE. What do you want me to do . . . put him in a home . . . lock him away so you and our Cathy and everybody else can stop feeling sorry for me?

PATSY. Why can you not see that all I want to do is try and make things easier for you?

JEANETTE. No . . . what yous all want is for me to give up . . . admit I can't cope . . . put him away . . . then she can gallivant off to Germany and not give us another thought and you can stop feeling you have to be some kind of interfering do-gooder.

PATSY. That's very hurtful, Jeanette.

JEANETTE. Maybe because it's the truth.

PATSY. People can only take so much Jeanette. You carry on the way you are going and you're right, it will be just you and him, and just you and him for a hell of a long time.

JEANETTE. Good . . . that is the way I want it. But you think you know it all . . . you think you can come round here and tell me just exactly how it's done . . . I'm lookin' forward to see how you cope when the time comes.

PATSY. I just hope to God I won't be as pigheaded as you . . . I hope I won't let stupid pride get in the way.

JEANETTE. Oh so what you are sayin' is Kenny is going to suffer because I'm not capable . . . because I'm too stupid to manage to get a hoist for him.

PATSY. I said stupid pride.

JEANETTE. Why don't you ring a social worker and tell them your sister is too stupid to look after her husband . . . go on . . . get him taken into a home . . .

PATSY. Why don't you bloody well listen.

JEANETTE. Why don't you just get the hell home and leave us alone!

PATSY. Alright, if that's the way you want it.

JEANETTE. Yes it is.

She stands looking at PATSY *until she leaves.*

JEANETTE *stays on alone.*

JEANETTE. I've decided something Kenny. Me and you are going out ... right now. Yes, everything is going to be absolutely normal.

Link into the next scene.

NORMAN *enters reading a paper.* PATSY *enters like a storm.*

PATSY. She is so bloody stubborn ... this is it. I'm not going back ... Norman ... Norman.

NORMAN (*sees* PATSY). Ack hallo love, are you back?

PATSY. She told me to get out.

NORMAN. Jeanette?

PATSY. That't the thanks you get for trying to help.

NORMAN. She wants to find her own feet, love.

PATSY. No ... No ... that's too easy ... she doesn't know where to look to find anything.

NORMAN. You can't help anybody that doesn't want to be helped.

PATSY. That's convenient isn't it, very convenient.

NORMAN. Patsy you are making me angry ... you have been unbearable since this happened to Kenny ... you're getting frustrated because you can't do anything to help, and yet you haven't come up with any suggestion that can help her ... what do you expect me to do eh ... why take it out on me?

PATSY. It's not fair ... they were happy, they had everything they wanted and look at them now ... what the hell is going to happen to their marriage for a start?

NORMAN. It might bring them closer together.

PATSY. Don't talk shite.

NORMAN. As far as I can see Jeanette and Kenny are doing fine at their marriage, maybe you should look in your own backyard.

PATSY. What do you mean?

NORMAN. There is more to this than Jeanette and Kenny . . . isn't there?

PATSY. Yes.

NORMAN. You think I don't know that.

PATSY. I dread what is in front of us.

NORMAN. Patsy, you have always known what I intended to do.

PATSY. I didn't let myself think about it.

NORMAN. It's not going to be that bad.

PATSY. How would you know that Norman? . . . you won't be the one that will have to be here all day.

NORMAN. What is the problem? . . . My Mother signed her house over to me so we wouldn't have any financial worries when she came to live with us. You've always wanted to leave work.

PATSY. I want to leave work because I'm tired being behind a shop counter for the last twenty years. I want to leave work so I can do all the things I've wanted to do and never had the time.

NORMAN. Is my Mother that big of a problem?

PATSY. Maybe not now, but what about when she becomes one?

NORMAN. We'll cross that bridge when it comes.

PATSY. I don't think I'll be any good looking after somebody . . . I'm not even that good with sick people . . . I'm not interested in being a nurse . . . If we really set down and thought about it Norman, you are better at it than me.

NORMAN. Don't be ridiculous.

PATSY. Why is it ridiculous.

NORMAN (*can't answer*). . . . Because it is, and you know it is.

PATSY. Good answer, Norman.

NORMAN. My Mother nursed her mother and father until they died, then she nursed my Da . . . what are you saying? . . . after she devotes her life to nursing other people that she herself has to be turned out to one of them homes to live with strangers?

PATSY. I don't know . . . I don't know what I'm saying.

NORMAN. I hope it's not what I think it is.

PATSY. I said I don't know . . . I can't think straight.

NORMAN. Let me remind you of one thing Patsy . . . we give our word and any man is only as good as his word . . . so I would prefer that this subject is not brought up again or it will come between us . . . Has that Cathy one put her trendy notions into your head?

PATSY. Trendy notions, what are you on about? She is twenty years old with a great future ahead of her that she is not prepared to sacrifice.

NORMAN. Well I hope she can sleep easy in her bed over in Germany or whatever it is.

PATSY. No she won't, and that is the price she is paying for what she did . . . can you not imagine, Norman, that saying 'No' might be just as hard.

NORMAN. Well I can tell you here and now we won't have that on our conscience. (*He exits.*)

Link into the next scene.

JEANETTE *is washing* KENNY.

JEANETTE. Kenny . . . we need to talk about something . . . you haven't . . . or not just you . . . we haven't . . . I don't know if you can anymore . . . or just don't want to . . . I mean . . . if there is a problem we can talk about it . . . or we could talk to somebody about it . . . I suppose we should have asked . . . but you know me: I couldn't really bring it up unless somebody said to me . . . well it sounds a bit ridiculous when somebody has just had what you had for me

to ask about sleeping together . . . is it a problem . . . tell me
. . . I mean I could help . . . talk to me, I understand . . . I'm
not saying that I feel deprived or that I'm going to go crazy if
I don't . . . it's just . . . well it used to be good . . . and . . . I
don't mind if you are not up to it yet . . . I can wait . . . it's
not the be-all-and-end-of-all of everything . . . it's just I
thought you might like to talk about it and maybe . . .

KENNY. Shut up . . . go and make me a cup of tea.

JEANETTE *walks out of the room. She wants to scream but can't
. . . she waits and then goes back into the room.*

Doorbell rings.

JEANETTE *is surprised and goes quickly to answer the door. As
usual* KENNY *pretends to be asleep.*

CATHY (enters). Can I get some things I left behind?

JEANETTE. I don't see why not.

CATHY. Hallo Daddy.

JEANETTE. He is asleep.

CATHY. How are you, Mammy?

JEANETTE (*desperately trying hard to be civil*). Me.

CATHY. Yes.

JEANETTE. Very well, thank you.

CATHY. I leave next weekend . . . I would like to come over
   before I go . . . maybe stay over on the Saturday night . . . It's
   Daddy's birthday.

JEANETTE. I really don't think it would be convenient . . . I
   have a routine and I don't like it disturbed.

CATHY. I could stay tonight.

JEANETTE. No you're alright, we prefer to be on our own.

CATHY. Can I go up and get these things?

JEANETTE. What is it?

CATHY. It's just a black plastic bag with some clothes in it I left
   it on the bed.

JEANETTE. I'll get them for you.

CATHY. Right.

CATHY *is left alone with* KENNY. *She just stares at the sleeping* KENNY.

JEANETTE *comes back with a plastic bag and hands it to her.*

CATHY. I'll write and let you know how it is.

JEANETTE. Only if you have the time.

CATHY. Of course I will.

JEANETTE. Cheerio then.

CATHY. I'll be home for term breaks.

JEANETTE. Sure won't that be nice for you.

CATHY. Aye . . . bye Daddy.

CATHY *exits* . . . JEANETTE *feels desperate but tries to behave as if nothing has happened.*

JEANETTE. It's alright you can wake up now . . .

CATHY *is outside and meets* FRANK McKINLEY.

FRANK. You must be Cathy then.

CATHY. Aye.

FRANK. I know all about you.

CATHY. Me.

FRANK. Aye, I work with your Da . . . Frank . . . Frank McKinley. Didn't you get a scholarship for somewhere?

CATHY. Yes, Germany.

FRANK. Your Da is a desperate bum . . . bragged about it for weeks.

CATHY. My Da bragged about me.

FRANK. Aye . . . you'd think the rest of us has no kids . . . my Cathy this and my Cathy that . . . you did him proud, love. He maintained you got your brains from him. But I'll tell you this, you got your looks from your Mother.

CATHY. Thanks . . . are you going in to visit?

FRANK. Aye . . . don't want him to think the boys have forgot about him.

CATHY. Well, it's nice to meet you Frank. I just hope you have better luck than me . . . see ya . . . (*She leaves.*)

Doorbell rings.

JEANETTE. There is one good thing Kenny ... you don't have to waste your energy to go asleep again.

FRANK. Hallo ... Jeanette? ... Frank McKinley ... I work with Kenny.

JEANETTE. Hallo Frank ... I'm afraid he's asleep ...

FRANK. Don't worry ... How is he?

JEANETTE. Not so bad.

FRANK. It was a desperate shock to us all ... Donkey was the fittest one of the lot of us.

JEANETTE. Sure it could happen to anybody ... I'll wake him up.

FRANK. Ack, no, I'm sure he doesn't want to be bothered with me. I brought him this ... you can give it to him.

Hands JEANETTE *a parcel.*

JEANETTE. What is it?

FRANK. It's only a laugh.

JEANETTE *begins to open it.*

FRANK (*embarrassed*). ... You're not going to open it are you?

JEANETTE. Certainly I am.

FRANK. It is only a laugh ... I swear.

JEANETTE *opens it ... it is a hardback writing pad ... she reads the title.*

JEANETTE. 'Confessions of a Long Distance Lorry Driver by Kenny Duncan'.

FRANK. It was the wee girls in the office ... they asked all of us to write a page as if we were Kenny ... then they typed it all up ... they're desperate cases.

JEANETTE (*she flicks through and reads*). 'Arrived in Calais and was greeted by six screamin' wee French nubiles ... oo la la la Kenny give us your body for a lilo ... I flashed my teeth, threw them the label of my Y-fronts, one caught it in her teeth and then threw herself in front of the lorry ... unfortunately I didn't see her as I was too busy atin' my Yorkie ... and then

there were five . . . Five wee screamin' French nubiles' . . .
What is this?

FRANK. Don't pay no heed to any of it . . . the laugh with
Kenny was he was all gong and no dinner . . . I mean . . . he
was all talk.

JEANETTE. Well I hope so . . .

FRANK. Sure what would he be looking at other weemin for
when you were at home?

JEANETTE. You don't have to say that you know.

FRANK. I'm serious . . . Is he giving you a hard time?

JEANETTE. He has his off days.

FRANK. He can be a humpy big bugger . . . I know him.

JEANETTE. Sure he's my husband . . . your wife would do the
same for you.

FRANK. I would doubt it.

JEANETTE. Certainly she would.

FRANK. No . . . I don't think so.

JEANETTE. Well, you would do it for her.

FRANK. I could but I don't think her boyfriend would approve.

JEANETTE. Oh God me and my big mouth . . . sorry.

FRANK. It's alright, we're divorced.

JEANETTE. Why don't you go in and see him?

FRANK. He'll get a laugh at this thing. It's just so hard to take
. . . Big Duncan in a wheelchair . . .

JEANETTE. Come on in . . . I'll wake him up.

FRANK. OK.

They go to where KENNY *is . . . His head is to the side as if he is
sleeping.*

JEANETTE. Kenny, look who's here.

He doesn't answer.

FRANK (*relieved*). . . . He's sleeping.

JEANETTE. Kenny . . . it's Frank.

FRANK. Leave him . . . don't annoy him.

JEANETTE. He couldn't be in a deep sleep . . . he was awake a minute ago.

JEANETTE *shakes him . . . and then lifts his head up . . . his eyes are open, but he is in a sort of trance.*

JEANETTE. Jesus Christ, Frank . . . there is something wrong . . . Kenny! . . . Kenny! . . . Frank get an ambulance . . . quick. (*She shakes him.*) . . . Kenny . . . Kenny . . . don't you die on me . . . don't you dare . . . don't you die . . . don't do it to me.

FRANK *dials as lights fade.*

Musical link into next scene.

JEANETTE *and district* NURSE.

JEANETTE. What do you mean it's not uncommon?

NURSE. A small number of stroke patients develop epilepsy as a result of a stroke.

JEANETTE. Well if it is so bloody common why did I not know what it was? . . . Why did somebody not tell me? . . . I'm the one that has to look after him . . . what good is it all yousins knowing about it when it's me has to deal with it?

NURSE. Now calm down Mrs Duncan.

JEANETTE. I am sick of yousins telling me to calm down . . . are you scared of me taking sick too and then you might have to take responsibility for Kenny? . . . Is that it? . . . Are you only concerned about me 'cos I'm doing your job for you?

NURSE. Mrs Duncan, I am not your enemy . . . I want your husband to get well . . . I don't wish for you to be in this situation.

JEANETTE. Then why did you not tell me how bloody awful it was going to be.

NURSE. I have tried to answer all your questions the best I can.

JEANETTE. That's not what I mean . . . I don't always know the questions to ask . . . it's like the secret bloody service.

NURSE. To be fair, in the early days it was difficult to tell you anything because you wouldn't accept your husband's illness.

JEANETTE. You should have made me . . . you should have told me everything.

NURSE. I told you to consult your family doctor . . . did you?

JEANETTE. I might as well have consulted the milkman . . . how long will he be like this? . . . It's difficult to say . . . will he be able to drive his lorry again? . . . It's difficult to say . . . could he take another stroke? . . . That's possible . . . will he make a full recovery? . . . That's a possibility also.

NURSE. The doctor is right . . . he doesn't want to give you any false hopes.

JEANETTE. I don't want false hope . . . I want more than a one-phrase answer . . . do you not think all this would be easier to accept if I knew exactly what it was he had? . . . And do you know why I didn't ask? . . . Because I felt like an eejit and didn't want to waste his time.

NURSE. Well you can't blame the doctor.

JEANETTE. Yes I do . . . I blame all of yis . . . you should know people like me don't know . . . youse are the ones with the information . . . how can we do your bloody job for yis if you don't tell us how? . . . I know . . . you're all scared we'd do it better and then youse wouldn't be able to treat us like imbeciles.

NURSE. I am really sorry you feel so bitter, Mrs Duncan.

JEANETTE. What do you expect? . . . Just tell me about these fits. Are they likely to occur often . . . and don't dare say . . . it's difficult to say.

NURSE (*timidly*). I am sorry but it is difficult to say.

JEANETTE. Why?

NURSE. Hopefully with the anti-convulsant tablets we will be able to control it.

JEANETTE. What if he takes one and I'm not in?

NURSE. I don't think it would be advisable to leave him unattended for a while . . . to be safe.

JEANETTE. You mean twenty-four hours a day.

NURSE. I can put you in touch with a volunteer organisation that can arrange for somebody to come and sit with Mr Duncan.

JEANETTE. Volunteer ... what is this? ... I could laugh ... youse are all the ones that are getting paid to be nurses and doctors ... I work in a school's canteen. I never wanted to be a nurse ... Everything is volunteer this and volunteer that ... what would happen if nobody volunteered? ... What would happen?

NURSE. I shudder to think.

JEANETTE. You're the one that's a nurse, but you go home at five o'clock.

NURSE. Please believe me I do understand ... and I just wish I could do more to help you.

JEANETTE. Yes ... I know you do ... sorry, I lost my temper.

NURSE. No don't apologise ... you needed to get it out.

JEANETTE. I'd better get back into him ... poor cratur ... all he ever hears is muffled voices in the background discussin' him.

NURSE. Perhaps you should be more open with him ... discuss things while he's there.

JEANETTE. One step at a time nurse ...

PATSY. It's only me ... am I allowed in?

JEANETTE (*smiles which means 'yes'*). Patsy, this is Kenny's nurse ... this is my sister.

PATSY. Pleased to meet you ... she is a desperate case my sister. She won't ask for nothing ... Jeanette, I have this address for you.

NURSE. I'll rush on here ... I have a few more patients to get round before I finish. (*She leaves*).

JEANETTE. You ask him to go.

PATSY. Me.

JEANETTE. Yes, he is more likely to go for you.

PATSY. I want you to be there too in case he thinks I'm interfering too much.

JEANETTE. Please, I'll use the opportunity to run up to the shop.

PATSY. Don't be long, I might need support.

JEANETTE. It won't take long . . . he'll probably say no . . . and that should take all of half a second.

PATSY *wheels Kenny in.*

KENNY. Where is Jeanette?

PATSY. She is away to the shop.

KENNY. Are you babysitting?

PATSY. Aye . . . and any oul gyp, and I'll put you over my knee.

KENNY. Promises . . . promises.

PATSY. I see you're getting back to your oul lecherous self. I want you to do somethin' for me.

KENNY. Does Norman know about this?

PATSY. Very funny . . . I am going to ask you something, and before you throw your head up I want you to let me finish.

KENNY. Shoot.

PATSY. And you'll hear me out.

KENNY. Yes.

PATSY. Promise.

KENNY. Promise.

PATSY. I have the address of a day centre here . . .

KENNY. No.

PATSY. You said you'd let me finish.

KENNY. I'll finish for you . . . you want to parcel me off to a ga-ga club.

PATSY. It is a centre where people are in the same boat as you . . . people who understand.

KENNY. I don't want to be treated like an invalid . . . I couldn't stand it.

PATSY. Kenny, she needs to get a break . . . do it for her.

KENNY. She can go out if she wants.

PATSY. What if you took a fit?

KENNY. I'm not going to take no fits; it's all in her head.

PATSY. Do you not think you are being a bit selfish?

KENNY. By wanting to stay in my own house?

PATSY. Jeanette is doing everything she can . . . you have to try and help yourself as well . . . like it or not you are disabled.

KENNY. Yes and I want to be disabled in my own home.

PATSY. You are a selfish pig.

KENNY. What is it to you?

PATSY. She is my sister.

KENNY. She is my wife.

PATSY. Then think about her for a change.

KENNY (*really angry*). . . . Look Patsy . . . do you think I don't know what a burden I am to her . . . what a burden I am to everybody? . . . Everyday I tell her I am. Every day she says I'm not . . . I want her to keep saying I'm not . . . but the more do-bloody-gooders keep insisting I am, someday she is going to agree. What am I supposed to do then?

PATSY. Then maybe you'd better give her a bit of space before that day comes.

KENNY. Maybe it would make youse all feel better if she said I *was* a burden . . . maybe it would suit you better if she did crack up.

PATSY. And just what the hell do you mean by that?

KENNY. Just what I said.

PATSY. You're saying plenty, but I want you to tell me what you mean.

KENNY. Do you want it translated . . . do you?

PATSY. I certainly bloody do.

KENNY. So you can get out of taking Norman's Mother . . . 'Oh look our Jeanette has cracked up' . . . do you want that to happen to me? . . .

PATSY. You are twisted Kenny Duncan, do you know that?

JEANETTE (*enters*). . . . Well.

KENNY. It's no . . . of course it is bloody no . . .

JEANETTE (*to* PATSY). I don't want to say I told you so, but I told you so.

PATSY. I was bloody doing it for you.

JEANETTE. I didn't ask you, did I?

PATSY. Maybe I should just keep my nose out . . . that way I'll keep it attached to my face.

JEANETTE. Did he snap at you?

PATSY. Snap at me . . . if he was a dog I'd get him put down.

JEANETTE (*laughing*). . . . He's a shocking case.

PATSY. Yes he is . . . just make him go.

JEANETTE. If he is going to go, he will do it in his own time. Anyway I haven't the energy to argue today.

PATSY. I'm wastin' my bloody time.

JEANETTE. You're not Patsy . . . it's just I can't just act on your demands immediately . . . I'll do it later.

PATSY. I give up . . . I just give up . . . (*Exits*).

JEANETTE *goes over to* KENNY.

JEANETTE. That was her idea love . . . I knew you wouldn't want to go.

KENNY. Right.

JEANETTE. And I wouldn't expect you to go.

KENNY. Good.

JEANETTE. It would not be fair.

KENNY. Correct.

JEANETTE. I know it would only be for a couple of hours until I got out to do some shopping but I'll manage . . . I'll just wheel you down to the shops . . . or better still, I have a wee tin of beans there should do us for the rest of the week.

KENNY. This is am . . . am . . . black . . .

JEANETTE. Blackmail . . . yes.

KENNY. You're getting too crafty for me.

JEANETTE. I have a good teacher ... well what shall we do tonight then?

KENNY. What's on ...

JEANETTE. I'm tired of that oul TV.

KENNY. Any better suggestions?

JEANETTE. Am ...

KENNY. No? ... that's good.

JEANETTE. Talk to me.

KENNY. What about?

JEANETTE. You never had any trouble before. TV or not, I never got you shut up.

KENNY. I had something to talk about. I was away all week. Sure you're with me all day. What is there to say? I wish I had been on the dole or something before this happened.

JEANETTE. What a thing to say.

KENNY. Then I wouldn't have had much to miss.

JEANETTE. Do you miss it a lot?

KENNY (*pause*). I miss the oul lorry.

JEANETTE. Do you?

KENNY. Me and her were soul mates.

JEANETTE. A lorry as a soul mate.

KENNY. I was a King and she was the Throne.

JEANETTE. It would be bad enough competing with another woman but a lorry is a bit much.

KENNY. I used to love getting off the ferry about four in the morning and driving through France ... Just me and her and the dawn.

JEANETTE. I'm jealous.

KENNY. Being so high up you could see for miles ... It was a great feeling ... I used to always stop the lorry in the same place and just sit and listen to the silence ... I loved it ... surrounded by miles and miles of mustard fields ... beautiful they are ... just this big yellow ocean for as far as your eyes could see . . . and away way in the distance you can see this wee stone farmhouse . . . I used to sit and stare with my eyes half closed. It didn't seem real . . . Then I used to fantasize about living in it. Gettin' up every morning and watching the acres and acres of gold . . . You know someday I'm going to find my way to that cottage. I'm going to knock on the door and say . . . tell me what it's like to live like this . . . I want to know . . . am I missing out on somethin' here?

JEANETTE. You never told me any of this before.

KENNY. Ack, by the time you get home and you've been hours at customs . . . all night slabbering with the boys on the ferry, it seems too far away to be important any more.

JEANETTE. I would love to see that place.

KENNY. Deal . . . as soon as I'm shipshape again I'll take you on the run.

JEANETTE. In the lorry?

KENNY. A King of the Road is allowed to bring his Queen now and again.

JEANETTE. What about the screamin' wee French Nubiles?

KENNY. Don't worry about them . . . I'll say you're my Ma.

JEANETTE *takes advantage of his good mood.*

JEANETTE. What about this day centre then?

KENNY. Don't know.

JEANETTE. If you love me, you'll go.

KENNY. More blackmail.

JEANETTE. You don't have to do anything you don't want to do.

KENNY. Yes I bloody do.

JEANETTE. Are you sure?

KENNY. No . . . but I'll go anyway.

End of scene as lights fade and music fades in.

ACT TWO

Musical link into the scene . . . JEANETTE *is carrying a supermarket basket. She is deciding between a cheap washing up liquid and Fairy* . . . *and can't decide* . . . FRANK McKINLEY *comes up behind her carrying a basket also.*

FRANK. Get the cheapie . . . that Fairy is an oul cod.

JEANETTE. God Frank . . . you scared the life out of me.

FRANK. Don't tell me I'm that bad.

JEANETTE. No it's just a thing I have about supermarkets . . . when anybody comes up behind me I think it's going to be somebody accusing me of shoplifting.

FRANK. Must have a guilty conscience.

JEANETTE. I have . . . when I was about eight I stole a hairpiece out of Woolies 'cos I wanted to have a ponytail.

FRANK. How have you been keeping?

JEANETTE. Not so bad . . . I never got thanking you for being so calm that night Kenny took the fit . . . I couldn't have coped if I had been on my own.

FRANK. Course you could . . . how has he been since?

JEANETTE. Great . . . he doesn't know he had one . . . he won't believe me he can't be left alone . . . so I have to find devious means of getting out for an hour or two.

FRANK. Hope you're not going to spend it deliberating over washing up liquid.

JEANETTE. I don't know what to do.

FRANK. Are you intending to wash three hundred boy scouts' greasy plates?

JEANETTE. I hadn't planned on it.

FRANK. Then get the cheap one.

JEANETTE. Great . . . I'm glad I didn't have to make that decision.

FRANK. Anything else you require, Madam?

JEANETTE. A sedative . . . I had my first driving lesson the day.

FRANK. Well I see you survived it, anyway.

JEANETTE. I'm still a wee bit jittery . . .

FRANK. How is the instructor?

JEANETTE. Said he was away for a large brandy.

FRANK. Not a bad idea. Do you fancy one?

JEANETTE. In the middle of the day?

FRANK. No law against it.

JEANETTE. Hey, why are you not at work?

FRANK. Compassionate leave to do my shoppin' . . . no, fortnight's holiday.

JEANETTE. Not going anywhere?

FRANK. No fun going on your own.

JEANETTE. To the pub then? . . . I haven't got long.

FRANK. Right I'll race you to the check-out.

They leave.

Link into the next scene.

JEANETTE *dashes in and looks at her watch . . . she throws her coat off.* KENNY *appears in his chair.*

JEANETTE. Well?

KENNY. I'm not going back to that nutter's club.

JEANETTE. Why?

KENNY. We've all one thing in common down there . . . if we were horses we would be cornbeef by now.

JEANETTE (*taking off* KENNY's *coat . . . trying not to go too near him in case he smells her breath*). Our Patsy said they played bowls and everything.

KENNY. I don't bloody play bowls.

JEANETTE (*irritated*). You could learn.

KENNY. Why?

JEANETTE. It will help strengthen your arm. Did you not meet anybody to talk to?

KENNY. You mean other cripples.

JEANETTE. I don't want to hear that word spoken in this house. What did you do all day?

KENNY. I got wheeled into a corner and left.

JEANETTE. Did you talk? I said did you speak? Do they know you can *talk*?

KENNY. No.

JEANETTE. Then what do you expect? . . . How are they supposed to know what you want if you don't tell them . . . I had my first driving lesson today . . . Can you imagine me in a car after all these years?

KENNY. You're not driving my car.

JEANETTE. Our car . . . my money paid for it too.

KENNY. Don't give a damn . . . you'll never drive . . . you're too . . . am too . . . am . . . damn.

JEANETTE. Stupid?

KENNY (*getting frustrated*). Too . . .

JEANETTE. Nervous.

KENNY. Yes.

JEANETTE. That will pass when I get used to it.

KENNY. What do you want to drive for?

JEANETTE. So I can take you places for a change.

KENNY. No . . . so you can . . . galli . . . am . . .

JEANETTE. Gallivant . . . I want us to be mobile again. I have a lesson every Thursday when you go to the centre.

KENNY. I'm not going back to that madhouse.

JEANETTE. Kenny, please, you might get to like it.

KENNY. Forget it.

JEANETTE. Kenny, you know I can't go out if you don't.

KENNY. I said forget it.

JEANETTE. No I won't. I'm doing it and that is that.

KENNY. You're not.

JEANETTE. You can't stop me.

KENNY. Well, if you are going to be so pigheaded about it. I
suppose you'd better. You just better bloody learn quick
before that place turns me ga-ga.

JEANETTE. No dear, I couldn't let that happen. (*She kisses him
on the cheek.*)

Pause.

JEANETTE. I saw Frank McKinley the day in the supermarket.

KENNY. Big Jinnie Anne.

JEANETTE. He is a very nice man.

KENNY. He's an oul woman . . . supermarkets suit him.

JEANETTE. How else is he going to feed himself if he doesn't
shop?

KENNY. No wonder his wife left him.

JEANETTE. It was him that left.

KENNY. How do you know that?

JEANETTE. He said.

KENNY. He said . . . what kind of conversation were you
having in the middle of a supermarket?

JEANETTE (*rambles nervously*). . . . Ack it was just I said is your
wife sick and he said he didn't have one 'cos he left her and
then I just bid him the time of day.

KENNY. So . . . you're gonna drive then . . . what brought this
on?

JEANETTE. So we can get out.

KENNY. You could have least left me that.

JEANETTE. Sure you can't . . . not yet.

KENNY. Do you ever stop to think what you're are doing to me.

JEANETTE. What?

KENNY. It's hard enough having to be washed and dressed ... but that's not enough ... I'm parcelled off to a crazy club so you can take away the last bit of independence I had. Could you not at least have waited until I'm better?

JEANETTE. What about *my* independence ... why can't I have any?

KENNY. You were happy enough before to sit back and let me do it all for you ... you didn't cry for your independence then.

JEANETTE. Because there wouldn't have been any point ... you knew it all ... I was too stupid to do anything ... maybe if you had given me a bit of encouragement before I wouldn't be in such a bloody mess ... have you forgotten that ... Oh don't you do that Jeanette, you'll make a balls of it ... leave it until I come home ... leave that to me you don't know nothing about money ... but who has to do it now?

KENNY. What do you have to do now?

JEANETTE. Alright do you want to know? ... I'll bloody tell you then ... in case you haven't noticed, I have no job at the moment ... in two months' time you will be dependent on invalidity and I will be dependent on you and the mortgage will be dependent on God because there will be nobody else to pay it ... We have a washing machine that is held together with sticky tape ... a biscuit tin full of bills that I'm frightened to pay ... but you haven't noticed any of these things have you ... because I didn't want you to worry.

KENNY. All the more reason why you shouldn't be wasting money on driving lessons.

JEANETTE. You bastard ... you selfish bastard ... I have had it with you ... I'm sick of you feeling sorry for yourself. Tired of being taken for granted. Me ... me ... me ... you can't get any further than that can you ... you were the same before and you haven't changed one bit ... well you listen here ... I am the one who is taking charge and if you don't like it you can go wherever the hell you like, but believe me nobody else would take the gift of you. (*She kicks the wheelchair and exits.*)

KENNY *sits alone . . . just staring . . .* JEANETTE *comes back in . . . after a long pause . . . and sits beside him.*

KENNY. Just don't have an accident . . .

JEANETTE. I love you.

KENNY. . . . or the insurance will go up.

Musical link into the next scene.

NORMAN *is reading the paper when* CATHY *enters . . . he is curt with her . . . She is carrying a case.*

CATHY. Hallo, Norman.

NORMAN. Oh, so you're back.

CATHY. Term break . . . Patsy out?

NORMAN. Shopping . . . she shouldn't be long.

CATHY. How is everybody?

NORMAN. Surviving.

CATHY (*pause*). . . . How's Patsy?

NORMAN. She shouldn't be long.

Pause.

CATHY. How is the cycling?

NORMAN. Not bad . . . not bad at all.

CATHY. Nice day, wasn't it?

NORMAN. Aye . . . not bad.

CATHY. How is your Mother?

NORMAN. She's holding up not bad.

CATHY. That's good . . . (*Tries to get away.*) Colin and Debrah upstairs?

NORMAN. No . . . nobody in but me. If you'll excuse me Cathy, I want to watch the sport. (*Switches the television on.*)

CATHY (*pause*). . . . Norman would you rather I left and came back?

NORMAN. Suit yourself.

CATHY *is about to leave, changes her mind and decides to take him on calmly and rationally.*

CATHY. What is your problem?

NORMAN. I beg your pardon?

CATHY. You're are having a real problem with me being here, Norman.

NORMAN. I'm having no problem . . . it is Saturday afternoon, my day off, and on Saturday afternoons I watch the sport.

CATHY. What is it?

NORMAN. I said I have no problem.

CATHY. Meaning *I* have.

NORMAN. Maybe you have . . . nothin' to do with me.

CATHY. Oh I know it hasn't . . . but I'm afraid I can't just sit here and let you judge me.

NORMAN. Am I asking you to sit here?

CATHY. Don't be so childish . . . are you not man enough to say what you think?

NORMAN. You know what I think . . . I think like your Ma and your Da and probably half the neighbourhood.

CATHY. I want to hear it from *you*, Norman.

NORMAN. Will it make any difference?

CATHY. No.

NORMAN. Well then.

CATHY. You have it all sorted out haven't you?

He ignores her.

CATHY. What do you think? . . . I'm interested.

NORMAN (*switches it off*). . . . I'll go upstairs and watch it. She shouldn't be long.

CATHY. Why are you running away from me?

NORMAN. I don't run away from nobody and not in my own house.

CATHY. Then why don't you tell me what you think?

NORMAN. It's not just what I think about you Cathy ... it's what I think would happen if there were more like you ... that scares me ... do you know that? ... It scares me.

CATHY. Why?

NORMAN. What the hell state are we going to be in if the next generation are so concerned with their own wants that any sense of duty or responsibility goes out the window ... what would happen eh?

CATHY. I've nothing against what my mother is doing ... I would do it if he were my husband, but only if I had no choice ...

NORMAN. What do you suggest then?

CATHY. That what she is doing shouldn't be expected of her ... that she should have been allowed to have an alternative ...

NORMAN. I'm listening Cathy ... I'm listening ... what's the alternative?

CATHY. Would you choose of your own free will to be an unpaid slave? ... She did have a choice, she could have decided not to give up her own life for somebody else. But because of some stupid narrow-minded principle she couldn't even consider it.

NORMAN. It's because of these so-called stupid narrow-minded principles that we have still some humanity left in this country ... (*Leaves*.)

CATHY (*after him*). And a lot of angry frustrated lonely people who have been taken advantage of.

NORMAN. Aye it's typical of your sort ... your education has taught you to criticise but damn the one of yis can come up with an answer.

CATHY. And your answer is not to think at all.

NORMAN. My answer is to do unto others as I would like done to me.

CATHY. So you are just as selfish as the rest of us.

NORMAN. Let me tell you about something Cathy ... looking after people isn't a new notion ... it's always been done ... I seen my mother when I was a wee lad running up and down the street with dinners for old ones that couldn't fend for themselves ... giving them the dignity of spending their last days in their own homes.

CATHY. Times have changed Norman ... we don't all run up and down the streets with plates of stew any more. I'm sure your Mother is a wonderful woman but then maybe she didn't have a lot to sacrifice in the first place.

PATSY (*enters with bags of shopping*). ...Cathy love ... (*Throws her arms around her.*) Welcome home ... Well how was it? ... Hope you didn't mention the War.

NORMAN. I'm away upstairs to watch the TV.

PATSY. Norman, I left a couple of bags at the door. Carry them in for me.

CATHY. It was alright.

PATSY. Did you meet any big blond sexy Germans?

CATHY. How are you?

PATSY. Same as ever ... Isn't she looking great Norman?

NORMAN (*sets bags down*). Oh aye ... a very important person is our Cathy now.

PATSY. What ... what do you mean?

NORMAN. Miss High and Mighty has just informed me that it befitted my mother to devote her life to looking after people because she wasn't much use for anything else.

CATHY. Stop twisting things to suit yourself ... I didn't say that.

PATSY. What is going on here?

NORMAN. I am trying to get peace on my day off, that is all.

PATSY. Have you annoyed Cathy?

NORMAN. Have I annoyed Cathy? ... She clears off ... deserts her Mother and then has the nerve to say it was because she was better than the rest of us.

PATSY. Norman, I think you had better go upstairs.

NORMAN. You're not so bloody special ... you go out there and you'll find that people have given up a hell of a lot more

than you to look after their loved ones . . . a scholarship in
Germany . . . it's not even a bloody job you're giving up . . .
it's not even bread and butter.

CATHY. You can't just measure everything against bread and
bloody butter.

PATSY. I said enough.

NORMAN. What then? . . . I could see me going to my Mother
and saying . . . Sorry Ma, you may have to look after yourself,
I have a wee notion that I might want to get a job in a few
years time so I'll just go off and have a holiday to think
about it.

CATHY. Were you ever young Norman, or were you born
forty-five?

PATSY. I think you should go Norman.

NORMAN. Let me remind you of one wee thing Cathy . . .
you're not going to be young forever . . . you might not be
healthy for ever, and little apples grow big.

CATHY. Yes and God forbid I don't do to my family what's
being done to me.

PATSY. I said Norman, I think you should go upstairs.

NORMAN. Hold on a minute . . . this is my home and I'm
being ordered about . . . I think it is maybe more in Cathy's
line to leave . . . if she doesn't like what I'm saying.

PATSY. Jesus she is only home . . . what kind of a family
welcome is this?

NORMAN. She started it.

CATHY. It's alright, I'll leave.

PATSY. Where are you going?

CATHY. Don't worry I'll be fine . . . (*She leaves*.)

NORMAN *sits down and puts the TV on defiantly.*

PATSY *takes off her coat and gathers up her bags in silence.*

NORMAN. She insulted my Mother . . . I won't have that in
my own home.

PATSY (*does not want to get into an argument*). . . . Yes Norman.

NORMAN. Sitting here minding my own business and next
thing that upstart comes in and gets at me . . . I wish you
would tell your family to keep me out of this.

PATSY. You're right Norman.

NORMAN. I've done nothing to nobody and the next thing she
is down my throat . . . what has it to do with me? . . .

PATSY. Nothing Norman . . . absolutely nothing . . . thought
you wanted to see the sport.

NORMAN (*mimics her*). . . . Nothing Norman, absolutely
nothing. Which means bloody everything.

PATSY. No, Norman you're right . . . my family has nothing
to do with you . . . and your family has nothing to do with
me . . . is that fair? . . . What would you like for lunch? (*Brings
pizzas out of a plastic bag.*)

NORMAN. Ah here we go again . . . my poor Mother is being
brought into this again.

PATSY. No she isn't . . . it's nothing to do with me . . . You
have three choices . . . mushroom and bacon . . . mixed
pepper or plain.

NORMAN. It's different . . . you are my wife . . . remember.

PATSY. And Cathy is my niece and Jeanette is my sister . . . it's
the old running up and down the street with plates of stew that
you're always on about . . . all muck in just like your Mother
did . . . Have you decided yet?

NORMAN. I'll help anybody that wants it . . . but I'm not
going to do it if it's going to be thrown back in my face.

PATSY. I don't want to hear any more . . . right . . . so if you
don't make up your mind it's mushroom and bacon . . .

Pause.

NORMAN. M'mother is not just going to disappear you know
. . . not talking about it won't solve it.

PATSY. I know . . . I know . . . but it is Saturday afternoon –
my day off as well Norman – and I have a mountain of things
to do.

Pause.

NORMAN. When I was round through the week I found the

teapot burning away . . . she put it on the stove and forgot about it.

PATSY. You never said.

NORMAN. I was scared to mention it . . . scared of your reaction if you want to know . . . you never ask about her any more.

PATSY. I know.

NORMAN. Why?

PATSY. Because I don't want to think about it . . . right, mushroom and bacon it is . . . (*She exits.*)

NORMAN (*shouts after her*). We are going to need to.

PATSY (*comes back*). Norman there is no point . . . you have made up your mind . . . what is the point in me saying anything . . . You were the one who said it could come between us . . . and it will . . . I think it already has . . . you know this and yet you still want to go ahead with this . . .

NORMAN. I have no choice.

PATSY. I should have . . . I should be allowed a choice.

NORMAN. And what about m'mother . . . if you said no, what choice has she?

PATSY. It's my life that is being affected.

NORMAN. Oh and hers wouldn't.

PATSY. You're doing alright out of this one Norman.

NORMAN. Meaning?

PATSY. If I say no then your Mother is affected . . . if I say yes I am affected . . . either way you do alright . . . what changes for you? . . . You still have your job . . . you'll still walk in here at six o'clock and read the paper and have your tea . . . you'll still have your Saturday afternoons glued to the telly . . . I'll be rushing about like a blue-arsed fly not only feeding you but your Mother as well.

NORMAN. It won't be like that . . . you'll have more time . . . you won't be working.

PATSY. What will I be doing? . . . Sitting on my arse? . . . What you mean is I'll have more time to do what I spend all day Saturday and Sunday doing . . . I would like some time to myself. One of these days.

NORMAN. Patsy, what in the name of God do you expect me to do?

PATSY. At this minute in time I want you to tell me what kind of pizza you want, or you'll get what you are given.

NORMAN. I don't care . . . any kind . . . I can't turn my Mother away . . . it would kill her.

PATSY. Maybe it won't . . . if she is going senile she won't know whether she is here or not.

NORMAN. I'll know.

PATSY. Are you bringing your Mother here for her sake or your sake?

NORMAN. What are you talking about, for my sake? . . . Do you think I'm not going to be put out as well?

PATSY. Being put out is a hell of a lot different from your whole life being turned upside down . . . you're missing the match Norman.

NORMAN. . . . Patsy, I want to talk to you.

PATSY. Norman, I don't have the time . . . you know what I am like on a Saturday . . . and anyway I don't want to compete with a football match.

NORMAN (*turns the TV off*). . . . You haven't mentioned any of this for months . . . I thought everything was alright.

PATSY. Well it isn't . . . (*Turns it back on*). . . . but there is no point in talking about it . . . you know how I feel.

NORMAN. You should have said.

PATSY. Would it make any difference?

NORMAN. I don't want this to come between us. I have said that.

PATSY. Too late: it has . . . and that is that.

NORMAN. Patsy, the last thing I want to do is to say to you whether you like it or not she is coming.

PATSY. Is there anything else to say?

NORMAN. No . . . but.

PATSY. Well then . . . I'm busy.

NORMAN. . . . I don't want her to come here with your attitude as it is.

PATSY. Tough . . . you can't have it every way.

NORMAN. . . . Have you no compassion? . . . I would do it for your Mother.

PATSY. Because you would not be the one who would be doing the looking after.

NORMAN. Alright then we will come back to the most important thing in all this . . . you gave me your word.

PATSY. Out of ignorance.

NORMAN. So it doesn't count then.

PATSY. No it doesn't.

NORMAN. In my book a promise is a promise.

PATSY. So all this arguing and fighting is a total waste of time because as soon as you are cornered you come out with the same old story . . . now do you want a pizza, or do you want to starve?

NORMAN. That same old story is what I happen to live by and it hasn't done me no harm yet.·

PATSY. What about the harm it might do me?

NORMAN. I'm sorry you weren't brought up with the same principles . . . because if you were we wouldn't be having this conversation.

PATSY. Yes it is a waste of time . . . you have wasted my valuable time . . . look, you've missed a goal.

Link into the next scene.

KENNY *is drawing on a sketch pad* . . . JEANETTE *is sitting for him.*

JEANETTE. Hurry up you, I've got a driving lesson.

KENNY. You can't hurry an artist.

JEANETTE. Hope this isn't ugly.

KENNY. I'm only drawing what I see.

JEANETTE. You could have stuck to vases and fruit bowls.

KENNY. I have progressed . . . don't smile.

JEANETTE. I dread what this is going to be like.

KENNY. You liked my fruit bowls.

JEANETTE. I didn't have to admit they looked like me . . .

KENNY. Now that could be a matter of opinion.

JEANETTE. Cheeky pig.

Phone rings.

JEANETTE *answers.*

JEANETTE. Hallo . . . yes . . . have you . . . is it bad? . . . It's just . . . well you know I can't get out if you don't . . . and my test is next week . . . OK, it can't be helped . . . cheerio. Shit.

KENNY. Can Mrs Greene not come?

JEANETTE. 'Flu.

KENNY. Do you want to go on? . . . It's only an hour or so.

JEANETTE. Kenny . . . No.

KENNY. Alright . . . alright . . . sit down again love and I'll get this finished.

JEANETTE *sits down.*

KENNY. This will turn out ugly if you don't cheer up.

JEANETTE. It was my last lesson before the test.

KENNY. You have been at it for near six months . . . you should be alright.

JEANETTE. It's not fair . . . Frank gives up his Saturday mornings especially to do it.

KENNY. Could we afford one lesson then the day before the test?

JEANETTE. That would mean going out with a stranger . . . Frank knows what I'm capable of . . . I have confidence in him . . . anyway we can't afford it.

KENNY. Away and get me a bowl of fruit – this is a waste of time.

CATHY *enters with her bag . . . all three of them don't really know what to say . . . tense and awkward.*

CATHY. Hallo . . . I'm back.

JEANETTE. Well . . . how was it?

CATHY. OK . . . how are yis?

JEANETTE. Great . . . your Daddy thinks he's an artist.

CATHY. Just thought I'd call and say hallo.

JEANETTE. Put that big bag down . . . (*Pause.*) . . . give me your coat.

KENNY. Do you fancy a portrait, Cathy? . . . Your mother is an awful subject.

CATHY. Sure.

JEANETTE. When did you get home?

CATHY. This morning.

Car horn sounds.

JEANETTE. Oh God, that's Frank . . . I'd better tell him.

KENNY. Away you go . . . sure Cathy is here.

JEANETTE. Do you mind Cathy? . . . It's just my last lesson before my test, and the woman who sits with your Daddy has 'flu.

CATHY. No, I don't mind.

JEANETTE (*brightens up*). . . . Thanks love . . . You can tell me all about it when I come back.

JEANETTE *leaves.*

CATHY. Where do you want me?

KENNY. Just sit there and turn your head to the side.

CATHY. I'm a mess.

KENNY. You look alright to me.

CATHY. When did you start this?

KENNY. The centre I go to . . . I tried bowls, but by the time everybody gets round to actually throwing the ball you could have drawn the pension.

CATHY. Enjoy it?

KENNY. Passes the time.

CATHY. Are you keeping alright?

KENNY. The best ... and yourself?

CATHY. OK.

KENNY. How was Germany?

CATHY. Alright.

KENNY. I never liked it much myself ... a humourless shower aren't they?

CATHY. A bit.

KENNY. I could never get the measure of them ... if you're sarcastic to them they take you serious ... can't even make Hitler jokes.

CATHY. I'm glad to be out of it for a while.

KENNY. Get homesick?

CATHY. Yes.

KENNY. Natural ... I was the same when I was working ... after five or six days with people talking gibberish in my ear it was great to see the oul Stranraer head up Belfast Lough.

CATHY *is trying to hold back the tears* ... KENNY *notices but pretends not to notice.*

KENNY. You can stay here if you want ... your room's still there.

CATHY. Thanks.

KENNY. This is going to look well ... hope you like it.

CATHY. I'm sure I will.

KENNY. What was the talent like ... any big romances?

CATHY. No ... not really ... well just one, sort of.

KENNY. Mess you around, did he?

CATHY. Just a bit.

KENNY. I'm having trouble with your nose Cathy ... I haven't come to terms with noses yet. ... Who was he then?

CATHY. Nobody really.

KENNY. Must have been somebody to make you that miserable.

CATHY. I'm not miserable.

KENNY. Hey you are talking to an artist here . . . we are trained to have a third eye . . . you know like . . . what's his name Cyclops.

CATHY. He wasn't worth it anyway.

KENNY. That's men for you . . . we can be right jerks.

CATHY. My fault too.

KENNY. Glad to hear you say that . . . we usually get all the blame.

CATHY. I suppose I just used him because I was desperate.

KENNY. You, desperate . . . come off it . . . that phone was like a date line some nights.

CATHY. This was different . . . strange place . . . knowing nobody so you cling to the first person you meet and then they end up becoming everything you left behind.

KENNY. Aye it doesn't do to depend too much on somebody else. It scares people away . . . it's too much to handle . . . somebody else's desperation . . .

CATHY. He ran alright.

KENNY. If he hadn't you'd have ended up disappointed anyway.

CATHY. Probably.

KENNY. Or if he hadn't he'd have put his price up . . . that's what happens when you're desperate for something . . . you pay for it through the nose . . . speaking of which . . . I'm sorry Cathy about this nose of yours . . . I just can't get it . . . I'll knock his teeth down his throat.

CATHY. There's no need . . . wouldn't give him the pleasure.

KENNY. Did you remind him who won the War?

CATHY (*laughs*). . . . What?

KENNY. Typical of them Krauts . . . we bate them and they

end up thinking they're still the Master Race . . . Hitler has a lot to answer for . . . dead or not.

CATHY. Daddy . . . He wasn't a German . . . he was from Belfast.

Link into the next scene.

FRANK *and* JEANETTE *standing in the street.*

FRANK (*outside the car*). . . . Now he'll ask you to read a registration number before you start . . . what is the number on that grey Astra parked just beyond the zebra crossing?

JEANETTE *takes a few steps forward to look.*

FRANK. Hey . . . Hey . . . where do you think you're going?

JEANETTE. I can't really see it.

FRANK. Failed.

JEANETTE (*determined*). . . . ABZ . . . 1347

FRANK (*takes a few paces forward to check.*). . . . Correct.

JEANETTE. You can't see it and you expect me to.

FRANK. *You* are doing the test . . . Right what is next?

JEANETTE. Get in the car.

FRANK. Wait until he tells you.

JEANETTE. Why?

FRANK. Just . . . they like you to know your place.

They sit down on two chairs.

FRANK. Next.

JEANETTE. Start the car.

FRANK. Failed.

JEANETTE. Fix the mirror.

FRANK. No.

JEANETTE. Introduce myself.

FRANK. Failed for arse-licking.

JEANETTE. Ah, for Christ sake.

FRANK. Failed for using abusive language.

JEANETTE. I'm going to be the first person that's failed without ever leaving the curb.

FRANK. Seat-belt.

JEANETTE. Of course . . . I knew that.

FRANK. Next.

JEANETTE. Start the car.

FRANK. Before you start the car.

JEANETTE. Fix the mirror.

FRANK. As well as fixing the mirror.

JEANETTE. Make sure he has his seat-belt on.

FRANK. As well as fixing the mirror and making sure he has his belt on.

JEANETTE. Check the wing mirror.

FRANK. As well as fixing the inside mirror and the outside mirror and making sure he has his seat-belt on.

JEANETTE (*baffled*). . . . Check that I have my keys with me.

FRANK. As well as fixing the inside mirror and the outside mirror and making sure he has his seat-belt on and checking you have your car keys.

JEANETTE. I don't bloody know . . . take a valium and offer him one.

FRANK. Check you're in neutral gear.

JEANETTE. I knew that . . . that's obvious.

FRANK. OK . . . next.

JEANETTE. Start the bloody car at last.

FRANK. No.

JEANETTE. No?

FRANK. No.

JEANETTE. I don't believe this . . . what do I do then . . . play him one of your Paddy Reilly tapes?

FRANK. There is no point in starting the car as you have failed
   ... If this was for real you would have jumped into the car
   giving him no time to put his seat-belt on ... started in gear
   ... jumped forward and as a result bashed his head off the
   windscreen giving him six stitches.

JEANETTE. I'll never get this.

FRANK. Of course you will ... let's start again.

JEANETTE. I'll fail, I know I will.

FRANK. You'd better not ... unfortunately I can't give you
   any more driving lessons.

JEANETTE. Why?

FRANK. This woman I've been seeing ... ack it was just casual
   at first ... the odd Sunday ... now it's gettin' a bit more
   serious and she wants me to spend most weekends with her
   now and she lives in Dublin.

JEANETTE. That's nice.

FRANK. So you better pass or I'll feel guilty.

JEANETTE. I didn't know you had a girlfriend.

FRANK. I hadn't for a while ... hard to have a relationship
   when you're away all the time ... never get a chance to meet
   anybody ... then one Sunday night in the pub she was there
   and that was that ... Here you, this isn't gettin' you passed
   your test.

JEANETTE. Is she jealous of you taking another woman out?

FRANK. No ... she knows I'm doing it for m'mate.

JEANETTE. You're dead decent Frank.

JEANETTE. I enjoyed it ... you were a good pupil, I'm sure
   Kenny would have done the same for me.

JEANETTE. Yes ... I'm sure he would ... start again then.

FRANK. The blue Mini parked outside that shoe shop.

JEANETTE. L0I 6768 ... wait until I'm asked to get into the
   car, put on my seat belt, check he has his on, position the
   mirror, check the gears and put the key in the ignition.

FRANK. Passed that bit.

JEANETTE. I'll pass more than that bit . . . I'll pass the whole bloody lot.

Link into the next scene.

KENNY *is looking out the window impatiently.*

CATHY *comes in . . . with a bottle of champagne and three glasses.*

CATHY. No sign yet.

KENNY. Should be here soon . . . are you not a bit previous with that?

CATHY. She'll pass.

KENNY. I'll know by the look on her face . . . when I give the word . . . pop that thing.

CATHY. She will . . . she will . . . I know she will.

KENNY. She's determined anyway . . . this is it . . . here she comes . . .

CATHY. Well.

KENNY. Hard to say . . .

CATHY. Ack Daddy, you said you'd know.

KENNY. She is coming up the path . . . hide it.

CATHY. Ah frig.

JEANETTE (*comes in looking disappointed*). . . . I'm back.

KENNY. Well.

JEANETTE *puts her head down.*

KENNY (*puts his arms round her*). . . . Don't worry love . . . next time.

CATHY. Most people fail first time.

JEANETTE. Not me . . . (*Smiles.*) . . . I did it.

KENNY. Having me on.

CATHY. Champagne! . . . (*Gets the bottle.*)

JEANETTE. No . . . not when I'm driving.

KENNY. You're not driving now.

JEANETTE. Kenny I made a promise to myself when I passed that the first thing I was going to do was take you out . . . are you ready?

CATHY. Can I come? . . .

JEANETTE. Yes. We'll call and see our Patsy . . . I need to have a destination . . . I'm not that adventurous yet.

KENNY. It's only down the road.

JEANETTE. To you Kenny Duncan, but to me it is the Grand Prix. Come on.

KENNY. I want a crash helmet.

CATHY. Can I sit in the back? . . .

JEANETTE. You're all comedians I must say.

KENNY. Well done, love.

JEANETTE. Thanks . . . right, hit the road.

Link into the next scene

PATSY *and* NORMAN *are sitting in silence. Both watching television . . . saying nothing . . . speaking but saying nothing.* NORMAN *is innocently trying.*

NORMAN. Is this all that is on this side?

PATSY. Not much else.

Pause.

NORMAN. She was over the moon, wasn't she?

PATSY. Who?

NORMAN. Jeanette.

Long pause.

NORMAN. They seem to be gettin' on well.

PATSY. Yeah.

Pause.

NORMAN. In spite of it all.

PATSY. Yeah.

Pause.

NORMAN. He's lucky he has her.

PATSY. Yeah.

NORMAN. A lot of months ago she didn't know what end of her was up and now she has the whole thing under control . . . she's a trooper.

Pause.

NORMAN. I take my hat off to her . . . I never hardly ever heard her complain once . . . that Cathy one did all the complaining about her and now she comes running back.

PATSY. Aye . . . there ye go now.

NORMAN. And he is looking like a two year old . . . She's done wonders.

Pause.

NORMAN. Not much on, is there?

PATSY. No.

NORMAN. I think I might go to bed . . . only oul rubbish on this side.

PATSY. Yeah.

NORMAN. Tea?

PATSY. No thanks.

NORMAN. Anything?

PATSY. No thanks.

NORMAN. No tea or coffee?

PATSY. No thanks Norman.

NORMAN. Are you sure you wouldn't like one or the other?

PATSY. I am sure I wouldn't like one or the other. Or would you like to decide for me which one or the other I would far rather not have?

NORMAN. No tea . . . no coffee . . . that's fine . . . goodnight then.

PATSY. Goodnight.

PATSY *sits in silence . . . turns the TV off.*

NORMAN *comes back in.*

NORMAN. Have you finished with the *TV Times*?

PATSY. Why?

NORMAN. I would like to watch TV in bed.

PATSY. I wouldn't.

NORMAN. Then you go up to bed and I will stay here and watch it.

PATSY. I am not ready to go to bed yet.

NORMAN. Then I shall watch it until you are ready to and then I will continue to watch it down here . . . is that fair?

PATSY. Yeah.

NORMAN. Goodnight.

PATSY *goes to the phone and dials . . . she waits . . . There is no answer and she can't understand it. She sits down again still not understanding why she didn't get an answer. She dials again . . . still no answer.*

PATSY (*shouts*). . . . Norman . . . Norman . . . quick . . . Norman.

NORMAN (*enters*). . . . What's wrong?

PATSY. There is no answer from Jeanette and Kenny's.

NORMAN. Is that a problem?

PATSY. Yes it is only half ten.

NORMAN. They could be still out.

PATSY. Kenny goes to bed at half nine . . . he gets too tired to stay up longer . . .

NORMAN. Maybe Jeanette is in bed too.

PATSY. No . . . never at this time . . . Cathy should be there . . . the phone is beside the bed anyway.

NORMAN. Maybe she just isn't answering.

PATSY. No she wouldn't do that.

NORMAN. Well . . . what do you think?

PATSY. Norman . . . ring the hospital.

NORMAN. The hospital?

PATSY. Norman please . . . there is something wrong . . . please Norman. I can't face it . . . please . . . you do it.

NORMAN *lifts phone and dials.*

Link into the next scene.

JEANETTE *is sitting alone on a chair . . . hospital waiting room.*

CATHY *brings on two plastic cups of coffee.*

CATHY. Sorry . . . I had to walk about a mile to get it. Anybody come yet?

JEANETTE. No.

CATHY. At least he's conscious.

JEANETTE. Aye . . . might not be that bad.

CATHY. Just another fit maybe.

JEANETTE. Yes. His eyes were open when they wheeled him in Cathy . . . wasn't just me . . . they *were* open.

JEANETTE. Yes they were.

CATHY. Why does nobody come to tell you anything?

JEANETTE. Everybody is scared of telling you the worst so they tell you nothing, or they have about twenty different phrases they use . . . but when you learn to decode it . . . it actually means nothing anyway.

CATHY. They haven't given us any indication.

JEANETTE. I hope it wasn't the shock of me taking him out in the car . . . too much excitement in one day.

CATHY. Stop blaming yourself.

JEANETTE. I'm responsible for him.

CATHY. We've been here hours.

JEANETTE. You're right Cathy . . . If you don't ask . . . you'd be here all night . . . I'll go and find the doctor.

JEANETTE *leaves.*

CATHY *waits* . . . NORMAN *and* PATSY *come in.*

PATSY. What's wrong . . . what is it?

CATHY. He collapsed just before he got into bed. Don't know what it is . . . she thinks he may just have taken a fit and didn't come out of it properly.

PATSY (*sits down*). . . . I phoned . . . when I got no answer I panicked.

NORMAN. Where is Jeanette?

CATHY. Marching up there to find the doctor.

PATSY. Will he be alright?

CATHY. They won't tell her anything yet.

NORMAN. I suppose they have to be sure, right enough.

CATHY. Oh God, I hope it's what she thinks it is.

PATSY. So do I . . . for her sake . . . your mother shouldn't have to go through all that again.

NORMAN. That's the thing with strokes . . . you cud be back to square one at the drop of a hat . . . (*Realises he shouldn't have said it.*) . . . stuffy oul place this.

PATSY. If it is . . . God forbid . . . this time she is well armed.

CATHY. She's wiser alright . . . will it make any difference?

NORMAN. A little knowledge can be dangerous . . .

PATSY. Pardon?

NORMAN. What I mean is . . . are you better off just going ahead in ignorance and making the most of it, than spending your life being frustrated at what happens?

PATSY. Maybe trying to make it easier might be an option.

NORMAN. Aye Patsy . . .

Pause.

CATHY. He was doing brilliant . . . he's a different person . . . just getting to know him really.

NORMAN. You should be proud of your mother.

CATHY. I am . . . but maybe for not the same reasons as you.

Pause.

JEANETTE (*enters*). . . . Another stroke . . . a massive stroke.

PATSY. Jeanette . . .

Nobody can say anything.

JEANETTE. So . . . back to square one. (*She sits down.*)

JEANETTE. This time he'll stay here until he's better.

PATSY. Yes . . . they owe you that.

CATHY. Mammy I'll stay home . . . I'll help.

JEANETTE. No . . . this is not going to ruin your life . . . No
. . . He'll stay here until he can walk out.

PATSY. I'll stand by you Jeanette . . . you can't go through that
again . . .

NORMAN. Yes . . . they owe you something.

Blackout.

Next scene . . . JEANETTE *sits alone and flicks through the TV
channels, walks around feeling his absence . . . sits in the wheelchair . . .
Hamster Wheel tunes fades in and continues.*

Lights fade.

JEANETTE *and* CATHY *wheel* KENNY *on as in first scene. They
wheel him round to front stage and both lift him into the chair . . . same as
beginning.*

Blackout.